DC UNIVERSE
REBIRTH

THE DELUXE EDITION

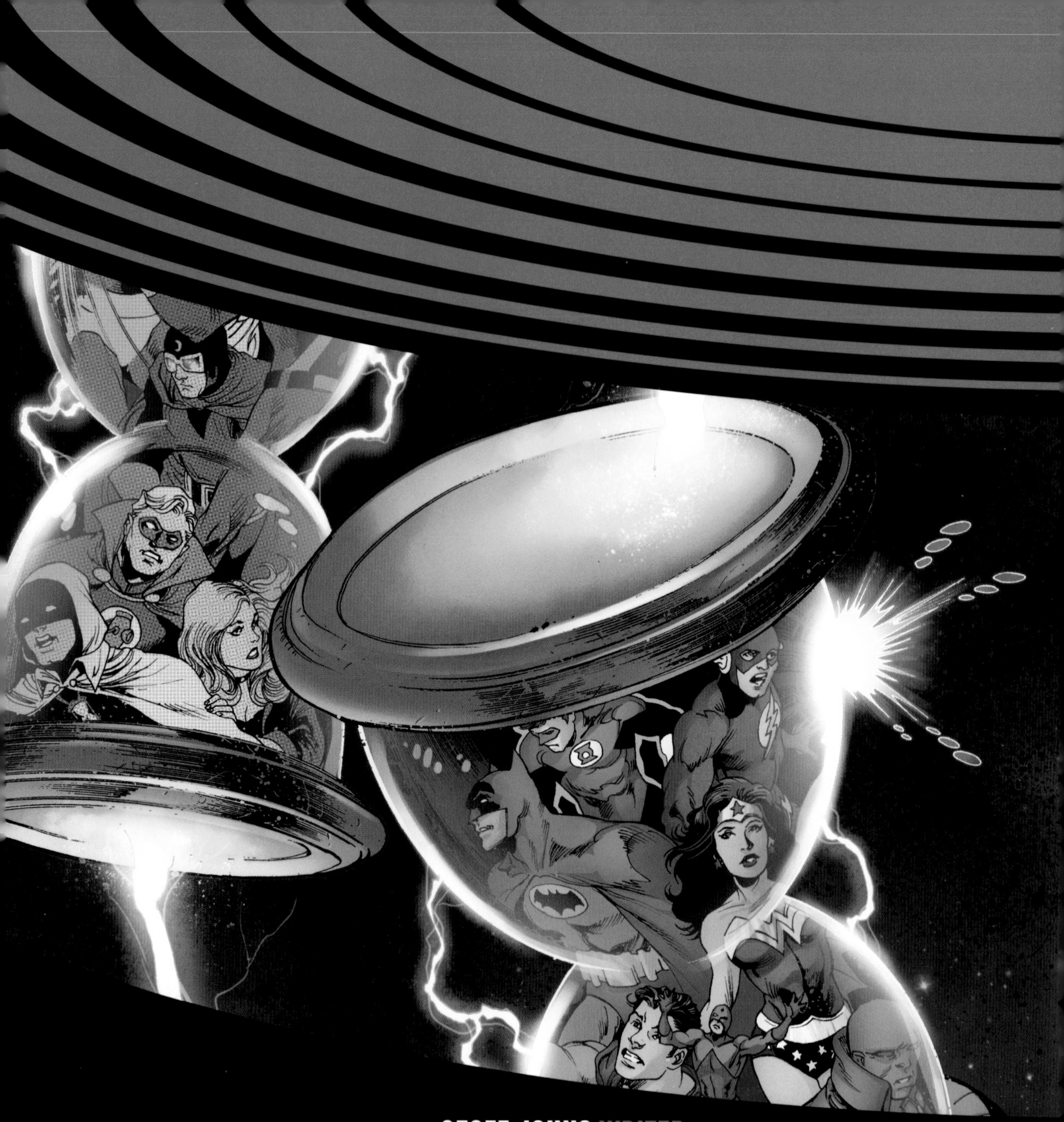

GEOFF JOHNS WRITER

CHAPTER 1 LOST

GARY FRANK and **ETHAN VAN SCIVER** artists * **BRAD ANDERSON** and **JASON WRIGHT** colorists

CHAPTER 2 LEGACY

GARY FRANK artist * **BRAD ANDERSON** colorist

CHAPTER 3 LOVE

IVAN REIS penciller * **JOE PRADO** and **IVAN REIS** inkers * **HI-FI** colorist

CHAPTER 4 LIFE

PHIL JIMENEZ and **GARY FRANK** pencillers * **MATT SANTORELLI** and **GARY FRANK** inkers
GABE ELTAEB and **BRAD ANDERSON** colorists

EPILOGUE

GARY FRANK and **IVAN REIS** pencillers * **GARY FRANK** and **JOE PRADO** inkers
BRAD ANDERSON and **HI-FI** colorists

NICK J. NAPOLITANO letterer

GARY FRANK and **BRAD ANDERSON** collection cover artists

SUPERMAN created by **JERRY SIEGEL** and **JOE SHUSTER**
By special arrangement with the Jerry Siegel family

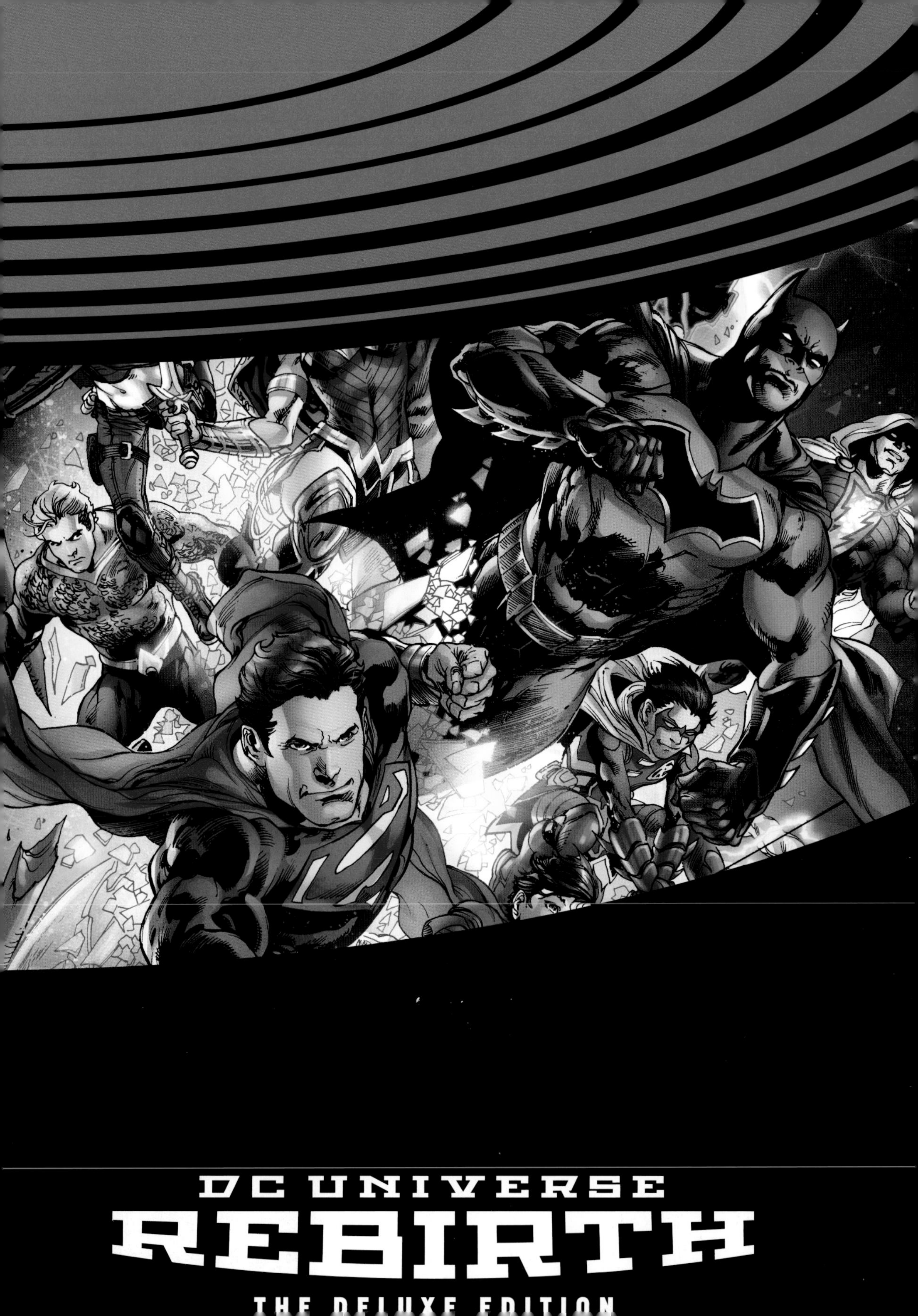

DC UNIVERSE REBIRTH

THE DELUXE EDITION

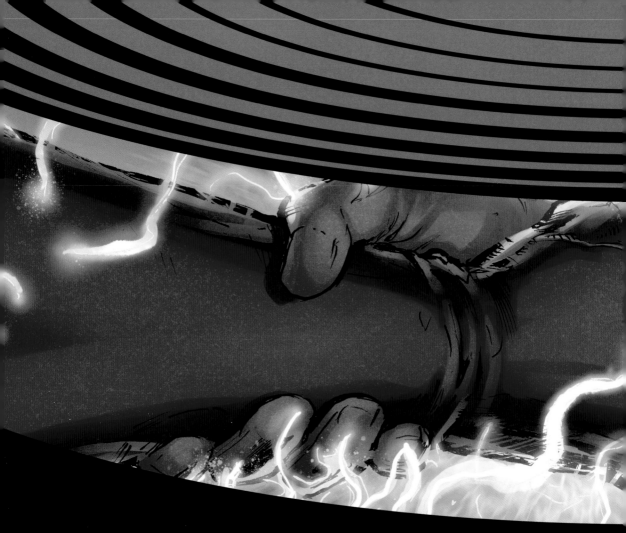

EDDIE BERGANZA Editor - Original Series ⬦ **ANDREW MARINO** Assistant Editor - Original Series
JEB WOODARD Group Editor - Collected Editions ⬦ **STEVE COOK** Design Director - Books ⬦ **DAMIAN RYLAND** Publication Design

BOB HARRAS Senior VP - Editor-in-Chief, DC Comics

DIANE NELSON President ⬦ **DAN DiDIO** Publisher ⬦ **JIM LEE** Publisher ⬦ **GEOFF JOHNS** President & Chief Creative Officer
AMIT DESAI Executive VP - Business & Marketing Strategy, Direct to Consumer & Global Franchise Management ⬦ **SAM ADES** Senior VP - Direct to Consumer
BOBBIE CHASE VP - Talent Development ⬦ **MARK CHIARELLO** Senior VP - Art, Design & Collected Editions
JOHN CUNNINGHAM Senior VP - Sales & Trade Marketing ⬦ **ANNE DePIES** Senior VP - Business Strategy, Finance & Administration
DON FALLETTI VP - Manufacturing Operations ⬦ **LAWRENCE GANEM** VP - Editorial Administration & Talent Relations
ALISON GILL Senior VP - Manufacturing & Operations ⬦ **HANK KANALZ** Senior VP - Editorial Strategy & Administration
JAY KOGAN VP - Legal Affairs ⬦ **THOMAS LOFTUS** VP - Business Affairs
JACK MAHAN VP - Business Affairs ⬦ **NICK J. NAPOLITANO** VP - Manufacturing Administration
EDDIE SCANNELL VP - Consumer Marketing ⬦ **COURTNEY SIMMONS** Senior VP - Publicity & Communications
JIM (SKI) SOKOLOWSKI VP - Comic Book Specialty Sales & Trade Marketing ⬦ **NANCY SPEARS** VP - Mass, Book, Digital Sales & Trade Marketing

Special thanks to **MIKE COTTON**, **BRIAN CUNNINGHAM** and **AMEDEO TURTURRO**

DC UNIVERSE: REBIRTH - THE DELUXE EDITION

DC Comics, 2900 West Alameda Ave., Burbank, CA 91505. Printed by Transcontinental Interglobe, Beauceville, QC, Canada. 11/4/16.
First Printing.
ISBN: 978-1-4012-7072-8   LCSD ISBN: 978-1-4012-7251-7

Library of Congress Cataloging-in-Publication Data

Names: Johns, Geoff, 1973- author. | Frank, Gary, 1969- artist, penciller. |
Van Sciver, Ethan, artist. | Reis, Ivan, artist. | Jimenez, Phil,
penciller.
Title: DC Universe : rebirth / Geoff Johns, writer ; chapter 1 /Lost, Gary
Frank and Ethan Van Sciver, artists ; chapter 2/Legacy, Gary Frank, artist;
chapter 3/Love, Ivan Reis, artist ; chapter 4/Life, Phil Jimenez and
Gary Frank, pencillers.
Description: Deluxe edition. | Burbank, CA : DC Comics, [2016]
Identifiers: LCCN 2016042491 | ISBN 9781401270728 (hardback)
Subjects: LCSH: Comic books, strips, etc. | BISAC: COMICS & GRAPHIC NOVELS /
Superheroes.
Classification: LCC PN6728.D35334 J64 2016 | DDC 741.5/973–dc23
LC record available at https://lccn.loc.gov/2016042491

PEFC Certified
Printed on paper from
sustainably managed
forests and controlled
sources
PEFC/01-31-106   www.pefc.org

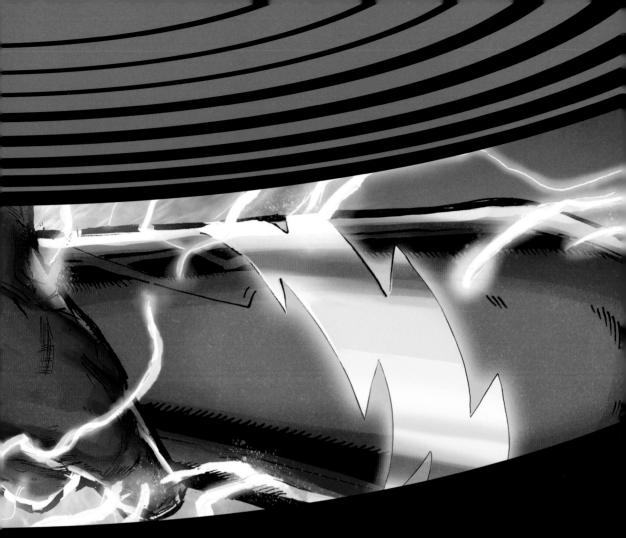

Introduction by **Diane Nelson**

I was flattered to be asked to write an introduction to one of DC Comics' books. This is my first introduction, and I feel like there's a lovely serendipity to it being for DC UNIVERSE: REBIRTH #1, as this week marks seven years since I had the honor to take over DC Comics, creating DC Entertainment and embarking on our own company-wide rebirth of sorts.

There are few books I'd feel comfortable having meaningful words to contribute to an introduction, as there are many who have loved these characters far longer than I. But REBIRTH is special to me, and obviously to so many fans, for a variety of reasons.

I have watched and worked with Dan DiDio, Jim Lee and Geoff Johns since putting them in place as my executive leadership team in 2010. I have seen firsthand the passion and dedication they bring to this business and the art of comic book storytelling. As had been my intent in hiring them, they each bring uniquely complementary skills and perspectives to one another, and share a deep and lifelong love of DC and all of its characters.

REBIRTH and the subsequent books that launched after have reinforced for me the delicate balance we face as a publisher in this industry. How do we continue to deliver the characters and stories that fans have loved for decades while pushing ourselves and our talent to innovate, to bring fresh and diverse perspectives, to address timely social and cultural issues? And how do we try new things in the face of what is often brutal (and fanatical) criticism if we don't get it right? That's the

definition of fandom, and we dust ourselves off and keep trying because everyone at DC is also a fan. We do all this in the face of an often-struggling print and direct market—one we work hard to keep vibrant and strong. We do this in an environment of tough, but invigorating, competition with our fellow publishers.

When launched in 2011, the New 52 was controversial for many in tone and storytelling, with some arguing that it was not successful from a business standpoint. I argue that, while there were aspects of the storytelling that many fans disagreed with, the New 52 was an unmitigated success. It brought new readers to retailers, helped boost DC's business, and has been suggested to have helped re-energize the industry overall. We all win when that happens. And it can only happen by taking risks and trying new things. There was strong storytelling in the New 52 and we are all proud of it.

Rebirth has been another example of rethinking how to approach the DC Universe, with its success to date unprecedented, and there are very clear reasons for that. Dan, Jim and Geoff collaborated across the entire line in a way that has not been done at DC over the past seven years. This cooperation continued what worked with the New 52 while returning to what many felt was missing from the DC Universe. Their shared vision is inspiring.

Which brings me to the architect of this book and the key driver of the overall execution of the Rebirth line: Geoff Johns

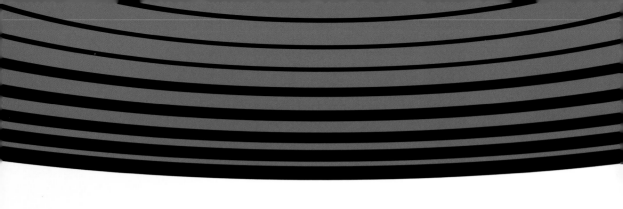

Geoff has always had his own superhuman powers, and I've been amazed to watch what he's capable of since hiring him. His encyclopedic knowledge of DC characters, dating back to their beginning, is obvious (and he comes pretty close to having similar knowledge of Marvel characters). His work ethic is inspiring. He continues to write powerful stories–comics, screenplays, TV scripts and so much more–while holding down a "day job" as Chief Creative Officer for DC Entertainment because he loves to create.

The thing about Geoff that this book demonstrates so clearly is his love for the core attributes of the DC Universe and its characters. They are, by the way, attributes he personally shares: optimism, hope, idealism and selflessness. It is clear that these characters have brought a smile to Geoff's face since he was a young boy, and I know he takes pride in continuing to bring that same happiness–the heroism, aspiration and joy of these characters–to fans old and new.

I find it hard to believe that anyone reading this deluxe edition of DC UNIVERSE: REBIRTH has not yet read it in another form, be it print or digital. Nonetheless, I will minimize spoilers with the hope that this edition is a gift to at least some new fans. There are, however, a handful of moments–of beautifully written words and gorgeously illustrated art–that are worth calling out for what they represent about the DC Universe.

Within the first panels of the book, our key protagonist describes "the day I met my *hero*." In so doing, he found "hope and inspiration" and became part of a "legacy." That, to my mind, sums up what superheroes are all about. Certainly over time and throughout various periods in our culture, they've taken on different perspectives and motivations that reflect our world or the vision of the creator imagining their newest story. But at its heart, this is what our heroes are all about, what the DC Universe is about. REBIRTH shows us that the world is ready to embrace those positive and inspiring attributes again.

The book itself is broken into chapters, beginning with Chapter 1 and what has been "Lost," continuing to Chapter 2 and "Legacy," then Chapter 3's "Love," the "Life" of Chapter 4, and finally an epilogue that drops your jaw to the ground and guarantees to leave you wanting more. This is how Geoff thinks about the DC Universe and the role Rebirth is playing in bringing our storytelling back to its core strengths.

My love for this business comes from a deep-rooted appreciation and respect for creators. They put their heart and soul into what they do every day and then they put it out into the world to be embraced or rejected, often by people they will never know personally. People who pay little regard (at times) to the part of themselves these creators have given as a gift to us all. This has to be the most stressful thing a creative person can choose to do, but when they do it well, it leaves a legacy and an impact that lives on for generations.

I happen to know that Geoff, like any creative talent, felt terrible anxiety about this book and how it would be received. He cares desperately about the quality of everything he does, but this book meant something very personal for him. That anxiety– maybe even fear–of how fans would feel about the creation he and REBIRTH's remarkable team of artists produced was nearly overwhelming for Geoff, particularly as he knew this was kicking off a much bigger line.

On our way back from a business trip, before the story even saw color, I had the unique opportunity to walk through the book's pencils with Geoff. This was before the pressure of imminent release was upon him. And, as I have reminded him since, there was no anxiety; there was confidence, pride and passion. He knew exactly which moments would make fans cry. Which moments would make them cheer. When they would gasp and when they would sigh with relief. He pointed out each and every scene and character that I have since read about in fan and retailer feedback as the most powerful and welcome moments of this book. Geoff Johns knows this world. He knows these characters–what makes them so powerful and what has made so many of them last and resonate for decades. He knows how to tell a story that leaves you wanting more–how to create anticipation or set up something (or someone) new at the same time that he shows us the characters we've always loved.

Finally, I can't end this introduction without far too few words about the artists who worked so closely with Geoff to develop and bring this story to life: Gary Frank, Ethan Van Sciver, Ivan Reis, Phil Jimenez and so many talented inkers, colorists and letterers. They are among the very, very best in our business. They each bring a unique and stunning style and talent to their work, yet it feels seamless in this book. Geoff has always been one to acknowledge and closely collaborate with his artist partners. This book is a tribute to that, and I congratulate all of them on a creation that will undoubtedly leave a legacy for generations and that has been a true Rebirth for the DC Universe.

Diane Nelson
President of DC Entertainment
September 2016

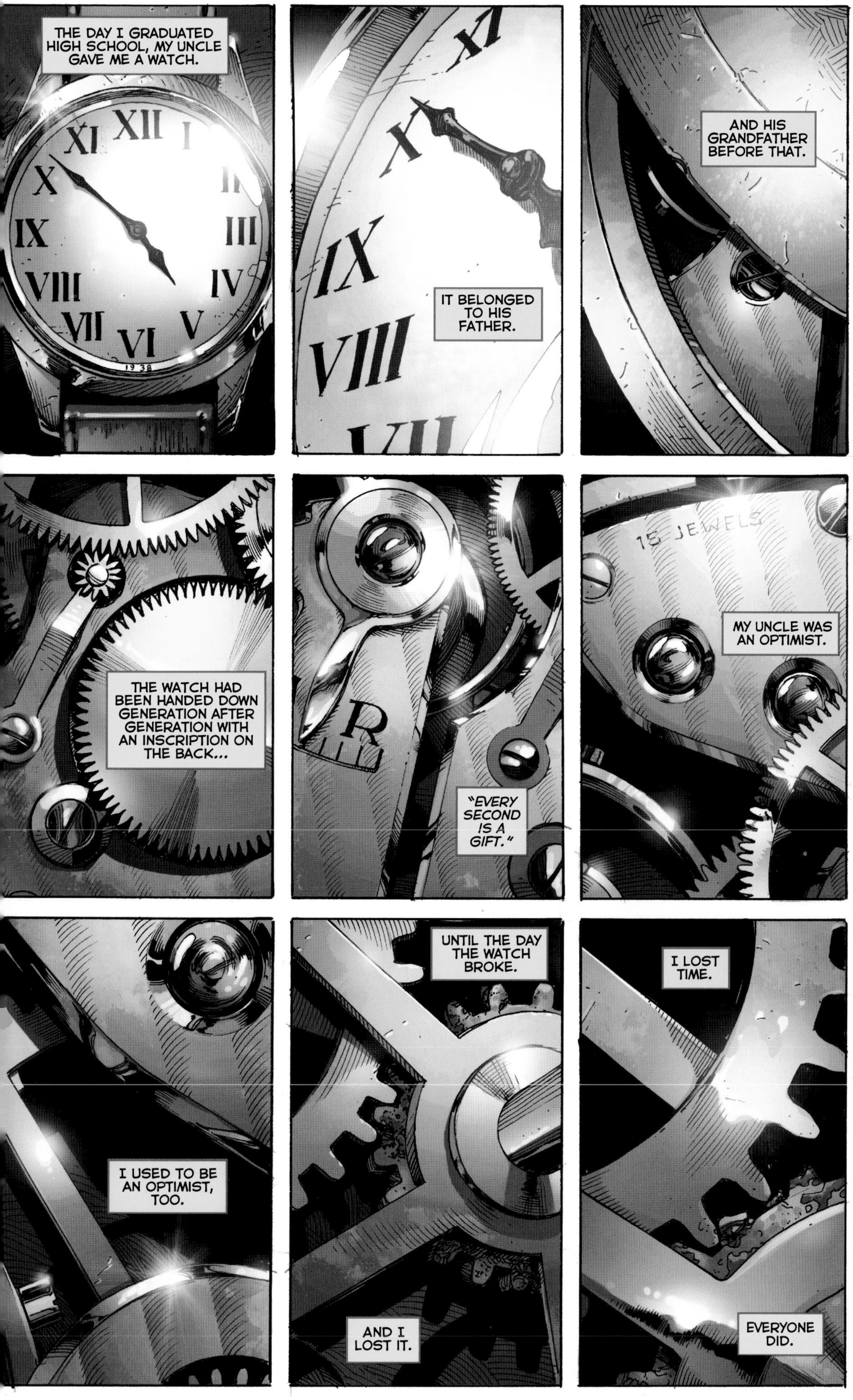
THE DAY I GRADUATED HIGH SCHOOL, MY UNCLE GAVE ME A WATCH.
1938
IT BELONGED TO HIS FATHER.
AND HIS GRANDFATHER BEFORE THAT.
THE WATCH HAD BEEN HANDED DOWN GENERATION AFTER GENERATION WITH AN INSCRIPTION ON THE BACK...
"EVERY SECOND IS A GIFT."
15 JEWELS
MY UNCLE WAS AN OPTIMIST.
I USED TO BE AN OPTIMIST, TOO.
UNTIL THE DAY THE WATCH BROKE.
AND I LOST IT.
I LOST TIME.
EVERYONE DID.

I LOOK DOWN AT IT AND KNOW WITHOUT QUESTION: I LOVE THIS WORLD.

BUT THERE'S SOMETHING MISSING.

GROWING UP, I HAD A FATHER WHO WAS MORE FOCUSED ON GETTING RICH QUICK THAN RAISING A SON--

--AND A MOTHER TOO BUSY WORRYING ABOUT WHAT EVERYONE THOUGHT OF HER TO WORRY ABOUT ME.

I HAD NO BROTHERS OR SISTERS. NO REAL FRIENDS.

UNTIL THE DAY I MET MY *HERO.* I FOUND HOPE AND INSPIRATION. I WAS BLESSED WITH POWER AND A PURPOSE. I BECAME PART OF A *LEGACY.*

MY LIFE WAS BETTER THAN I EVER IMAGINED IT COULD BE.

BUT IT WAS ALL RIPPED AWAY.

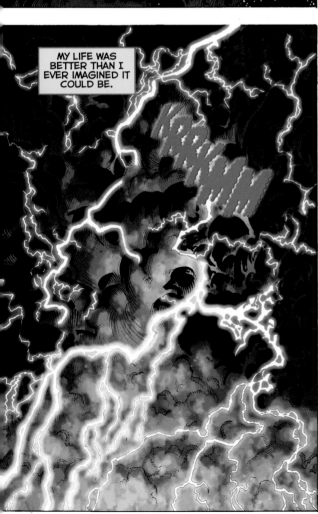

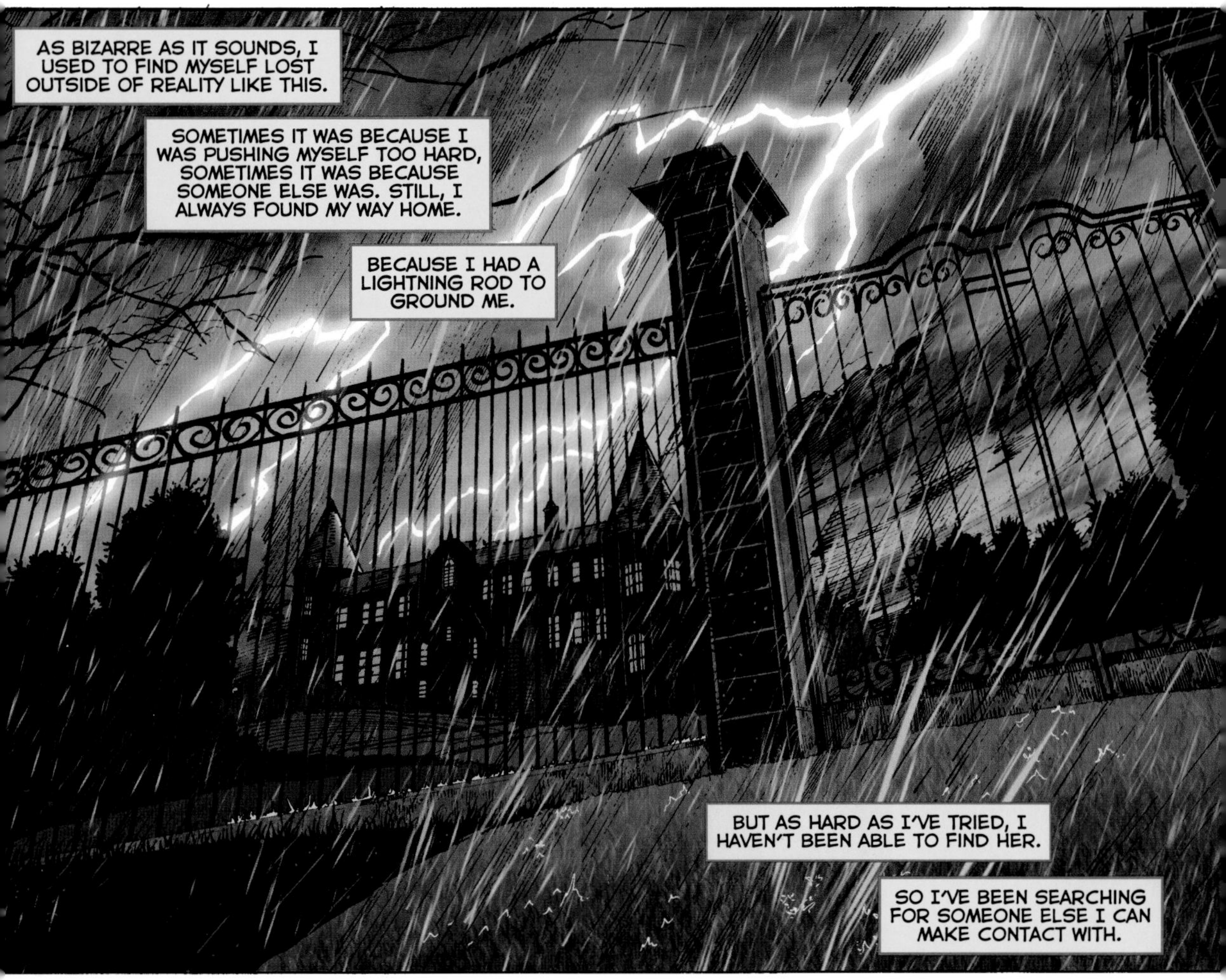

AS BIZARRE AS IT SOUNDS, I USED TO FIND MYSELF LOST OUTSIDE OF REALITY LIKE THIS.
SOMETIMES IT WAS BECAUSE I WAS PUSHING MYSELF TOO HARD, SOMETIMES IT WAS BECAUSE SOMEONE ELSE WAS. STILL, I ALWAYS FOUND MY WAY HOME.
BECAUSE I HAD A LIGHTNING ROD TO GROUND ME.
BUT AS HARD AS I'VE TRIED, I HAVEN'T BEEN ABLE TO FIND HER.
SO I'VE BEEN SEARCHING FOR SOMEONE ELSE I CAN MAKE CONTACT WITH.

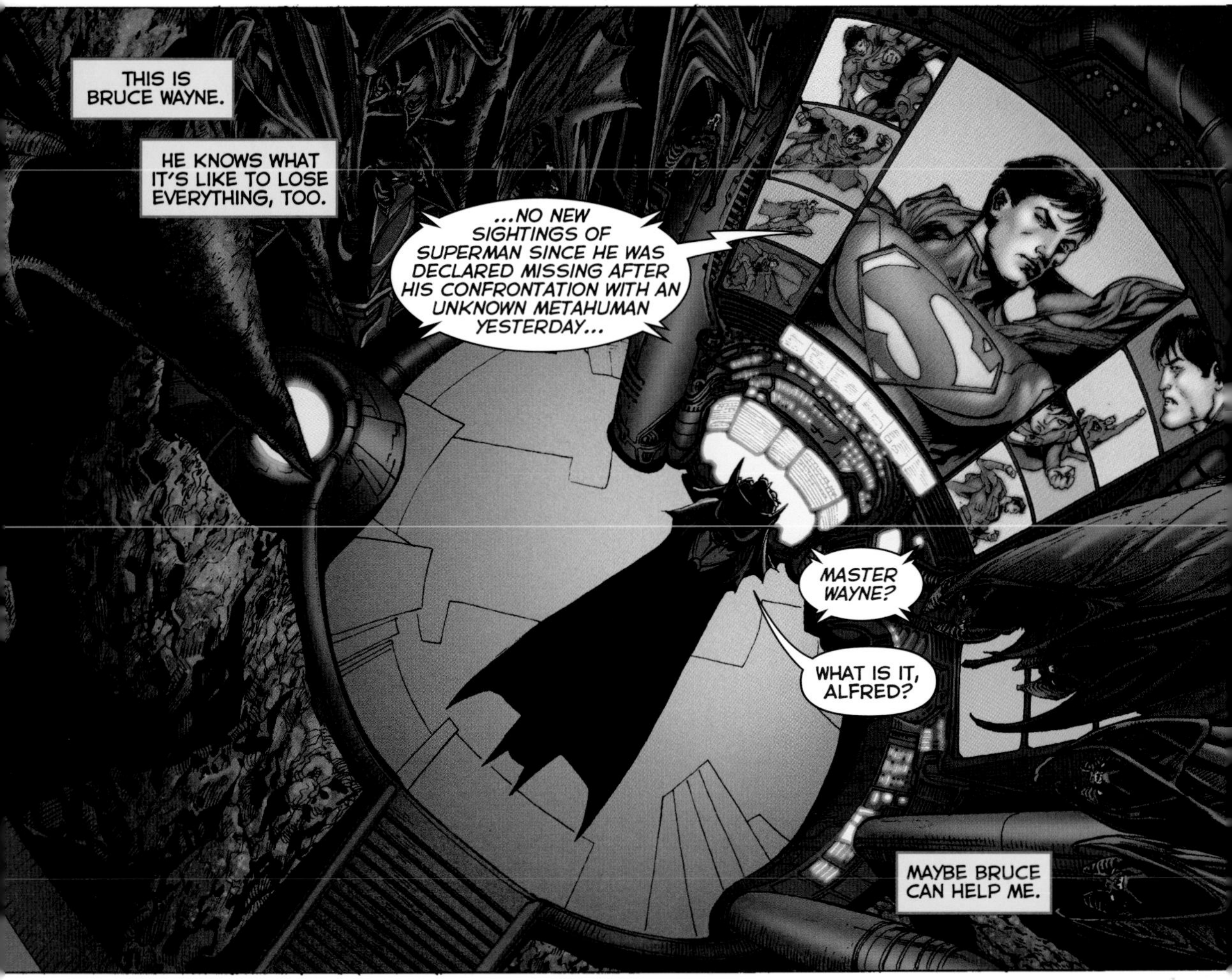

THIS IS BRUCE WAYNE.
HE KNOWS WHAT IT'S LIKE TO LOSE EVERYTHING, TOO.
...NO NEW SIGHTINGS OF SUPERMAN SINCE HE WAS DECLARED MISSING AFTER HIS CONFRONTATION WITH AN UNKNOWN METAHUMAN YESTERDAY...
MASTER WAYNE?
WHAT IS IT, ALFRED?
MAYBE BRUCE CAN HELP ME.

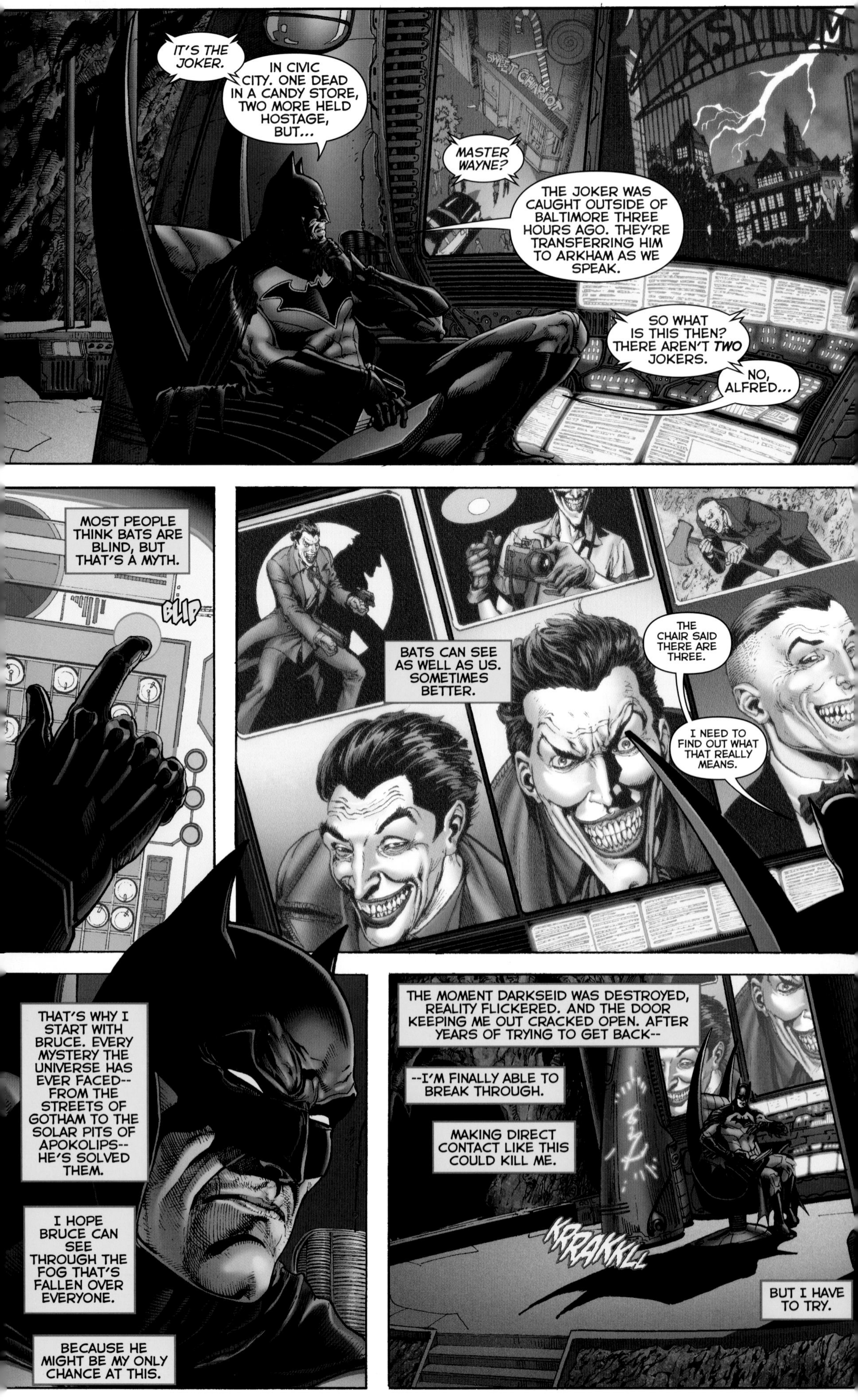
IT'S THE JOKER.
IN CIVIC CITY. ONE DEAD IN A CANDY STORE, TWO MORE HELD HOSTAGE, BUT...
SWEET CHARIOT
ASYLUM
MASTER WAYNE?
THE JOKER WAS CAUGHT OUTSIDE OF BALTIMORE THREE HOURS AGO. THEY'RE TRANSFERRING HIM TO ARKHAM AS WE SPEAK.
SO WHAT IS THIS THEN? THERE AREN'T TWO JOKERS.
NO, ALFRED...
MOST PEOPLE THINK BATS ARE BLIND, BUT THAT'S A MYTH.
BLIP
BATS CAN SEE AS WELL AS US. SOMETIMES BETTER.
THE CHAIR SAID THERE ARE THREE.
I NEED TO FIND OUT WHAT THAT REALLY MEANS.
THAT'S WHY I START WITH BRUCE. EVERY MYSTERY THE UNIVERSE HAS EVER FACED-- FROM THE STREETS OF GOTHAM TO THE SOLAR PITS OF APOKOLIPS-- HE'S SOLVED THEM.
I HOPE BRUCE CAN SEE THROUGH THE FOG THAT'S FALLEN OVER EVERYONE.
BECAUSE HE MIGHT BE MY ONLY CHANCE AT THIS.
THE MOMENT DARKSEID WAS DESTROYED, REALITY FLICKERED. AND THE DOOR KEEPING ME OUT CRACKED OPEN. AFTER YEARS OF TRYING TO GET BACK--
--I'M FINALLY ABLE TO BREAK THROUGH.
MAKING DIRECT CONTACT LIKE THIS COULD KILL ME.
KRRAKKL!
BUT I HAVE TO TRY.

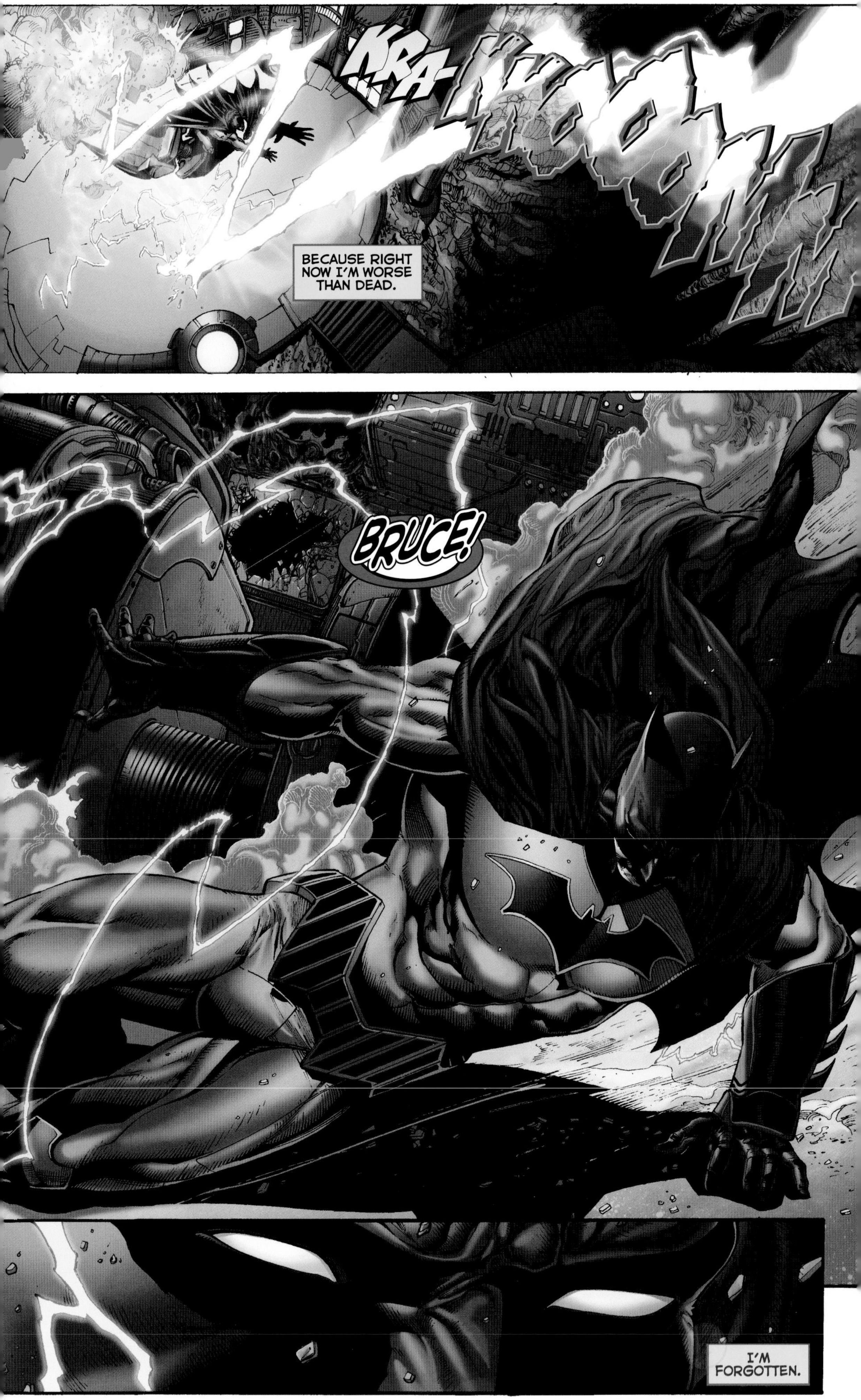
KRA-KOOOM
BECAUSE RIGHT NOW I'M WORSE THAN DEAD.
BRUCE!
I'M FORGOTTEN.

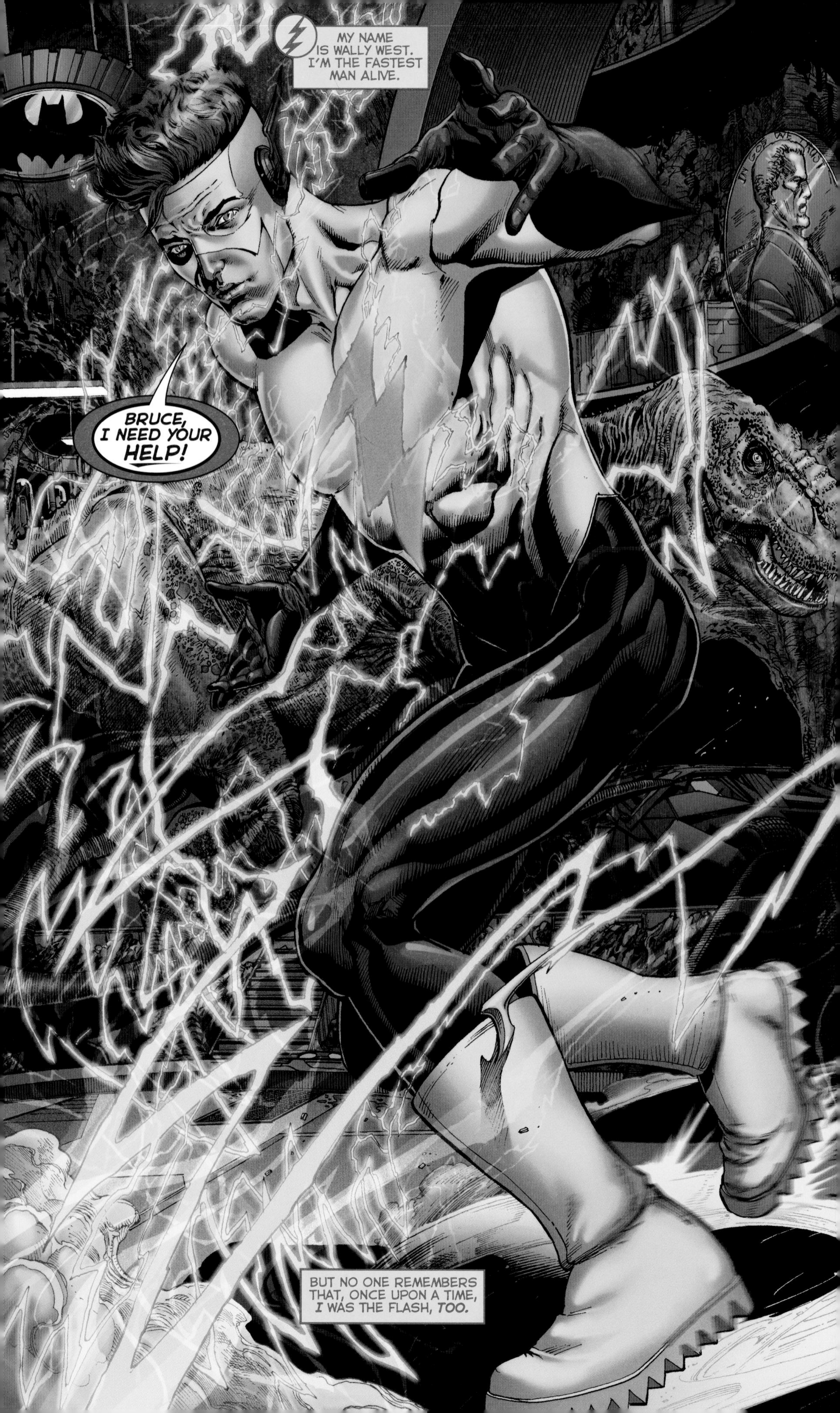
MY NAME IS WALLY WEST. I'M THE FASTEST MAN ALIVE.
BRUCE, I NEED YOUR HELP!
BUT NO ONE REMEMBERS THAT, ONCE UPON A TIME, I WAS THE FLASH, TOO.

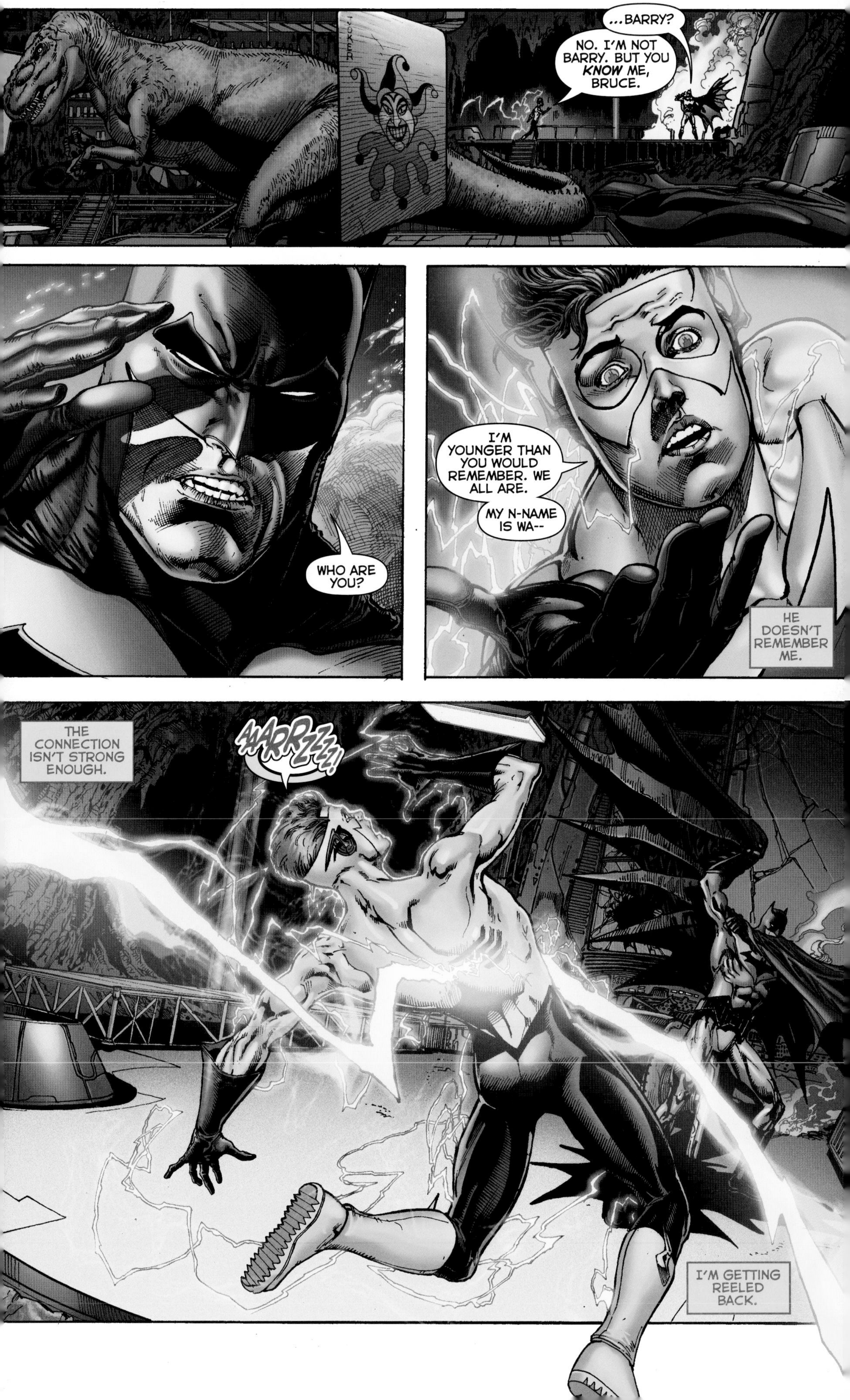
...BARRY?
NO. I'M NOT BARRY. BUT YOU KNOW ME, BRUCE.
WHO ARE YOU?
I'M YOUNGER THAN YOU WOULD REMEMBER. WE ALL ARE.
MY N-NAME IS WA--
HE DOESN'T REMEMBER ME.
THE CONNECTION ISN'T STRONG ENOUGH.
AAARRZZZ!
I'M GETTING REELED BACK.

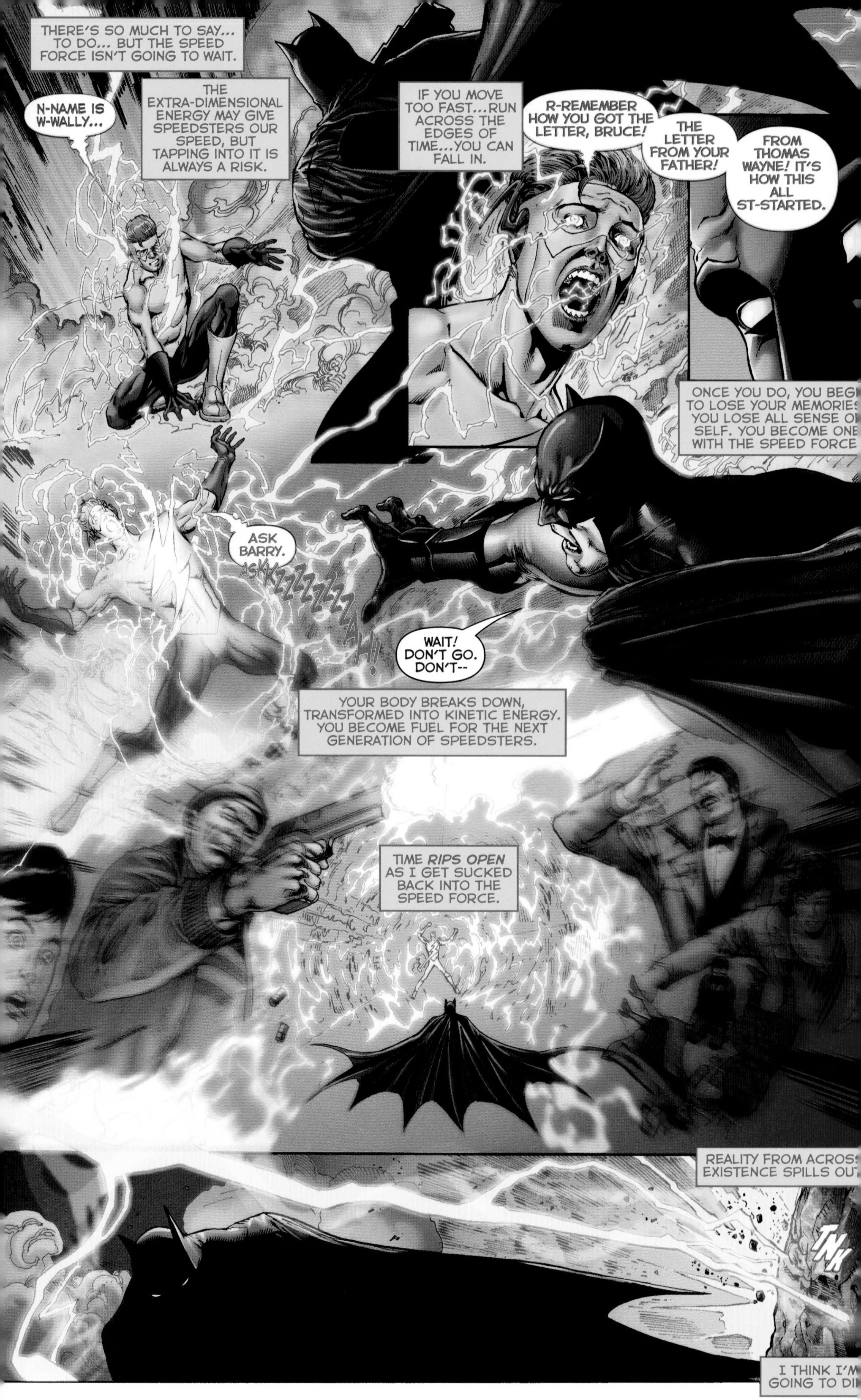

THERE'S SO MUCH TO SAY... TO DO... BUT THE SPEED FORCE ISN'T GOING TO WAIT.
N-NAME IS W-WALLY...
THE EXTRA-DIMENSIONAL ENERGY MAY GIVE SPEEDSTERS OUR SPEED, BUT TAPPING INTO IT IS ALWAYS A RISK.
IF YOU MOVE TOO FAST...RUN ACROSS THE EDGES OF TIME...YOU CAN FALL IN.
R-REMEMBER HOW YOU GOT THE LETTER, BRUCE!
THE LETTER FROM YOUR FATHER!
FROM THOMAS WAYNE! IT'S HOW THIS ALL ST-STARTED.
ONCE YOU DO, YOU BEG
TO LOSE YOUR MEMORIES
YOU LOSE ALL SENSE O
SELF. YOU BECOME ONE
WITH THE SPEED FORCE
ASK BARRY.
ASKKZZZZZZZZAH!
WAIT! DON'T GO. DON'T--
YOUR BODY BREAKS DOWN, TRANSFORMED INTO KINETIC ENERGY. YOU BECOME FUEL FOR THE NEXT GENERATION OF SPEEDSTERS.
TIME RIPS OPEN AS I GET SUCKED BACK INTO THE SPEED FORCE.
REALITY FROM ACROSS
EXISTENCE SPILLS OUT
TNK
I THINK I'M
GOING TO DI

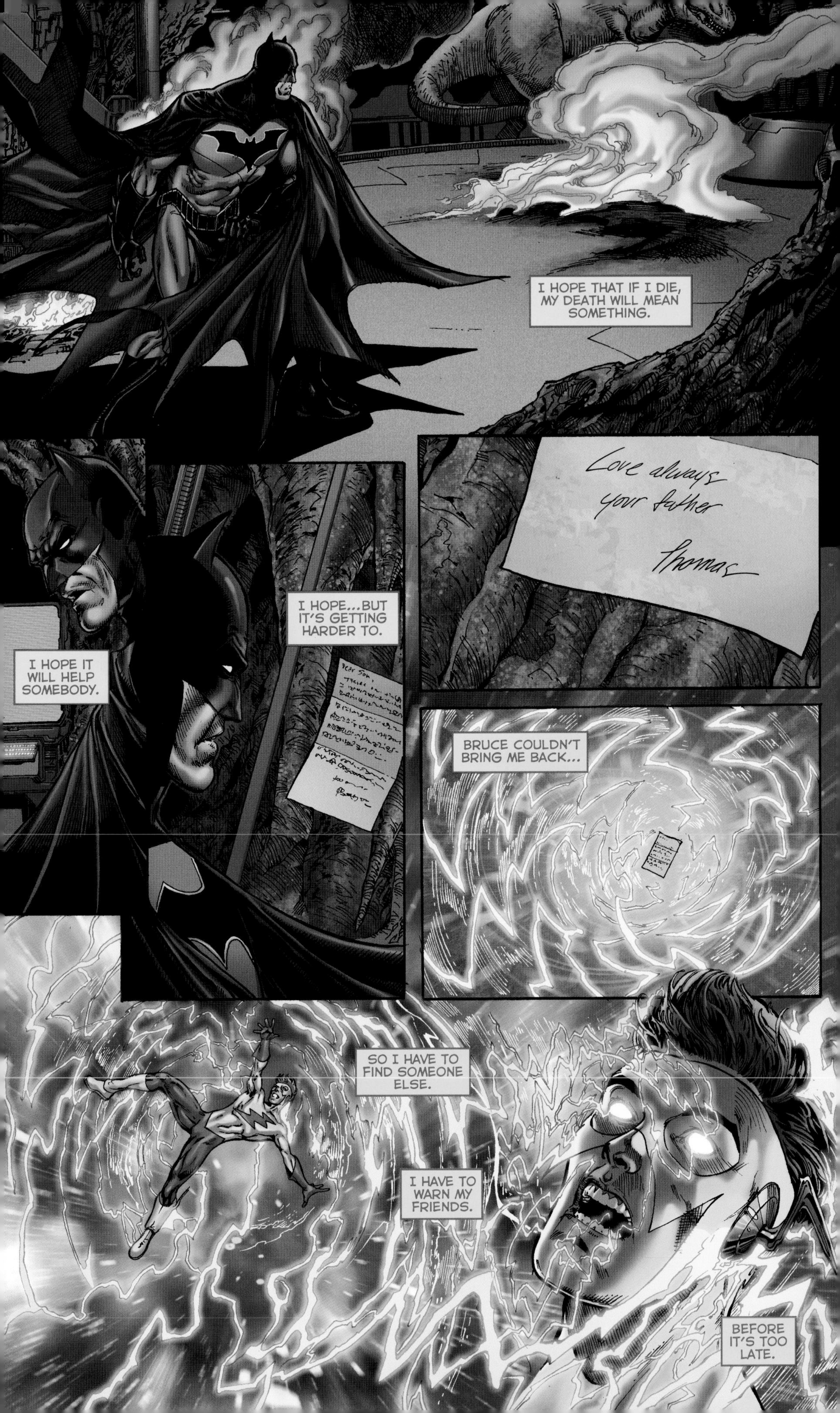
I HOPE THAT IF I DIE, MY DEATH WILL MEAN SOMETHING.
I HOPE IT WILL HELP SOMEBODY.
I HOPE...BUT IT'S GETTING HARDER TO.
Love always your father Thomas
BRUCE COULDN'T BRING ME BACK...
SO I HAVE TO FIND SOMEONE ELSE.
I HAVE TO WARN MY FRIENDS.
BEFORE IT'S TOO LATE.

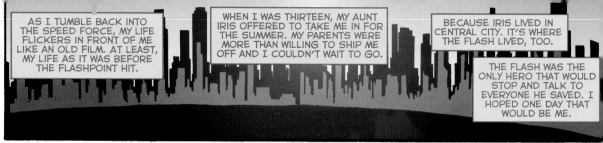

AS I TUMBLE BACK INTO THE SPEED FORCE, MY LIFE FLICKERS IN FRONT OF ME LIKE AN OLD FILM. AT LEAST, MY LIFE AS IT WAS BEFORE THE FLASHPOINT HIT.

WHEN I WAS THIRTEEN, MY AUNT IRIS OFFERED TO TAKE ME IN FOR THE SUMMER. MY PARENTS WERE MORE THAN WILLING TO SHIP ME OFF AND I COULDN'T WAIT TO GO.

BECAUSE IRIS LIVED IN CENTRAL CITY. IT'S WHERE THE FLASH LIVED, TOO.

THE FLASH WAS THE ONLY HERO THAT WOULD STOP AND TALK TO EVERYONE HE SAVED. I HOPED ONE DAY THAT WOULD BE ME.

BARRY, I WANT YOU TO MEET MY NEPHEW WALLY! HE'S THE PRESIDENT OF THE FLASH FAN CLUB IN HIS HOMETOWN!

PRESIDENT AND ONLY MEMBER.

HMM! HI, WALLY...

EVERYTHING WAS SO SIMPLE BACK THEN.

IRIS AND HER BOYFRIEND INTRODUCED ME TO THE FLASH. AT THE TIME, I DIDN'T KNOW HE AND BARRY ALLEN WERE ONE AND THE SAME.

I THOUGHT MEETING HIM WOULD BE THE GREATEST MOMENT OF MY LIFE.

BUT IT GOT BETTER.

I WAS STRUCK BY A BOLT OF LIGHTNING AND DOUSED IN CHEMICALS--THE SAME ACCIDENT THAT TRANSFORMED BARRY ALLEN INTO THE FLASH HAPPENED TO ME.

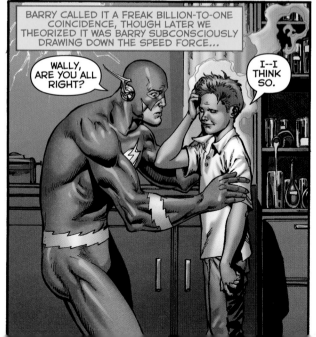

BARRY CALLED IT A FREAK BILLION-TO-ONE COINCIDENCE, THOUGH LATER WE THEORIZED IT WAS BARRY SUBCONSCIOUSLY DRAWING DOWN THE SPEED FORCE...

WALLY, ARE YOU ALL RIGHT?

I--I THINK SO.

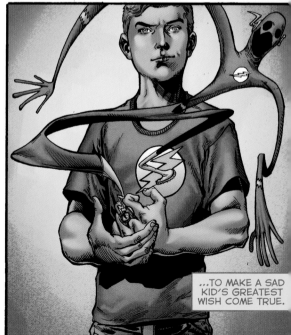

...TO MAKE A SAD KID'S GREATEST WISH COME TRUE.

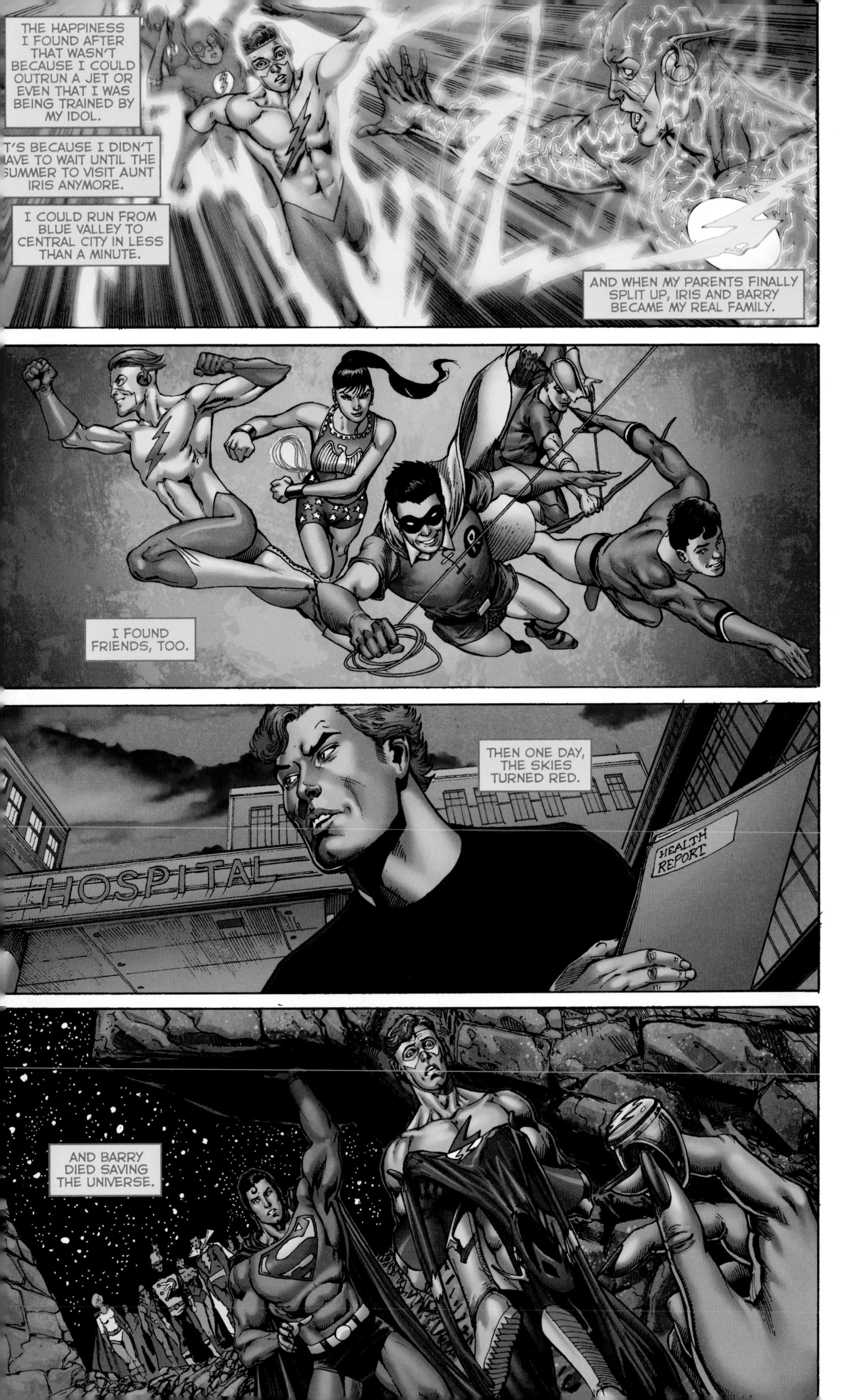

THE HAPPINESS I FOUND AFTER THAT WASN'T BECAUSE I COULD OUTRUN A JET OR EVEN THAT I WAS BEING TRAINED BY MY IDOL.
IT'S BECAUSE I DIDN'T HAVE TO WAIT UNTIL THE SUMMER TO VISIT AUNT IRIS ANYMORE.
I COULD RUN FROM BLUE VALLEY TO CENTRAL CITY IN LESS THAN A MINUTE.
AND WHEN MY PARENTS FINALLY SPLIT UP, IRIS AND BARRY BECAME MY REAL FAMILY.
I FOUND FRIENDS, TOO.
THEN ONE DAY, THE SKIES TURNED RED.
HOSPITAL
HEALTH REPORT
AND BARRY DIED SAVING THE UNIVERSE.

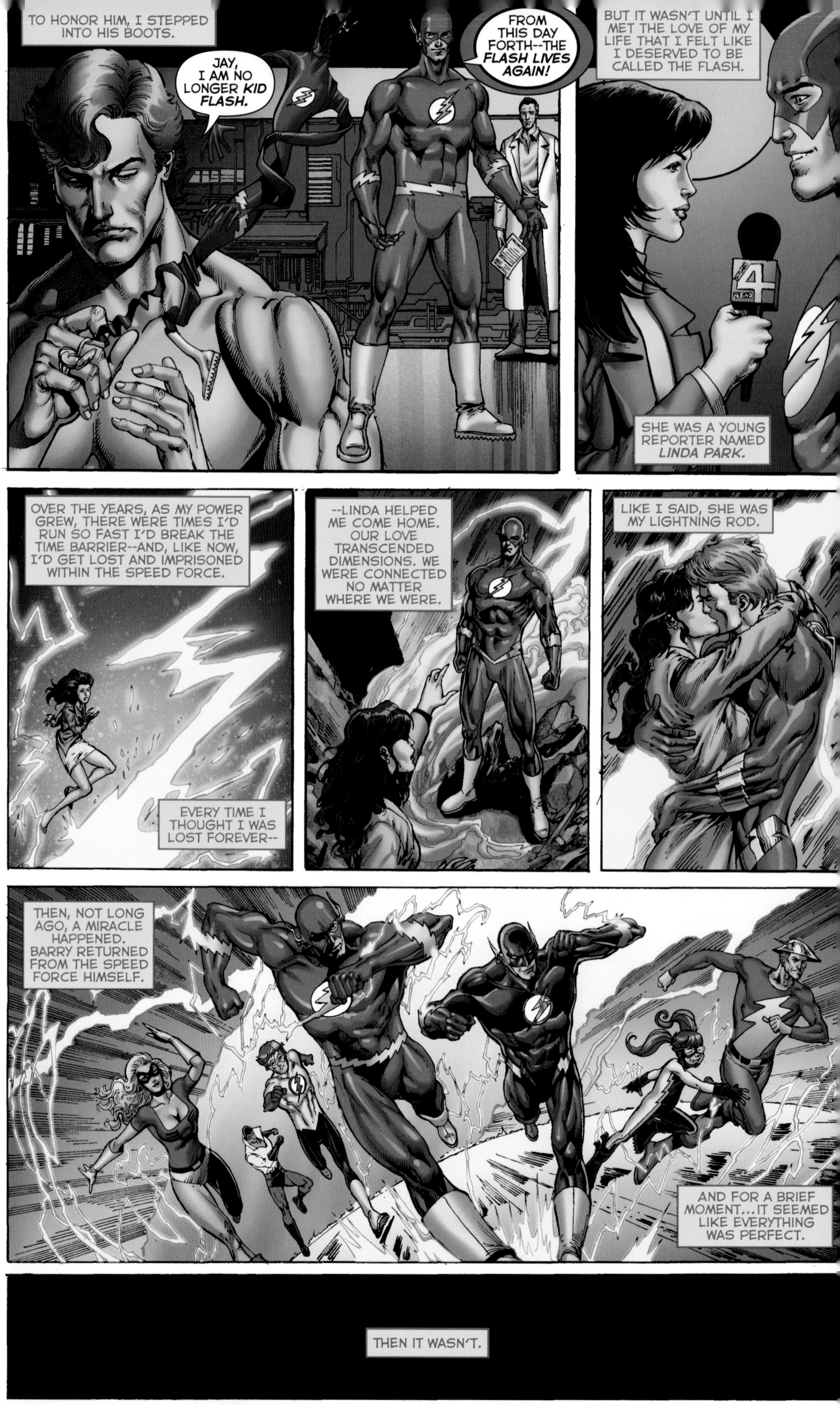
TO HONOR HIM, I STEPPED INTO HIS BOOTS.
JAY, I AM NO LONGER KID FLASH.
FROM THIS DAY FORTH--THE FLASH LIVES AGAIN!
BUT IT WASN'T UNTIL I MET THE LOVE OF MY LIFE THAT I FELT LIKE I DESERVED TO BE CALLED THE FLASH.
4 NEWS
SHE WAS A YOUNG REPORTER NAMED LINDA PARK.
OVER THE YEARS, AS MY POWER GREW, THERE WERE TIMES I'D RUN SO FAST I'D BREAK THE TIME BARRIER--AND, LIKE NOW, I'D GET LOST AND IMPRISONED WITHIN THE SPEED FORCE.
EVERY TIME I THOUGHT I WAS LOST FOREVER--
--LINDA HELPED ME COME HOME. OUR LOVE TRANSCENDED DIMENSIONS. WE WERE CONNECTED NO MATTER WHERE WE WERE.
LIKE I SAID, SHE WAS MY LIGHTNING ROD.
THEN, NOT LONG AGO, A MIRACLE HAPPENED. BARRY RETURNED FROM THE SPEED FORCE HIMSELF.
AND FOR A BRIEF MOMENT...IT SEEMED LIKE EVERYTHING WAS PERFECT.
THEN IT WASN'T.

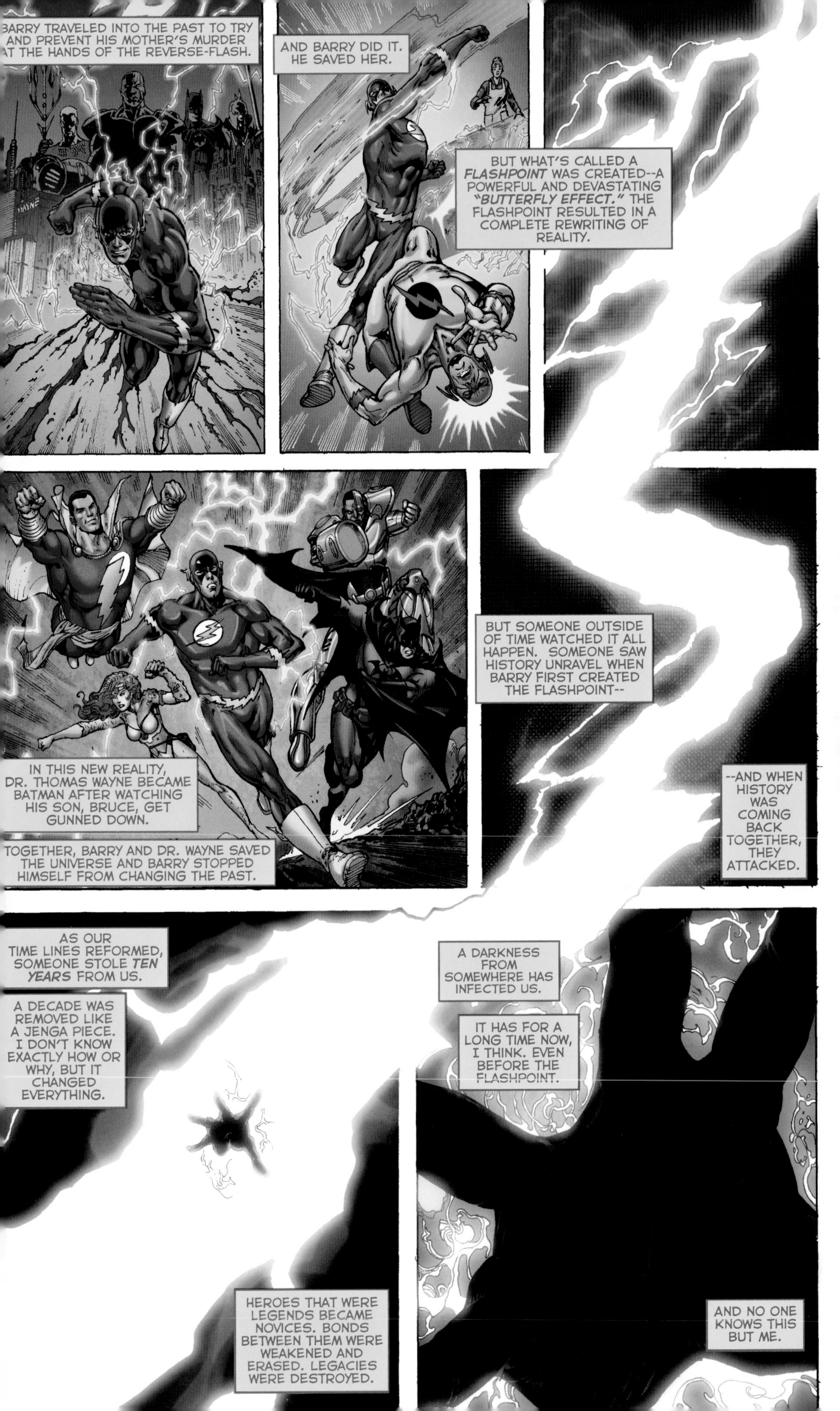
BARRY TRAVELED INTO THE PAST TO TRY AND PREVENT HIS MOTHER'S MURDER AT THE HANDS OF THE REVERSE-FLASH.
AND BARRY DID IT. HE SAVED HER.
BUT WHAT'S CALLED A *FLASHPOINT* WAS CREATED--A POWERFUL AND DEVASTATING ***"BUTTERFLY EFFECT."*** THE FLASHPOINT RESULTED IN A COMPLETE REWRITING OF REALITY.
IN THIS NEW REALITY, DR. THOMAS WAYNE BECAME BATMAN AFTER WATCHING HIS SON, BRUCE, GET GUNNED DOWN.
TOGETHER, BARRY AND DR. WAYNE SAVED THE UNIVERSE AND BARRY STOPPED HIMSELF FROM CHANGING THE PAST.
BUT SOMEONE OUTSIDE OF TIME WATCHED IT ALL HAPPEN. SOMEONE SAW HISTORY UNRAVEL WHEN BARRY FIRST CREATED THE FLASHPOINT--
--AND WHEN HISTORY WAS COMING BACK TOGETHER, THEY ATTACKED.
AS OUR TIME LINES REFORMED, SOMEONE STOLE ***TEN YEARS*** FROM US.
A DECADE WAS REMOVED LIKE A JENGA PIECE. I DON'T KNOW EXACTLY HOW OR WHY, BUT IT CHANGED EVERYTHING.
HEROES THAT WERE LEGENDS BECAME NOVICES. BONDS BETWEEN THEM WERE WEAKENED AND ERASED. LEGACIES WERE DESTROYED.
A DARKNESS FROM SOMEWHERE HAS INFECTED US.
IT HAS FOR A LONG TIME NOW, I THINK. EVEN BEFORE THE FLASHPOINT.
AND NO ONE KNOWS THIS BUT ME.

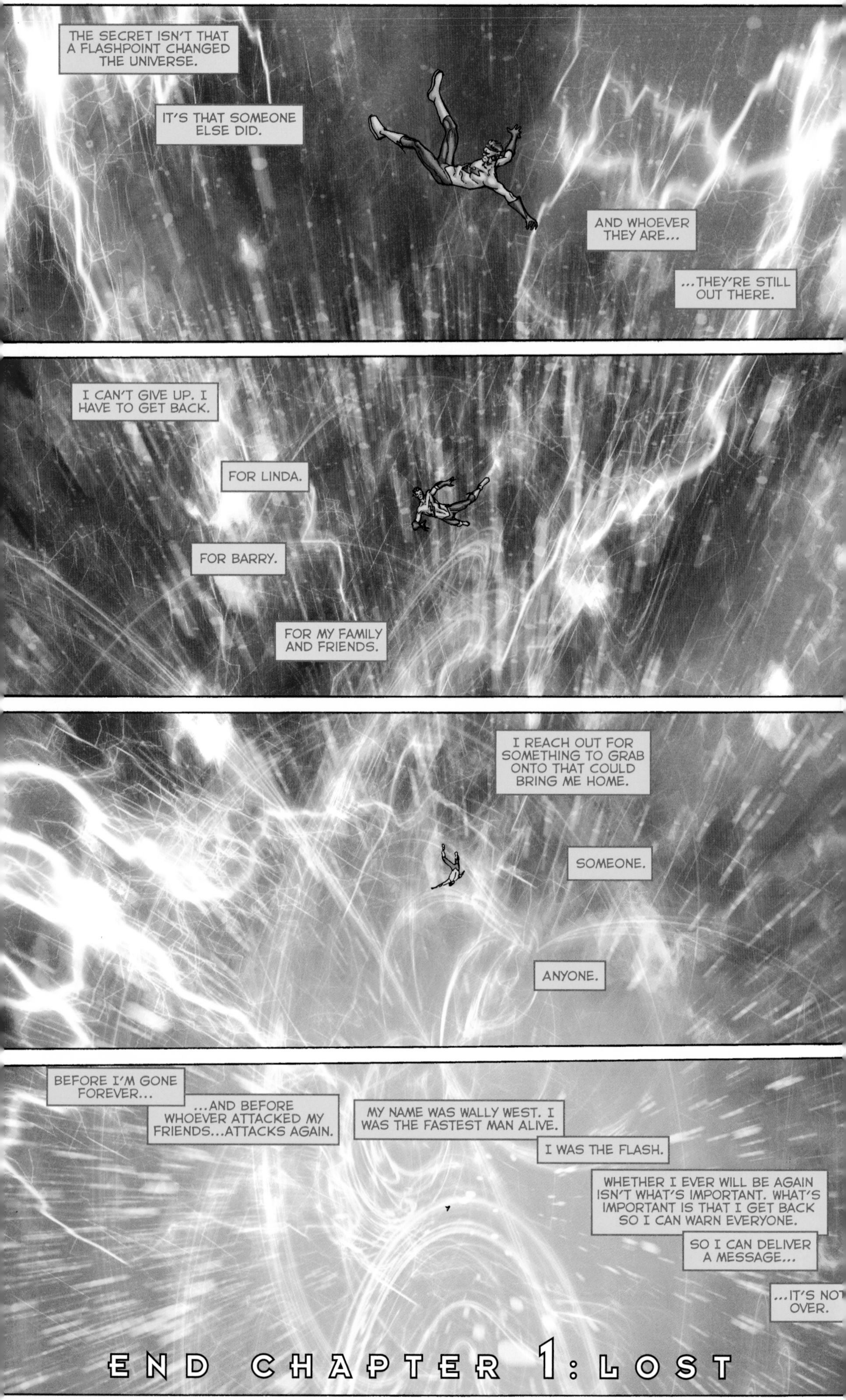
THE SECRET ISN'T THAT A FLASHPOINT CHANGED THE UNIVERSE.
IT'S THAT SOMEONE ELSE DID.
AND WHOEVER THEY ARE...
...THEY'RE STILL OUT THERE.
I CAN'T GIVE UP. I HAVE TO GET BACK.
FOR LINDA.
FOR BARRY.
FOR MY FAMILY AND FRIENDS.
I REACH OUT FOR SOMETHING TO GRAB ONTO THAT COULD BRING ME HOME.
SOMEONE.
ANYONE.
BEFORE I'M GONE FOREVER...
...AND BEFORE WHOEVER ATTACKED MY FRIENDS...ATTACKS AGAIN.
MY NAME WAS WALLY WEST. I WAS THE FASTEST MAN ALIVE.
I WAS THE FLASH.
WHETHER I EVER WILL BE AGAIN ISN'T WHAT'S IMPORTANT. WHAT'S IMPORTANT IS THAT I GET BACK SO I CAN WARN EVERYONE.
SO I CAN DELIVER A MESSAGE...
...IT'S NOT OVER.
END CHAPTER 1: LOST

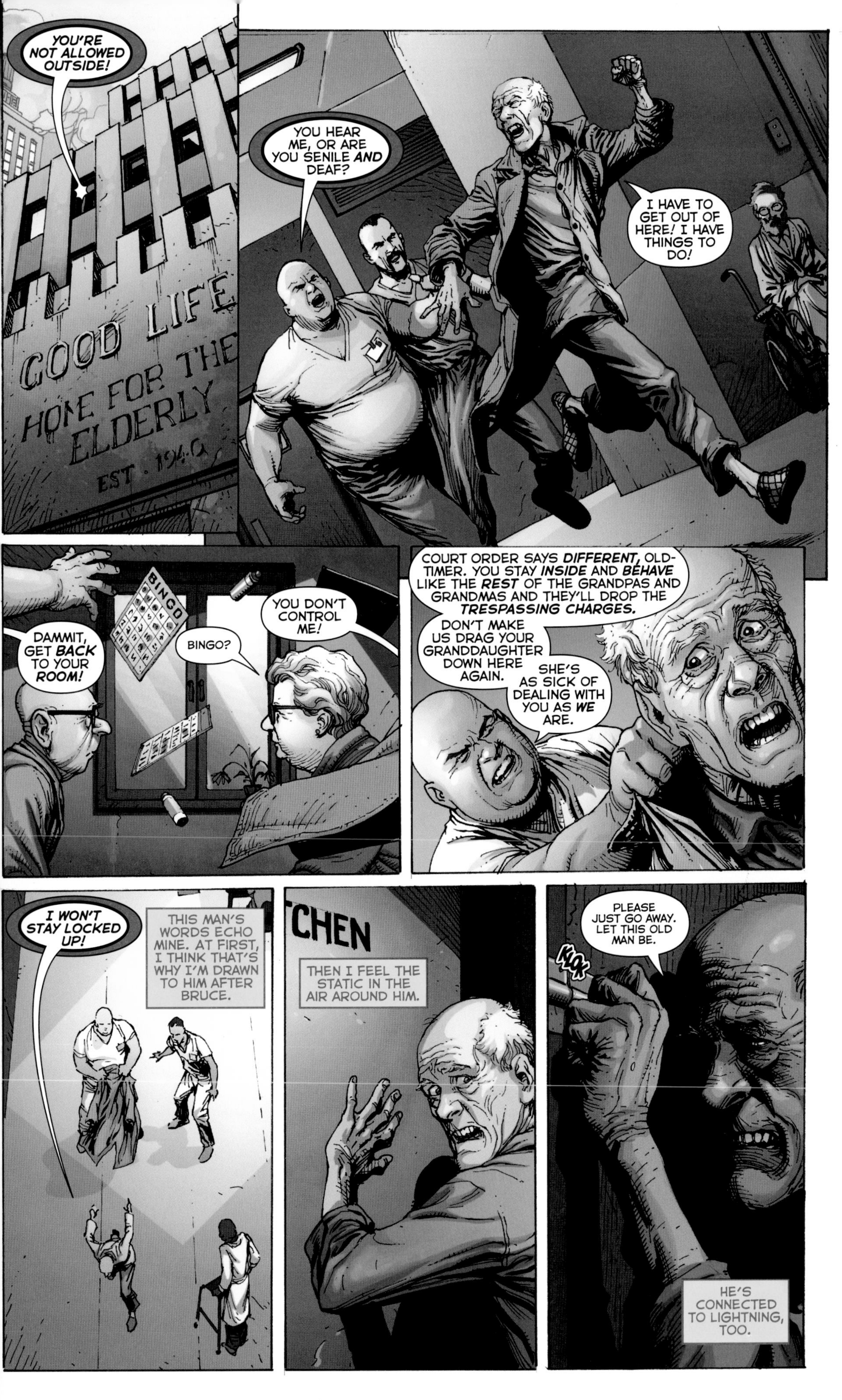
YOU'RE NOT ALLOWED OUTSIDE!
GOOD LIFE HOME FOR THE ELDERLY EST. 1940
YOU HEAR ME, OR ARE YOU SENILE AND DEAF?
I HAVE TO GET OUT OF HERE! I HAVE THINGS TO DO!
BINGO
DAMMIT, GET BACK TO YOUR ROOM!
BINGO?
YOU DON'T CONTROL ME!
COURT ORDER SAYS DIFFERENT, OLD-TIMER. YOU STAY INSIDE AND BEHAVE LIKE THE REST OF THE GRANDPAS AND GRANDMAS AND THEY'LL DROP THE TRESPASSING CHARGES.
DON'T MAKE US DRAG YOUR GRANDDAUGHTER DOWN HERE AGAIN.
SHE'S AS SICK OF DEALING WITH YOU AS WE ARE.
I WON'T STAY LOCKED UP!
THIS MAN'S WORDS ECHO MINE. AT FIRST, I THINK THAT'S WHY I'M DRAWN TO HIM AFTER BRUCE.
TCHEN
THEN I FEEL THE STATIC IN THE AIR AROUND HIM.
PLEASE JUST GO AWAY. LET THIS OLD MAN BE.
KLIK
HE'S CONNECTED TO LIGHTNING, TOO.

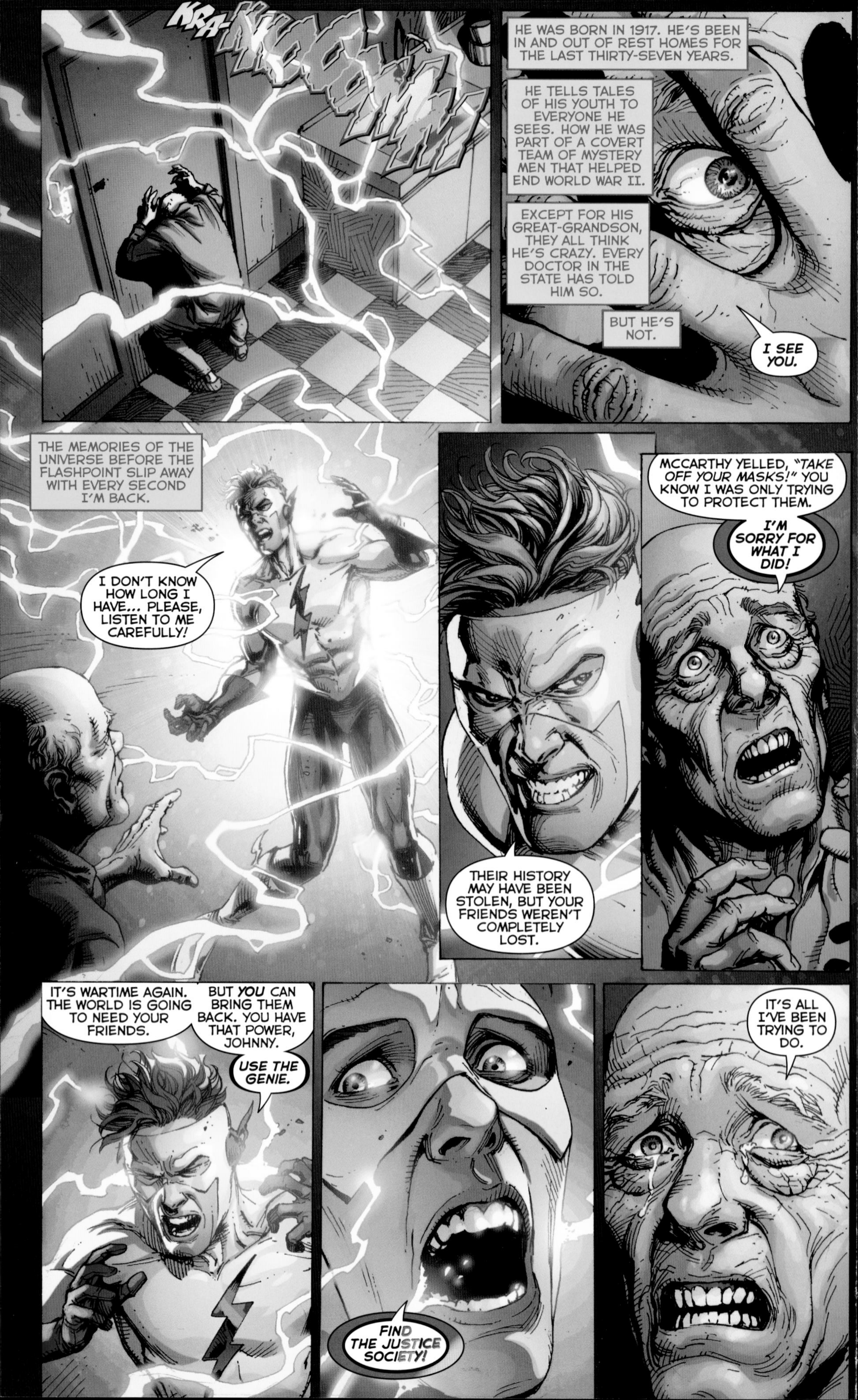
KRA-KOOOM!
HE WAS BORN IN 1917. HE'S BEEN IN AND OUT OF REST HOMES FOR THE LAST THIRTY-SEVEN YEARS.
HE TELLS TALES OF HIS YOUTH TO EVERYONE HE SEES. HOW HE WAS PART OF A COVERT TEAM OF MYSTERY MEN THAT HELPED END WORLD WAR II.
EXCEPT FOR HIS GREAT-GRANDSON, THEY ALL THINK HE'S CRAZY. EVERY DOCTOR IN THE STATE HAS TOLD HIM SO.
BUT HE'S NOT.
I SEE YOU.
THE MEMORIES OF THE UNIVERSE BEFORE THE FLASHPOINT SLIP AWAY WITH EVERY SECOND I'M BACK.
I DON'T KNOW HOW LONG I HAVE... PLEASE, LISTEN TO ME CAREFULLY!
THEIR HISTORY MAY HAVE BEEN STOLEN, BUT YOUR FRIENDS WEREN'T COMPLETELY LOST.
MCCARTHY YELLED, "*TAKE OFF YOUR MASKS!*" YOU KNOW I WAS ONLY TRYING TO PROTECT THEM.
I'M SORRY FOR WHAT I DID!
IT'S WARTIME AGAIN. THE WORLD IS GOING TO NEED YOUR FRIENDS.
BUT *YOU* CAN BRING THEM BACK. YOU HAVE THAT POWER, JOHNNY.
USE THE GENIE.
FIND THE JUSTICE SOCIETY!
IT'S ALL I'VE BEEN TRYING TO DO.

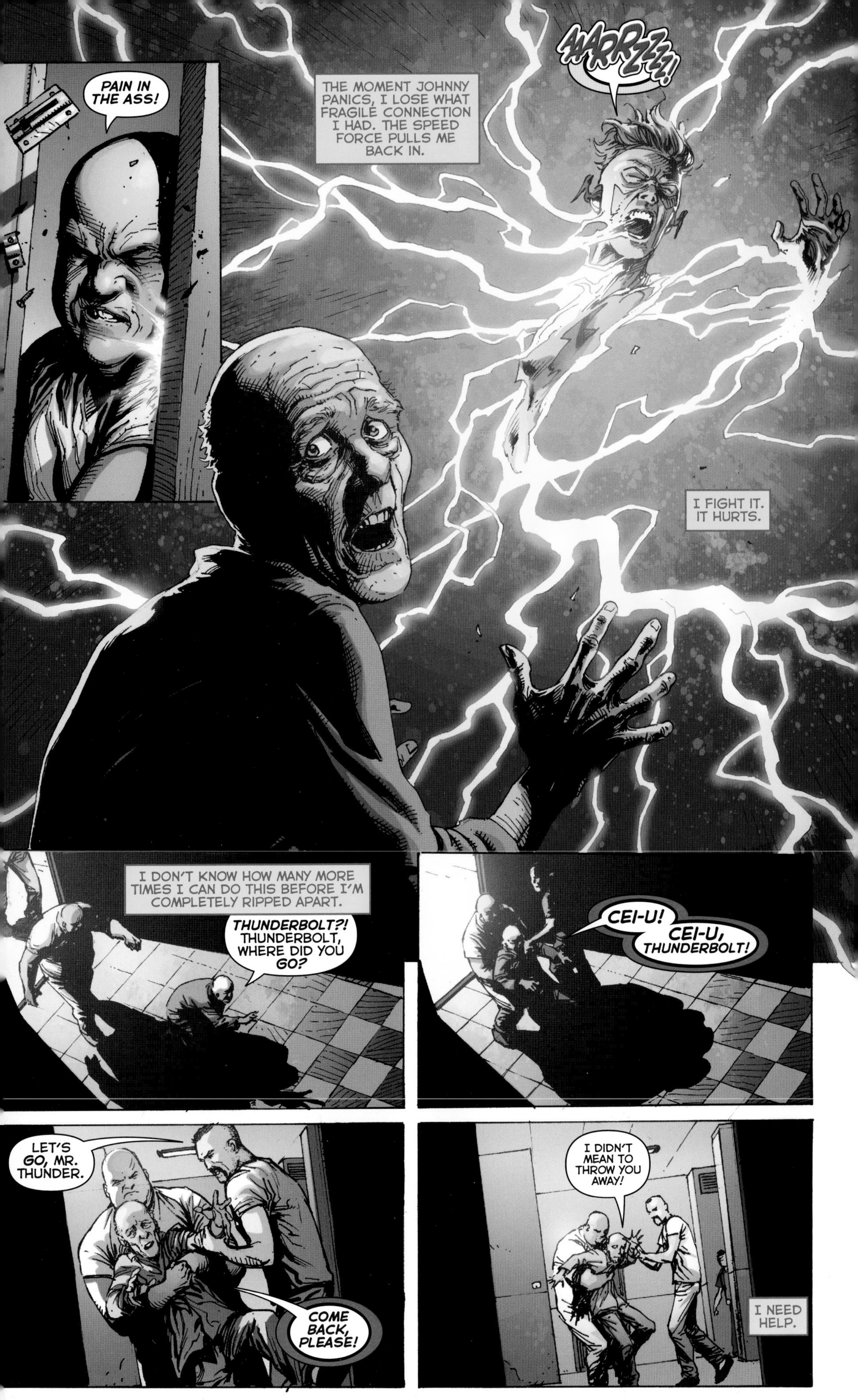
PAIN IN THE ASS!
THE MOMENT JOHNNY PANICS, I LOSE WHAT FRAGILE CONNECTION I HAD. THE SPEED FORCE PULLS ME BACK IN.
AARRZZZZ!
I FIGHT IT. IT HURTS.
I DON'T KNOW HOW MANY MORE TIMES I CAN DO THIS BEFORE I'M COMPLETELY RIPPED APART.
THUNDERBOLT?! THUNDERBOLT, WHERE DID YOU GO?
CEI-U!
CEI-U, THUNDERBOLT!
LET'S GO, MR. THUNDER.
COME BACK, PLEASE!
I DIDN'T MEAN TO THROW YOU AWAY!
I NEED HELP.

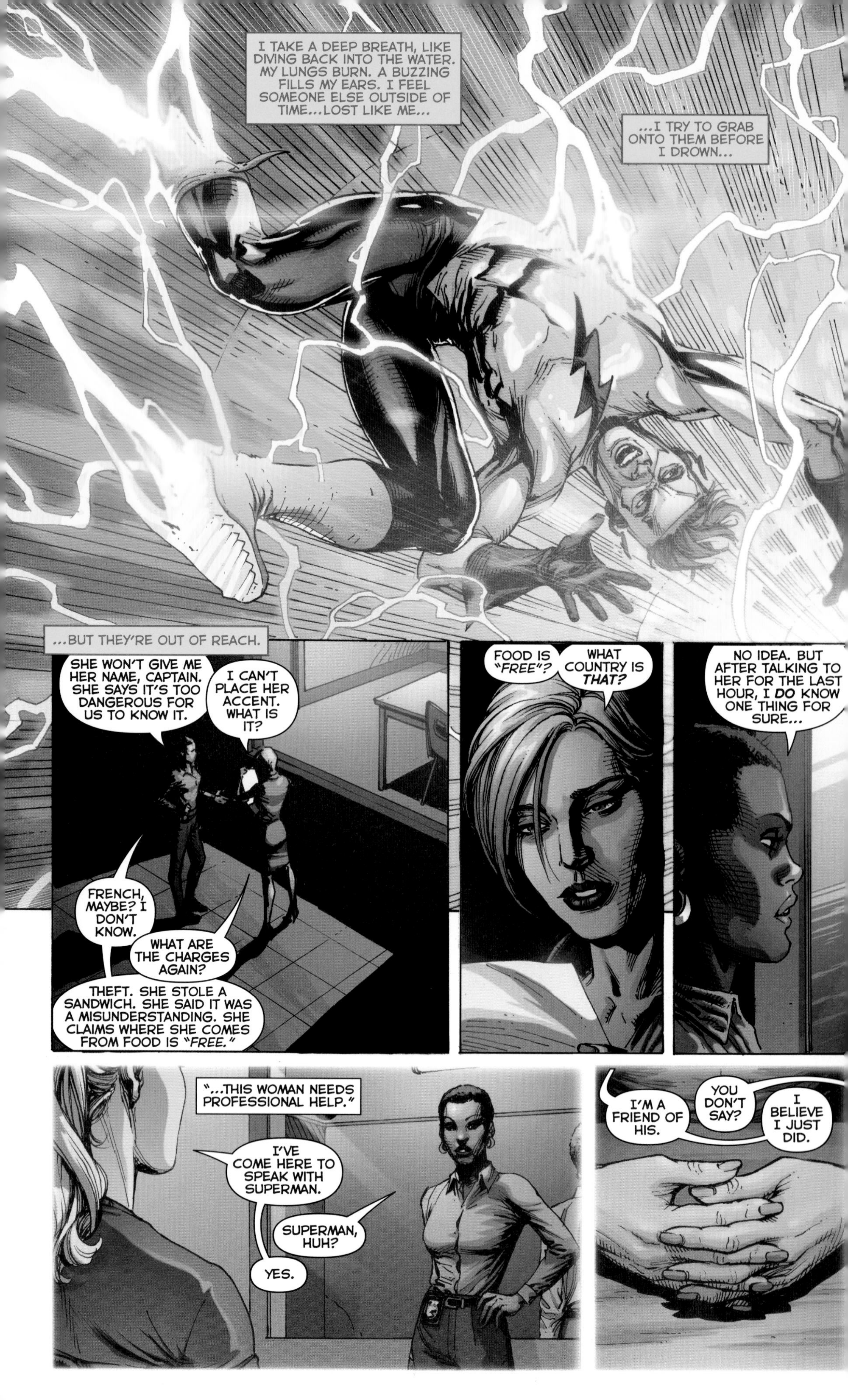

I TAKE A DEEP BREATH, LIKE DIVING BACK INTO THE WATER. MY LUNGS BURN. A BUZZING FILLS MY EARS. I FEEL SOMEONE ELSE OUTSIDE OF TIME...LOST LIKE ME...
...I TRY TO GRAB ONTO THEM BEFORE I DROWN...
...BUT THEY'RE OUT OF REACH.
SHE WON'T GIVE ME HER NAME, CAPTAIN. SHE SAYS IT'S TOO DANGEROUS FOR US TO KNOW IT.
I CAN'T PLACE HER ACCENT. WHAT IS IT?
FRENCH, MAYBE? I DON'T KNOW.
WHAT ARE THE CHARGES AGAIN?
THEFT. SHE STOLE A SANDWICH. SHE SAID IT WAS A MISUNDERSTANDING. SHE CLAIMS WHERE SHE COMES FROM FOOD IS "FREE."
FOOD IS "FREE"?
WHAT COUNTRY IS THAT?
NO IDEA. BUT AFTER TALKING TO HER FOR THE LAST HOUR, I DO KNOW ONE THING FOR SURE...
"...THIS WOMAN NEEDS PROFESSIONAL HELP."
I'VE COME HERE TO SPEAK WITH SUPERMAN.
SUPERMAN, HUH?
YES.
I'M A FRIEND OF HIS.
YOU DON'T SAY?
I BELIEVE I JUST DID.

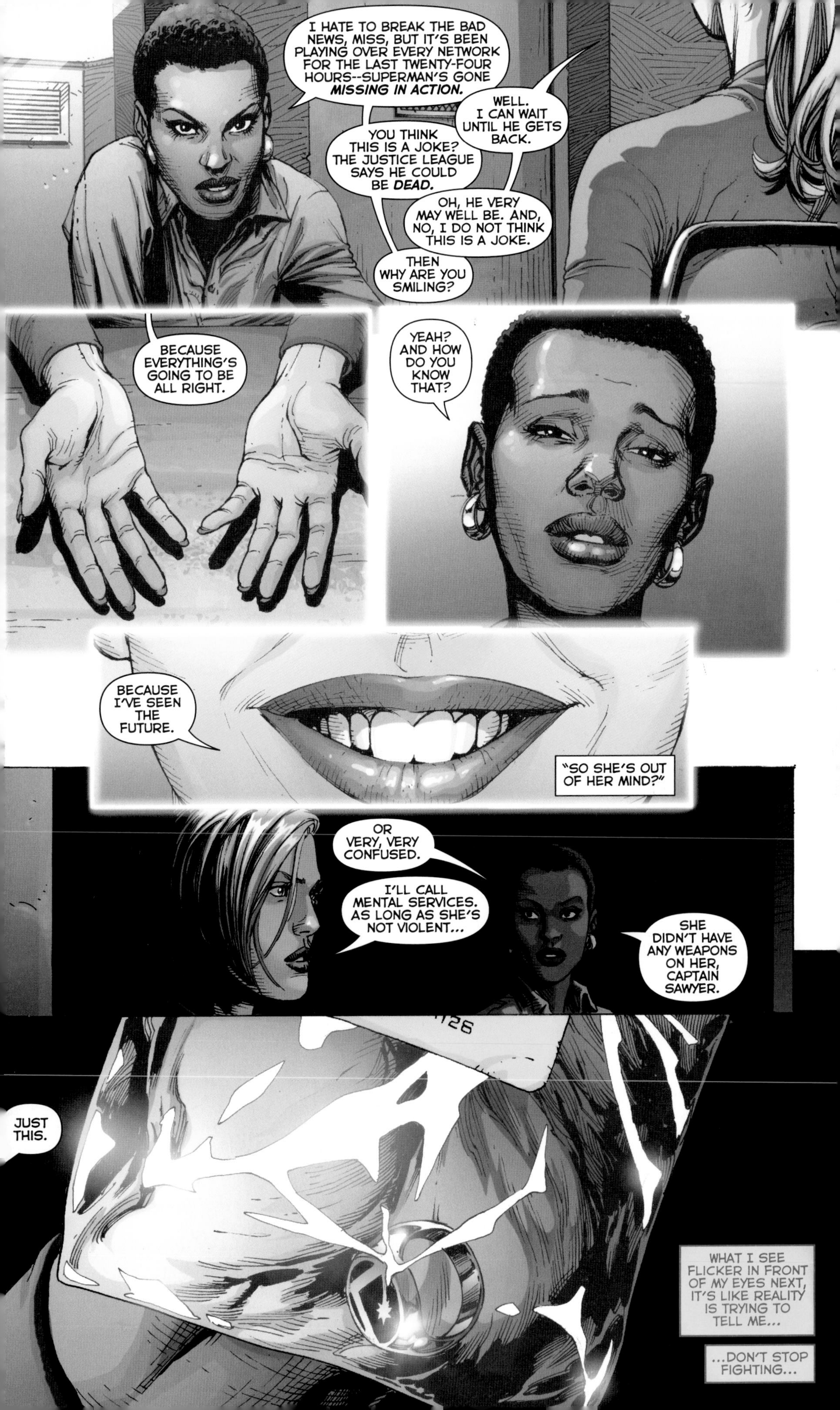

I HATE TO BREAK THE BAD NEWS, MISS, BUT IT'S BEEN PLAYING OVER EVERY NETWORK FOR THE LAST TWENTY-FOUR HOURS--SUPERMAN'S GONE MISSING IN ACTION.
WELL. I CAN WAIT UNTIL HE GETS BACK.
YOU THINK THIS IS A JOKE? THE JUSTICE LEAGUE SAYS HE COULD BE DEAD.
OH, HE VERY MAY WELL BE. AND, NO, I DO NOT THINK THIS IS A JOKE.
THEN WHY ARE YOU SMILING?
BECAUSE EVERYTHING'S GOING TO BE ALL RIGHT.
YEAH? AND HOW DO YOU KNOW THAT?
BECAUSE I'VE SEEN THE FUTURE.
"SO SHE'S OUT OF HER MIND?"
OR VERY, VERY CONFUSED.
I'LL CALL MENTAL SERVICES. AS LONG AS SHE'S NOT VIOLENT...
SHE DIDN'T HAVE ANY WEAPONS ON HER, CAPTAIN SAWYER.
JUST THIS.
WHAT I SEE FLICKER IN FRONT OF MY EYES NEXT, IT'S LIKE REALITY IS TRYING TO TELL ME...
...DON'T STOP FIGHTING...

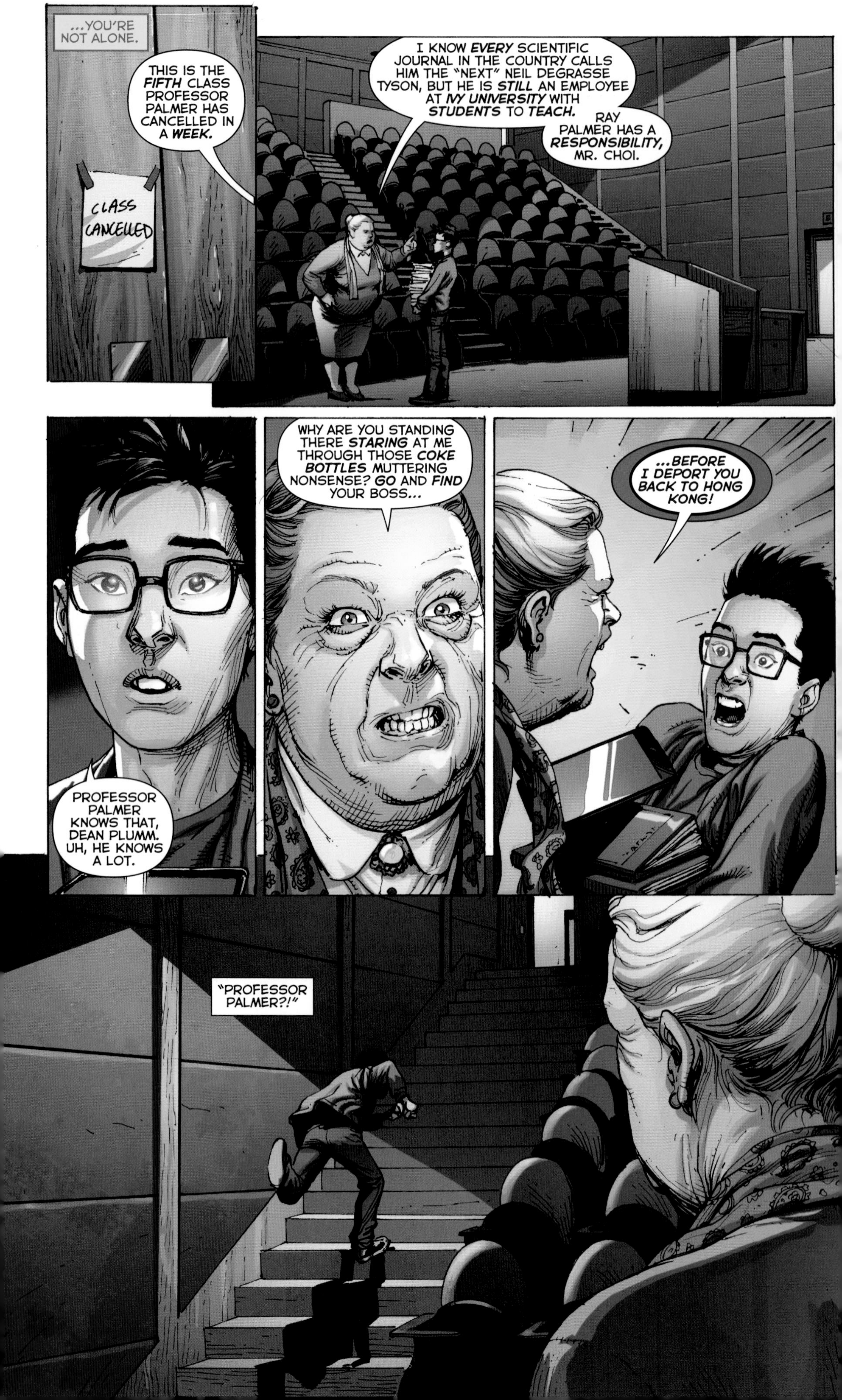
...YOU'RE NOT ALONE.
THIS IS THE FIFTH CLASS PROFESSOR PALMER HAS CANCELLED IN A WEEK.
CLASS CANCELLED
I KNOW EVERY SCIENTIFIC JOURNAL IN THE COUNTRY CALLS HIM THE "NEXT" NEIL DEGRASSE TYSON, BUT HE IS STILL AN EMPLOYEE AT IVY UNIVERSITY WITH STUDENTS TO TEACH.
RAY PALMER HAS A RESPONSIBILITY, MR. CHOI.
PROFESSOR PALMER KNOWS THAT, DEAN PLUMM. UH, HE KNOWS A LOT.
WHY ARE YOU STANDING THERE STARING AT ME THROUGH THOSE COKE BOTTLES MUTTERING NONSENSE? GO AND FIND YOUR BOSS...
...BEFORE I DEPORT YOU BACK TO HONG KONG!
"PROFESSOR PALMER?!"

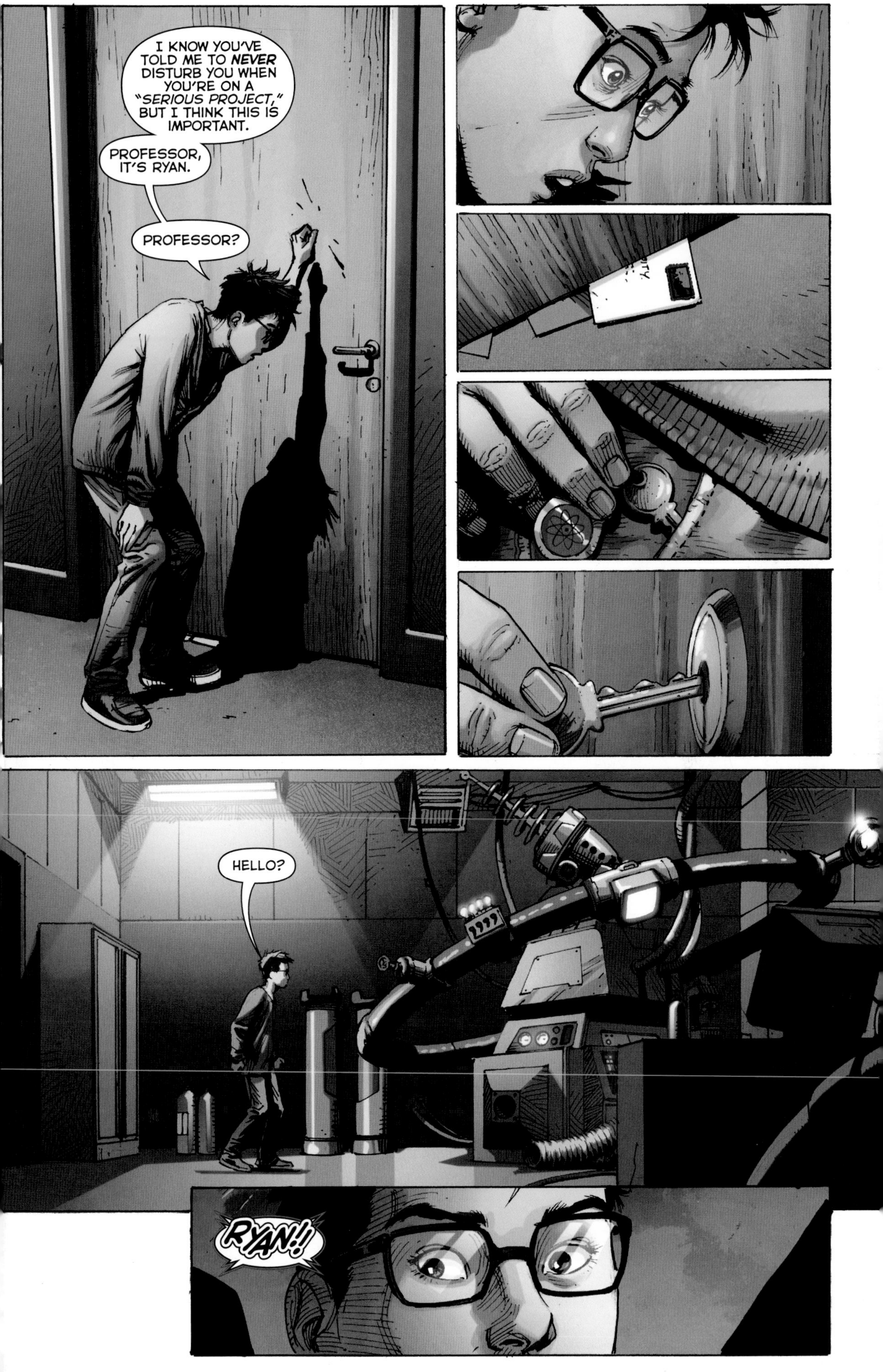

I KNOW YOU'VE TOLD ME TO ***NEVER*** DISTURB YOU WHEN YOU'RE ON A *"SERIOUS PROJECT,"* BUT I THINK THIS IS IMPORTANT.
PROFESSOR, IT'S RYAN.
PROFESSOR?
HELLO?
RYAN!!

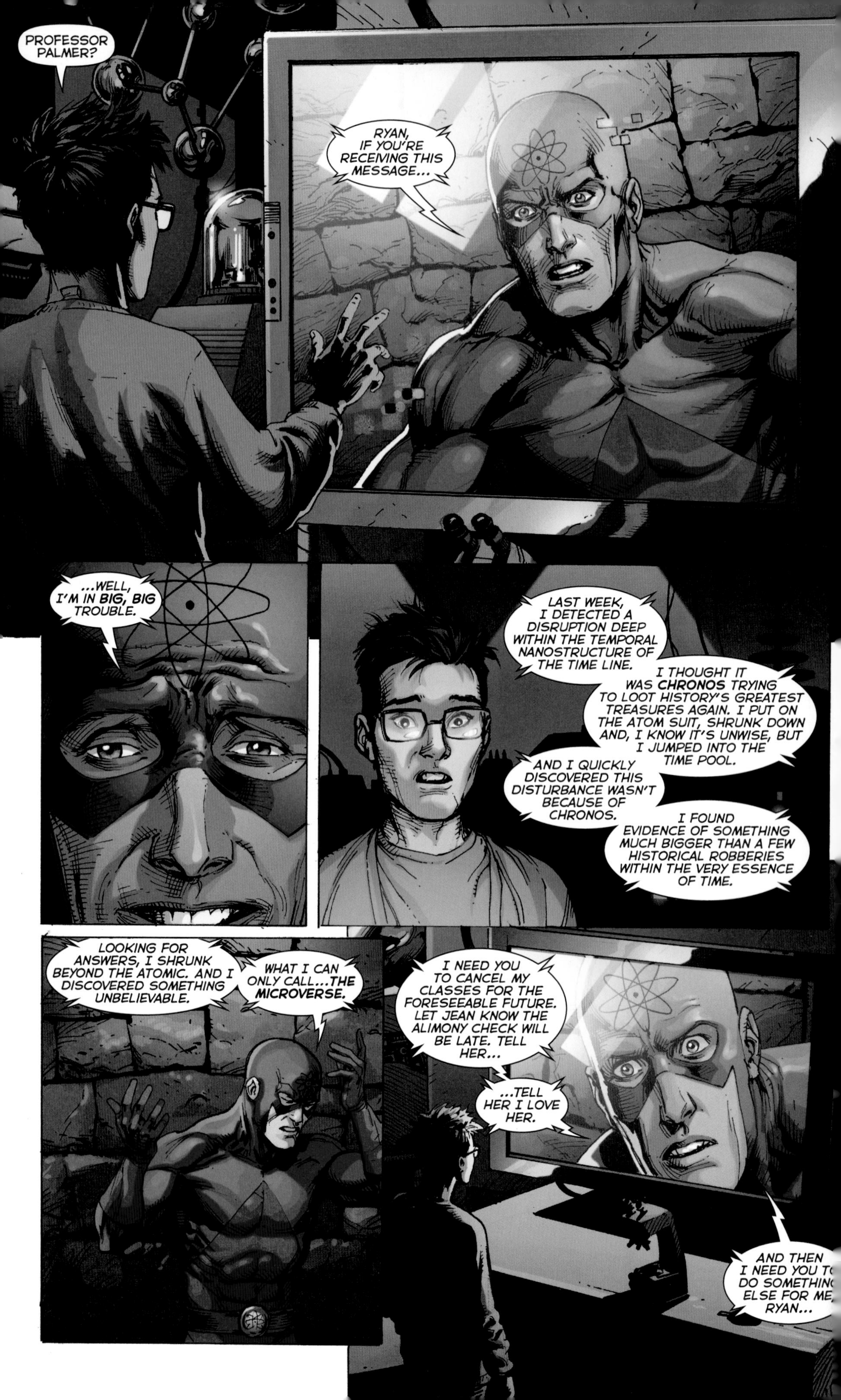
PROFESSOR PALMER?
RYAN, IF YOU'RE RECEIVING THIS MESSAGE...
...WELL, I'M IN BIG, BIG TROUBLE.
LAST WEEK, I DETECTED A DISRUPTION DEEP WITHIN THE TEMPORAL NANOSTRUCTURE OF THE TIME LINE.
I THOUGHT IT WAS CHRONOS TRYING TO LOOT HISTORY'S GREATEST TREASURES AGAIN. I PUT ON THE ATOM SUIT, SHRUNK DOWN AND, I KNOW IT'S UNWISE, BUT I JUMPED INTO THE TIME POOL.
AND I QUICKLY DISCOVERED THIS DISTURBANCE WASN'T BECAUSE OF CHRONOS.
I FOUND EVIDENCE OF SOMETHING MUCH BIGGER THAN A FEW HISTORICAL ROBBERIES WITHIN THE VERY ESSENCE OF TIME.
LOOKING FOR ANSWERS, I SHRUNK BEYOND THE ATOMIC. AND I DISCOVERED SOMETHING UNBELIEVABLE.
WHAT I CAN ONLY CALL...THE MICROVERSE.
I NEED YOU TO CANCEL MY CLASSES FOR THE FORESEEABLE FUTURE. LET JEAN KNOW THE ALIMONY CHECK WILL BE LATE. TELL HER...
...TELL HER I LOVE HER.
AND THEN I NEED YOU TO DO SOMETHING ELSE FOR ME, RYAN...

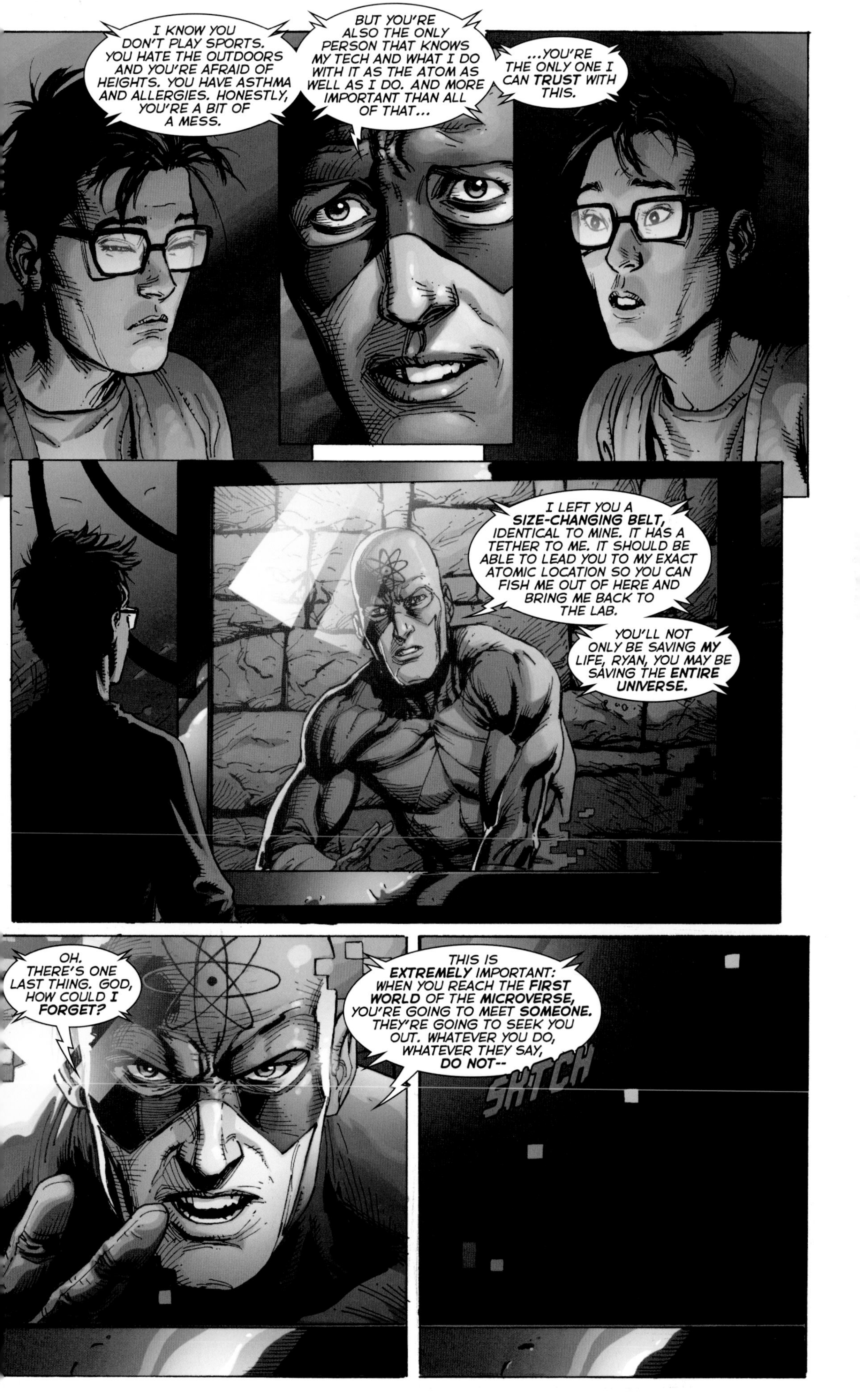
I KNOW YOU DON'T PLAY SPORTS. YOU HATE THE OUTDOORS AND YOU'RE AFRAID OF HEIGHTS. YOU HAVE ASTHMA AND ALLERGIES. HONESTLY, YOU'RE A BIT OF A MESS.
BUT YOU'RE ALSO THE ONLY PERSON THAT KNOWS MY TECH AND WHAT I DO WITH IT AS THE ATOM AS WELL AS I DO. AND MORE IMPORTANT THAN ALL OF THAT...
...YOU'RE THE ONLY ONE I CAN TRUST WITH THIS.
I LEFT YOU A SIZE-CHANGING BELT, IDENTICAL TO MINE. IT HAS A TETHER TO ME. IT SHOULD BE ABLE TO LEAD YOU TO MY EXACT ATOMIC LOCATION SO YOU CAN FISH ME OUT OF HERE AND BRING ME BACK TO THE LAB.
YOU'LL NOT ONLY BE SAVING MY LIFE, RYAN, YOU MAY BE SAVING THE ENTIRE UNIVERSE.
OH. THERE'S ONE LAST THING. GOD, HOW COULD I FORGET?
THIS IS EXTREMELY IMPORTANT: WHEN YOU REACH THE FIRST WORLD OF THE MICROVERSE, YOU'RE GOING TO MEET SOMEONE. THEY'RE GOING TO SEEK YOU OUT. WHATEVER YOU DO, WHATEVER THEY SAY, DO NOT--
SHTCH

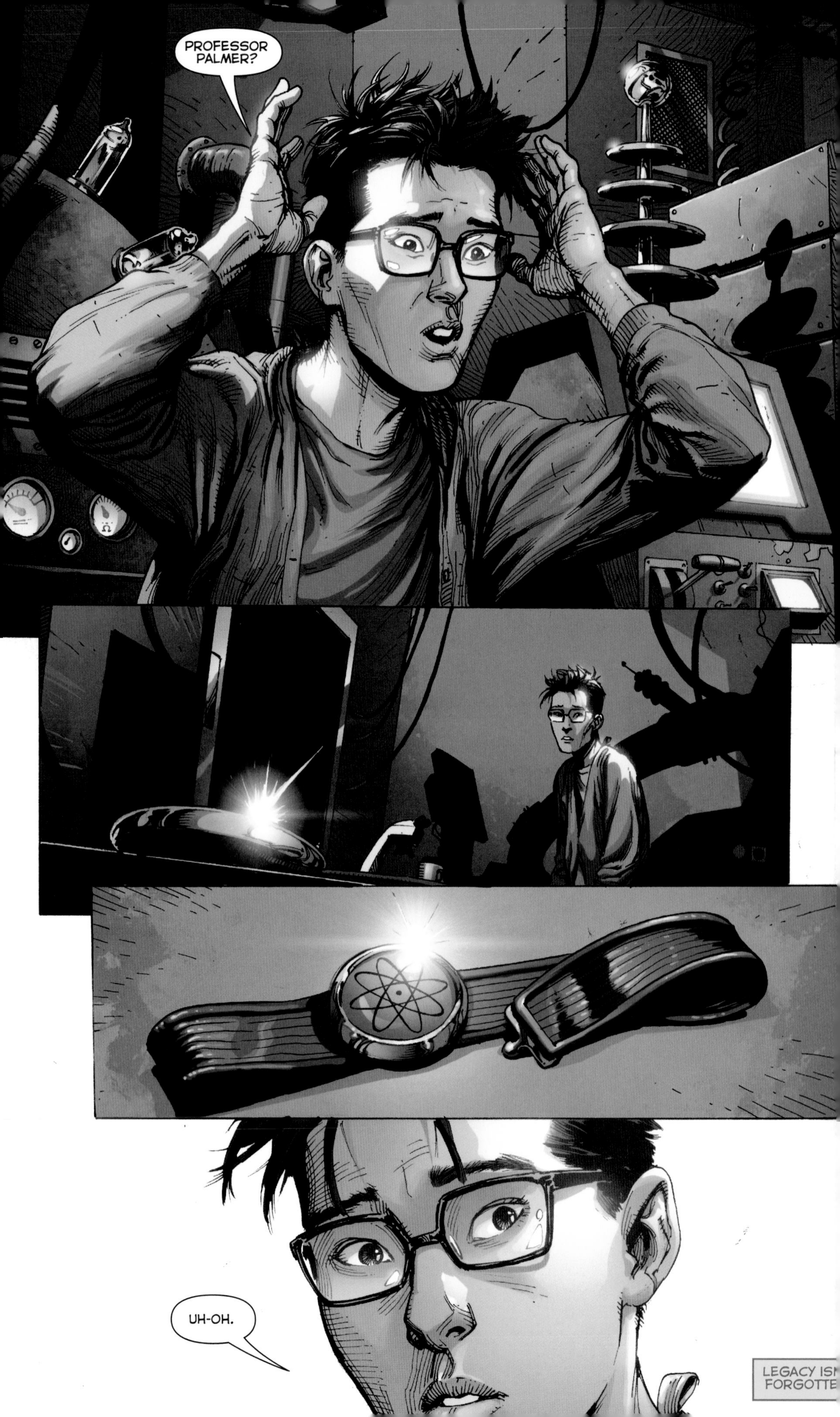
PROFESSOR PALMER?
UH-OH.

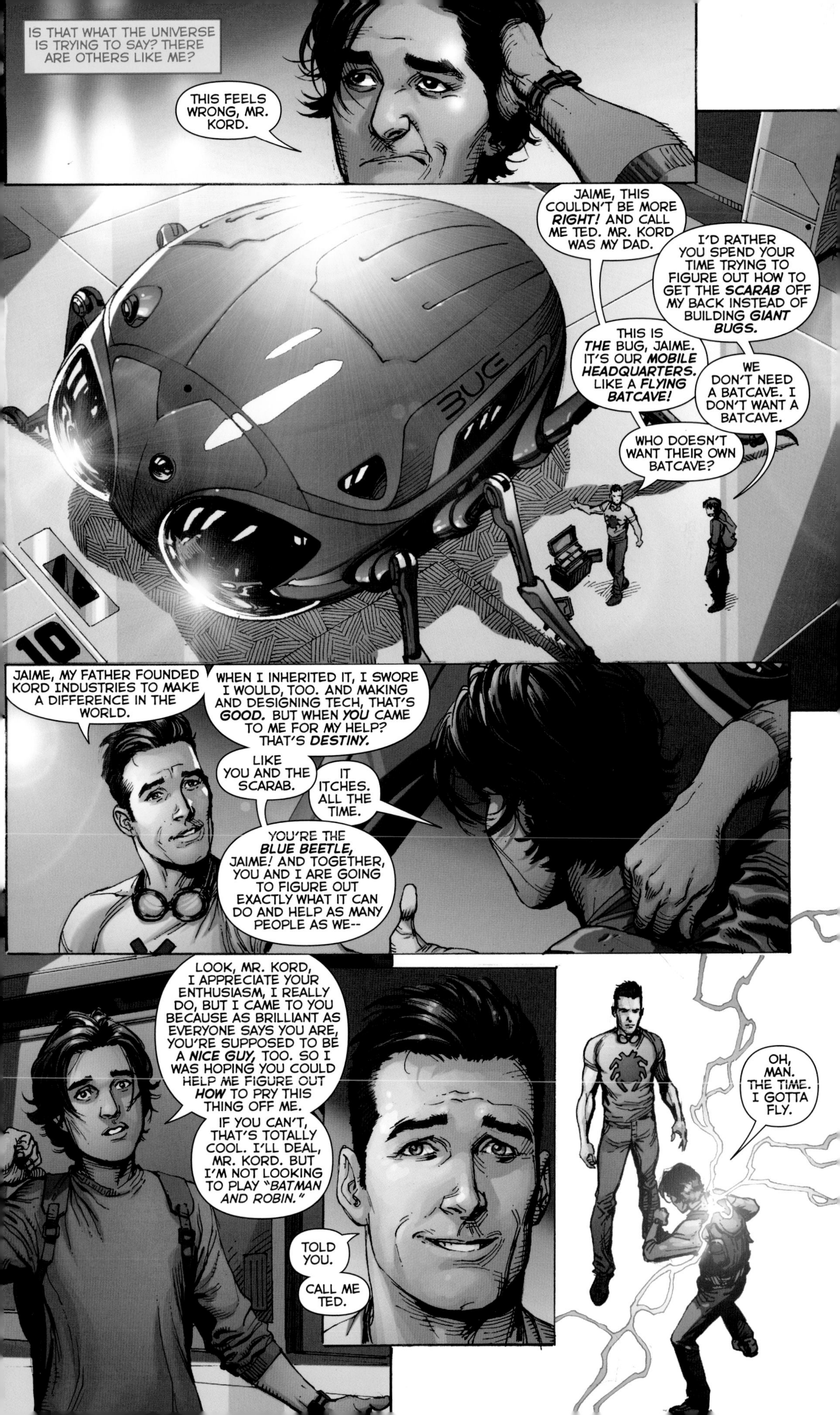
IS THAT WHAT THE UNIVERSE IS TRYING TO SAY? THERE ARE OTHERS LIKE ME?
THIS FEELS WRONG, MR. KORD.
JAIME, THIS COULDN'T BE MORE RIGHT! AND CALL ME TED. MR. KORD WAS MY DAD.
I'D RATHER YOU SPEND YOUR TIME TRYING TO FIGURE OUT HOW TO GET THE SCARAB OFF MY BACK INSTEAD OF BUILDING GIANT BUGS.
THIS IS THE BUG, JAIME. IT'S OUR MOBILE HEADQUARTERS. LIKE A FLYING BATCAVE!
WE DON'T NEED A BATCAVE. I DON'T WANT A BATCAVE.
WHO DOESN'T WANT THEIR OWN BATCAVE?
BUG
10
JAIME, MY FATHER FOUNDED KORD INDUSTRIES TO MAKE A DIFFERENCE IN THE WORLD.
WHEN I INHERITED IT, I SWORE I WOULD, TOO. AND MAKING AND DESIGNING TECH, THAT'S GOOD. BUT WHEN YOU CAME TO ME FOR MY HELP? THAT'S DESTINY.
LIKE YOU AND THE SCARAB.
IT ITCHES. ALL THE TIME.
YOU'RE THE BLUE BEETLE, JAIME! AND TOGETHER, YOU AND I ARE GOING TO FIGURE OUT EXACTLY WHAT IT CAN DO AND HELP AS MANY PEOPLE AS WE--
LOOK, MR. KORD, I APPRECIATE YOUR ENTHUSIASM, I REALLY DO, BUT I CAME TO YOU BECAUSE AS BRILLIANT AS EVERYONE SAYS YOU ARE, YOU'RE SUPPOSED TO BE A NICE GUY, TOO. SO I WAS HOPING YOU COULD HELP ME FIGURE OUT HOW TO PRY THIS THING OFF ME.
IF YOU CAN'T, THAT'S TOTALLY COOL. I'LL DEAL, MR. KORD. BUT I'M NOT LOOKING TO PLAY "BATMAN AND ROBIN."
TOLD YOU.
CALL ME TED.
OH, MAN. THE TIME. I GOTTA FLY.

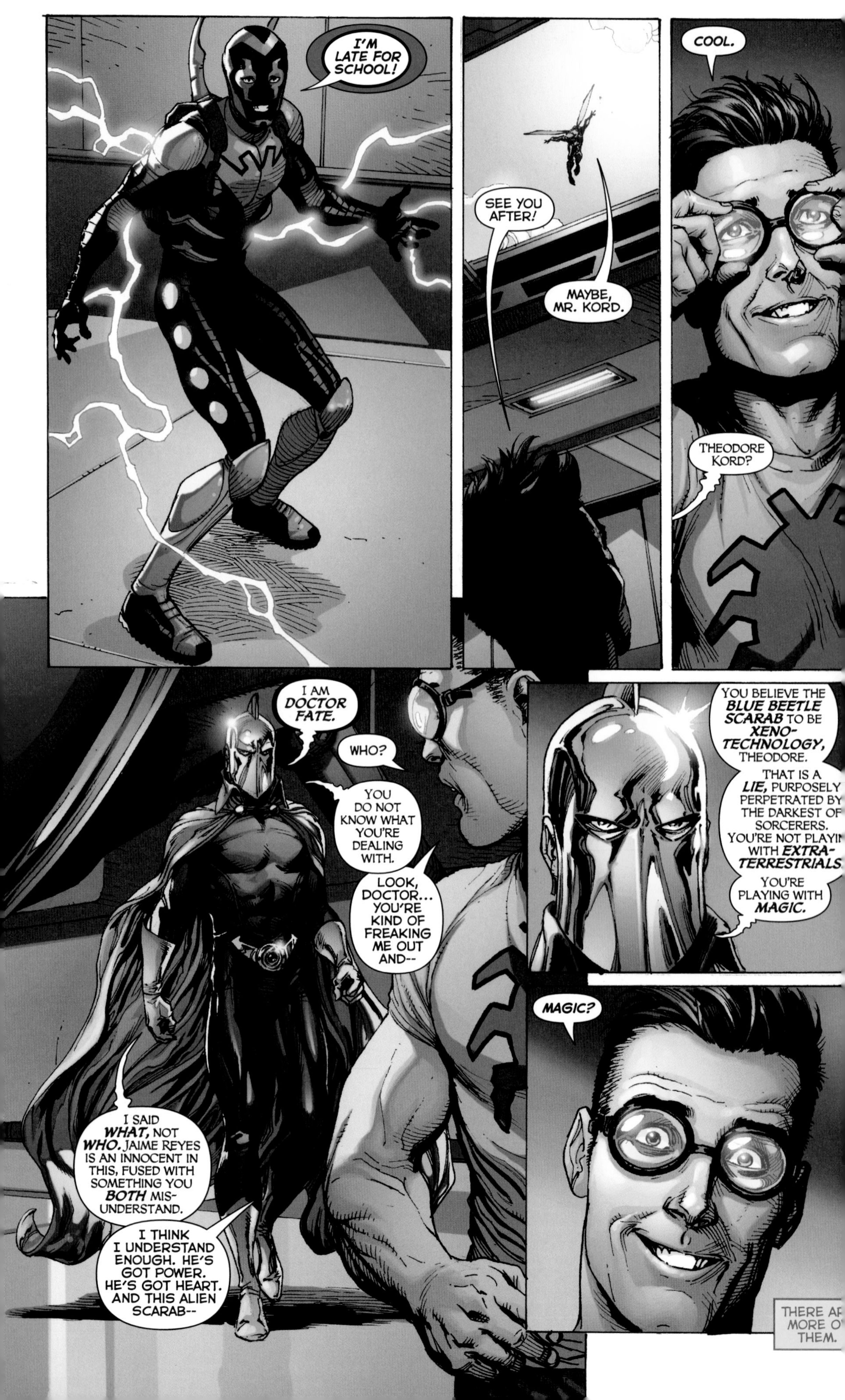
I'M LATE FOR SCHOOL!
SEE YOU AFTER!
MAYBE, MR. KORD.
COOL.
THEODORE KORD?
I AM DOCTOR FATE.
WHO?
YOU DO NOT KNOW WHAT YOU'RE DEALING WITH.
LOOK, DOCTOR... YOU'RE KIND OF FREAKING ME OUT AND--
I SAID WHAT, NOT WHO. JAIME REYES IS AN INNOCENT IN THIS, FUSED WITH SOMETHING YOU BOTH MIS-UNDERSTAND.
I THINK I UNDERSTAND ENOUGH. HE'S GOT POWER. HE'S GOT HEART. AND THIS ALIEN SCARAB--
YOU BELIEVE THE BLUE BEETLE SCARAB TO BE XENO-TECHNOLOGY, THEODORE.
THAT IS A LIE, PURPOSELY PERPETRATED BY THE DARKEST OF SORCERERS. YOU'RE NOT PLAYIN WITH EXTRA-TERRESTRIALS
YOU'RE PLAYING WITH MAGIC.
MAGIC?
THERE AR MORE O THEM.

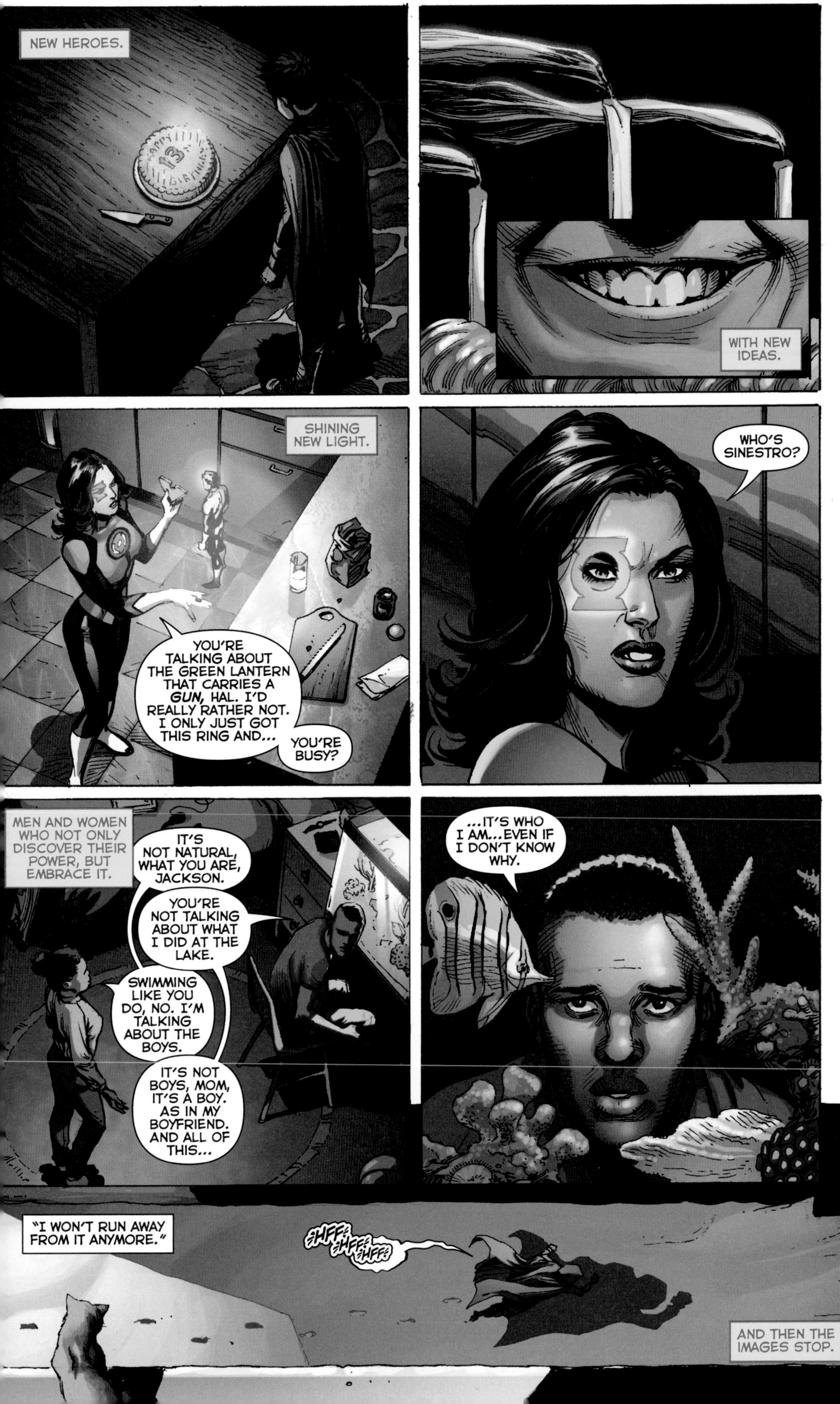
NEW HEROES.
WITH NEW IDEAS.
SHINING NEW LIGHT.
YOU'RE TALKING ABOUT THE GREEN LANTERN THAT CARRIES A GUN, HAL. I'D REALLY RATHER NOT. I ONLY JUST GOT THIS RING AND...
YOU'RE BUSY?
WHO'S SINESTRO?
MEN AND WOMEN WHO NOT ONLY DISCOVER THEIR POWER, BUT EMBRACE IT.
IT'S NOT NATURAL, WHAT YOU ARE, JACKSON.
YOU'RE NOT TALKING ABOUT WHAT I DID AT THE LAKE.
SWIMMING LIKE YOU DO, NO. I'M TALKING ABOUT THE BOYS.
IT'S NOT BOYS, MOM, IT'S A BOY. AS IN MY BOYFRIEND. AND ALL OF THIS...
...IT'S WHO I AM...EVEN IF I DON'T KNOW WHY.
"I WON'T RUN AWAY FROM IT ANYMORE."
HFF HFF HFF
AND THEN THE IMAGES STOP.

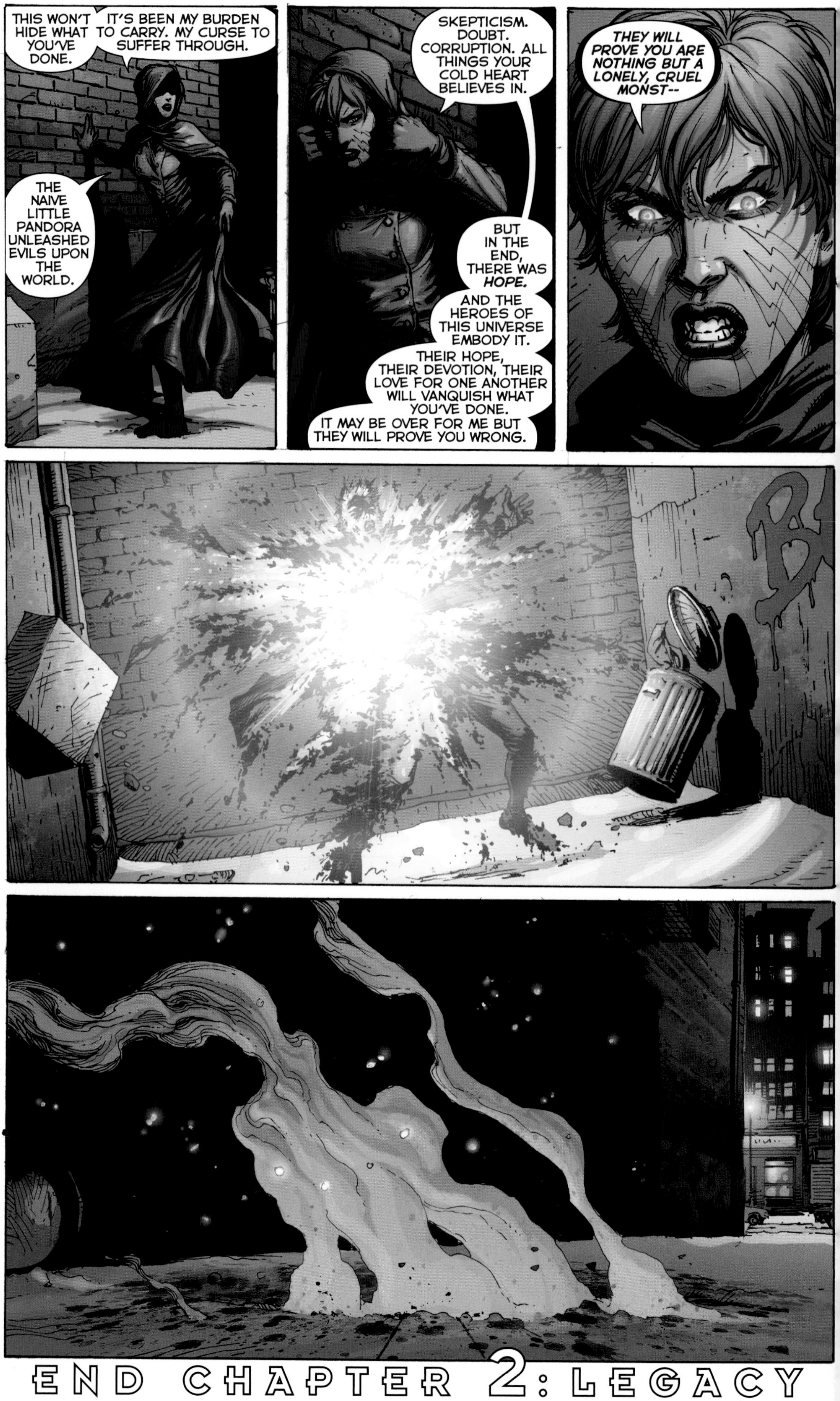
THIS WON'T HIDE WHAT YOU'VE DONE.
IT'S BEEN MY BURDEN TO CARRY. MY CURSE TO SUFFER THROUGH.
THE NAIVE LITTLE PANDORA UNLEASHED EVILS UPON THE WORLD.
SKEPTICISM. DOUBT. CORRUPTION. ALL THINGS YOUR COLD HEART BELIEVES IN.
BUT IN THE END, THERE WAS *HOPE.*
AND THE HEROES OF THIS UNIVERSE EMBODY IT.
THEIR HOPE, THEIR DEVOTION, THEIR LOVE FOR ONE ANOTHER WILL VANQUISH WHAT YOU'VE DONE.
IT MAY BE OVER FOR ME BUT THEY WILL PROVE YOU WRONG.
THEY WILL PROVE YOU ARE NOTHING BUT A LONELY, CRUEL MONST--

END CHAPTER 2: LEGACY

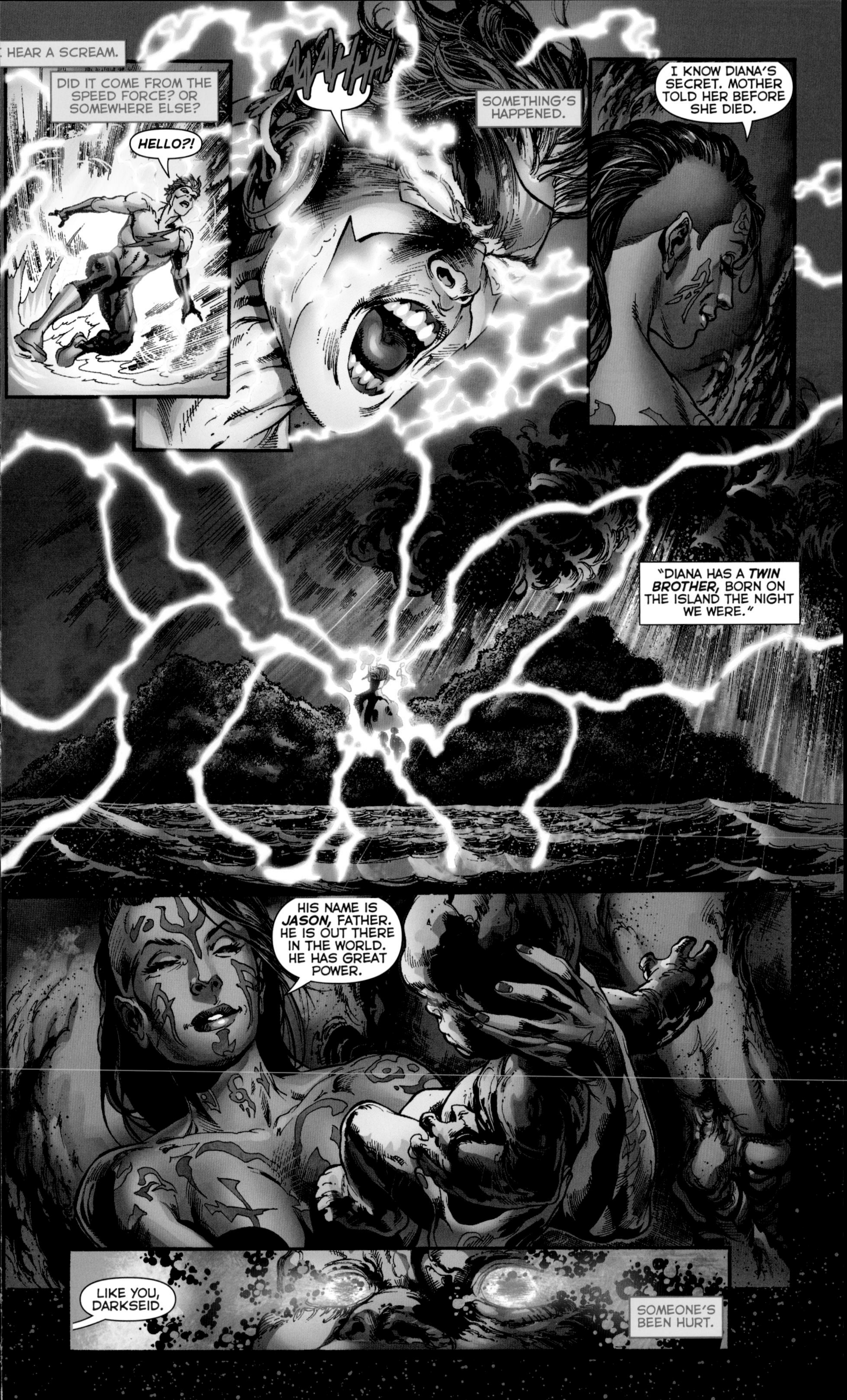
HEAR A SCREAM.
DID IT COME FROM THE SPEED FORCE? OR SOMEWHERE ELSE?
HELLO?!
AAAHHH!
SOMETHING'S HAPPENED.
I KNOW DIANA'S SECRET. MOTHER TOLD HER BEFORE SHE DIED.
"DIANA HAS A TWIN BROTHER, BORN ON THE ISLAND THE NIGHT WE WERE."
HIS NAME IS JASON, FATHER. HE IS OUT THERE IN THE WORLD. HE HAS GREAT POWER.
LIKE YOU, DARKSEID.
SOMEONE'S BEEN HURT.

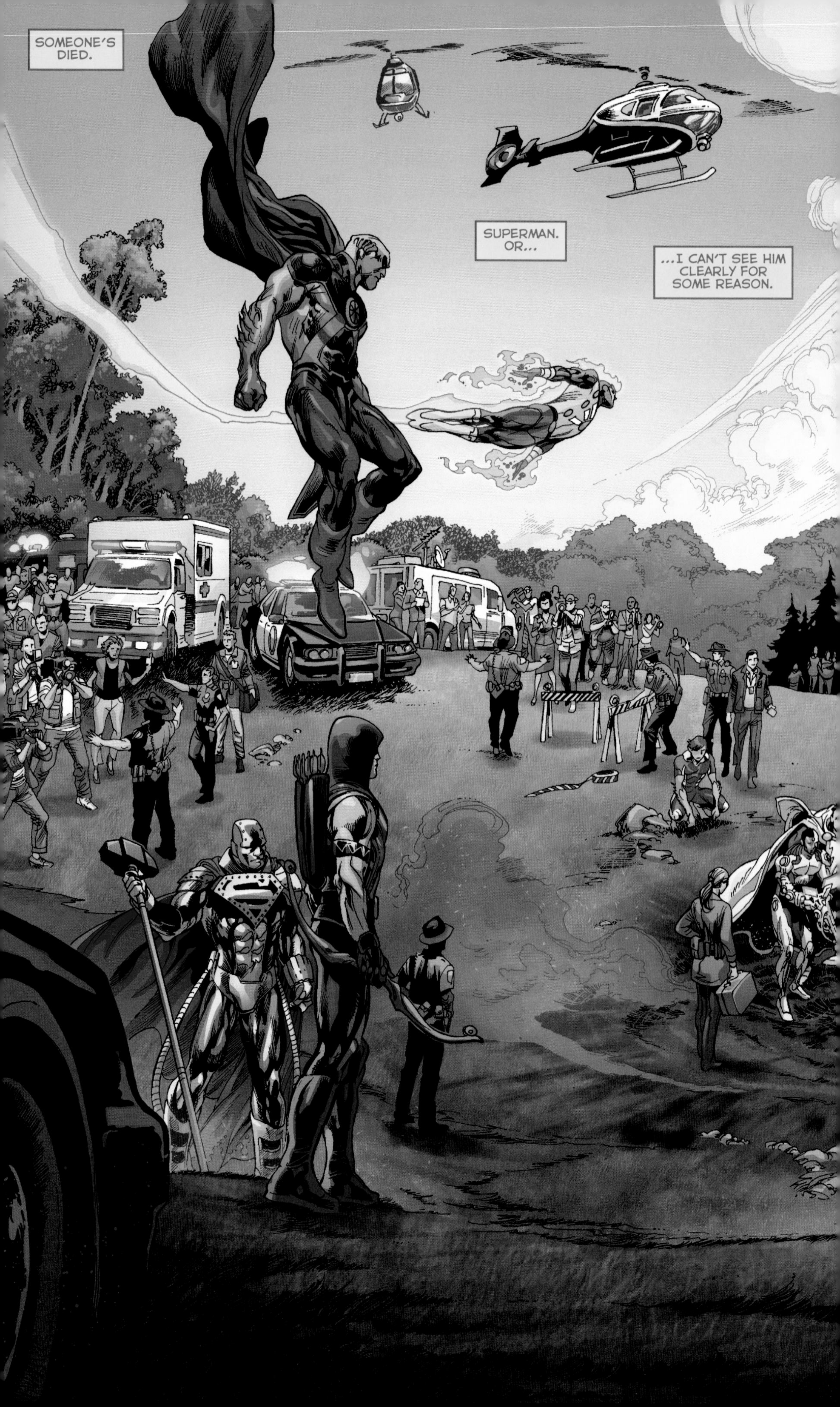
SOMEONE'S DIED.
SUPERMAN. OR...
...I CAN'T SEE HIM CLEARLY FOR SOME REASON.

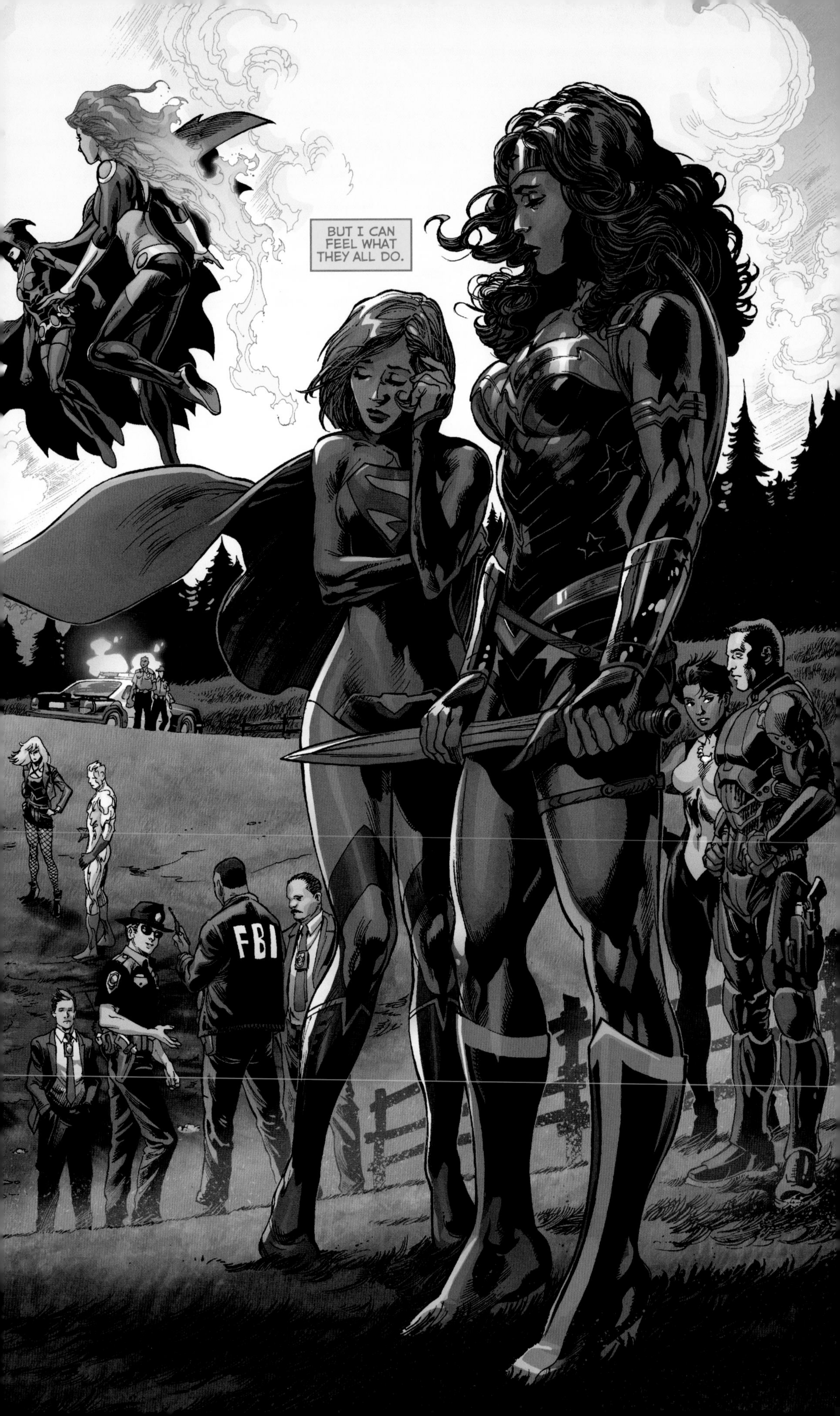
BUT I CAN FEEL WHAT THEY ALL DO.
FBI

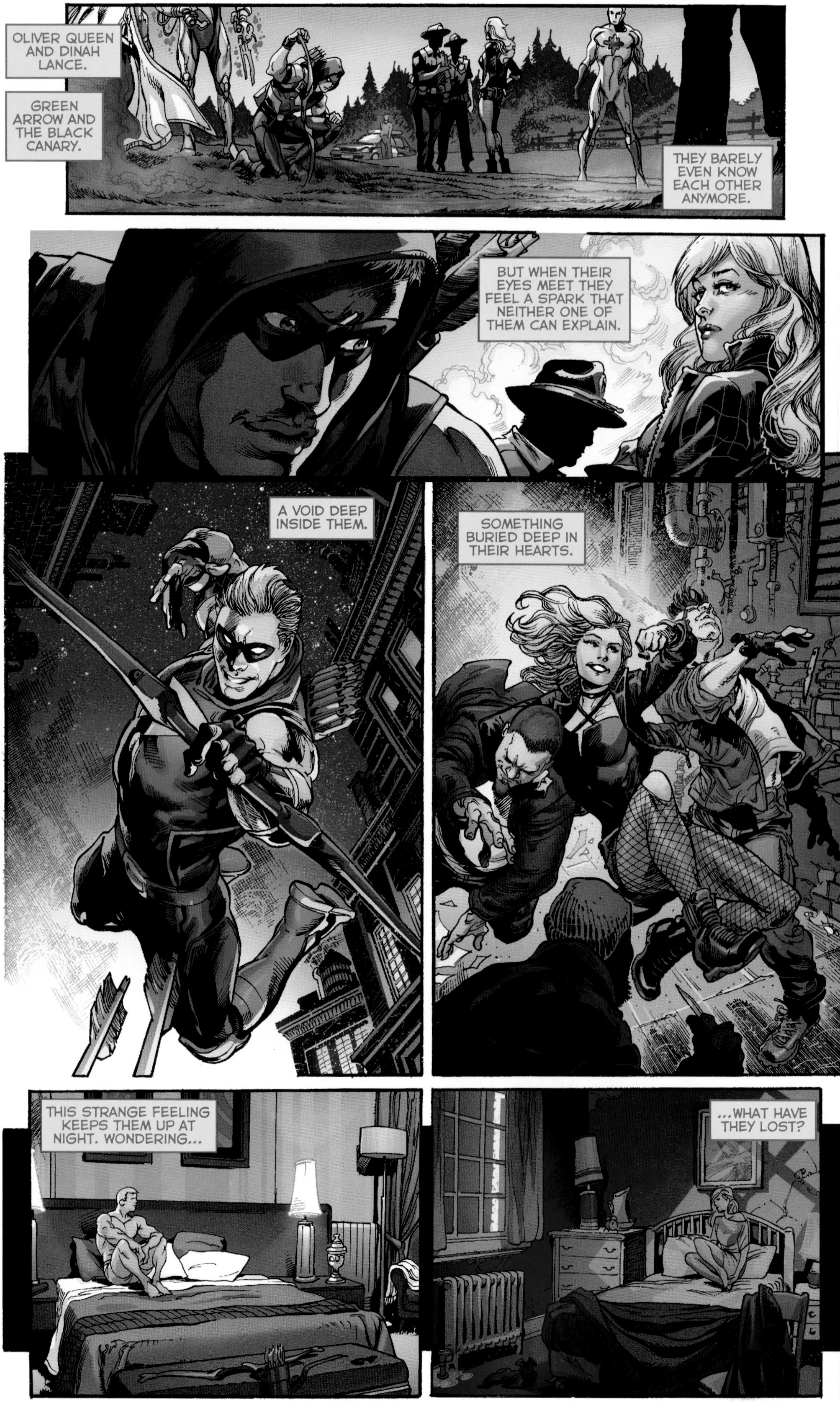
OLIVER QUEEN AND DINAH LANCE.
GREEN ARROW AND THE BLACK CANARY.
THEY BARELY EVEN KNOW EACH OTHER ANYMORE.
BUT WHEN THEIR EYES MEET THEY FEEL A SPARK THAT NEITHER ONE OF THEM CAN EXPLAIN.
A VOID DEEP INSIDE THEM.
SOMETHING BURIED DEEP IN THEIR HEARTS.
THIS STRANGE FEELING KEEPS THEM UP AT NIGHT. WONDERING...
...WHAT HAVE THEY LOST?

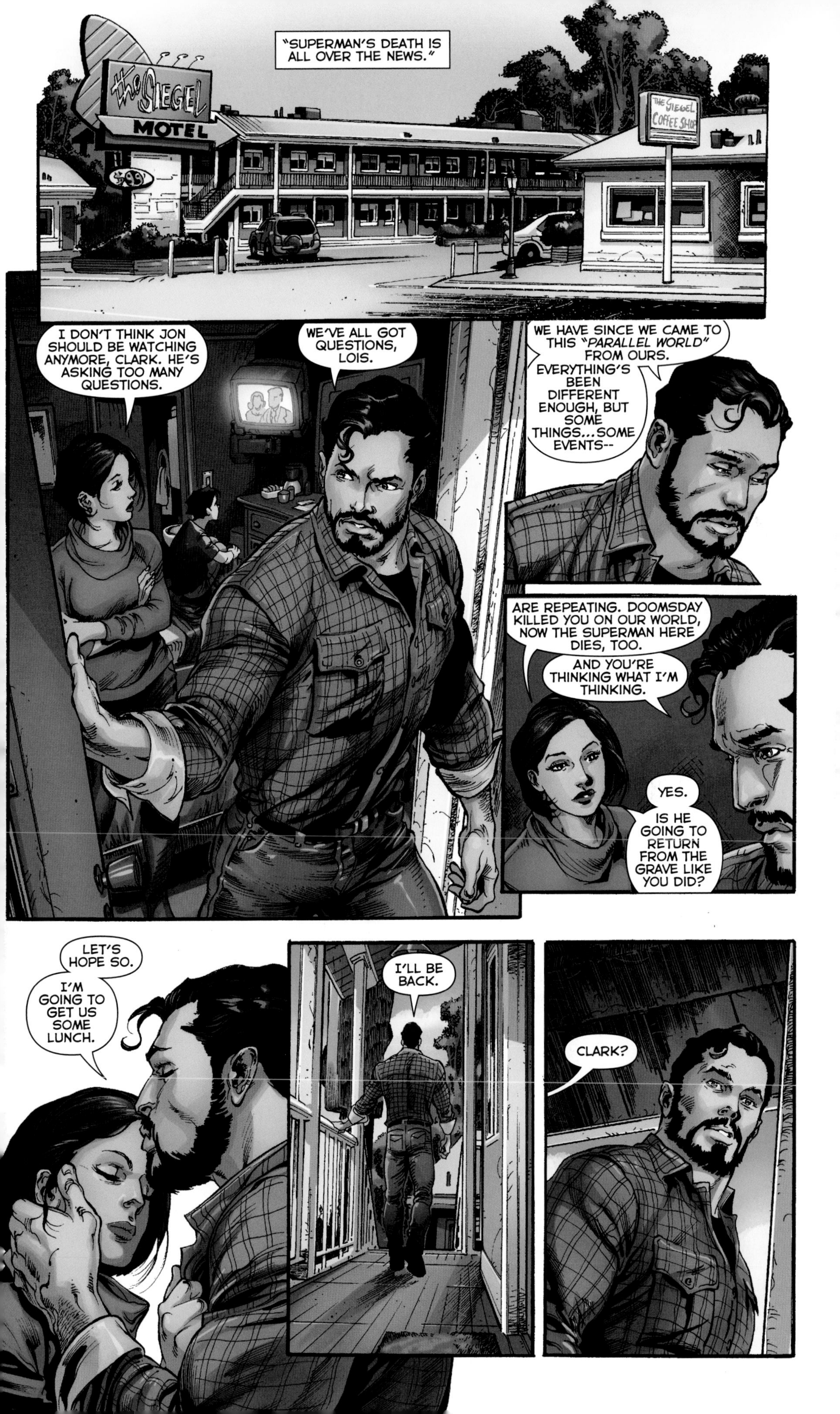
"SUPERMAN'S DEATH IS ALL OVER THE NEWS."
THE SIEGEL MOTEL
THE SIEGEL COFFEE SHOP
I DON'T THINK JON SHOULD BE WATCHING ANYMORE, CLARK. HE'S ASKING TOO MANY QUESTIONS.
WE'VE ALL GOT QUESTIONS, LOIS.
WE HAVE SINCE WE CAME TO THIS "PARALLEL WORLD" FROM OURS.
EVERYTHING'S BEEN DIFFERENT ENOUGH, BUT SOME THINGS...SOME EVENTS--
ARE REPEATING. DOOMSDAY KILLED YOU ON OUR WORLD, NOW THE SUPERMAN HERE DIES, TOO.
AND YOU'RE THINKING WHAT I'M THINKING.
YES.
IS HE GOING TO RETURN FROM THE GRAVE LIKE YOU DID?
LET'S HOPE SO.
I'M GOING TO GET US SOME LUNCH.
I'LL BE BACK.
CLARK?

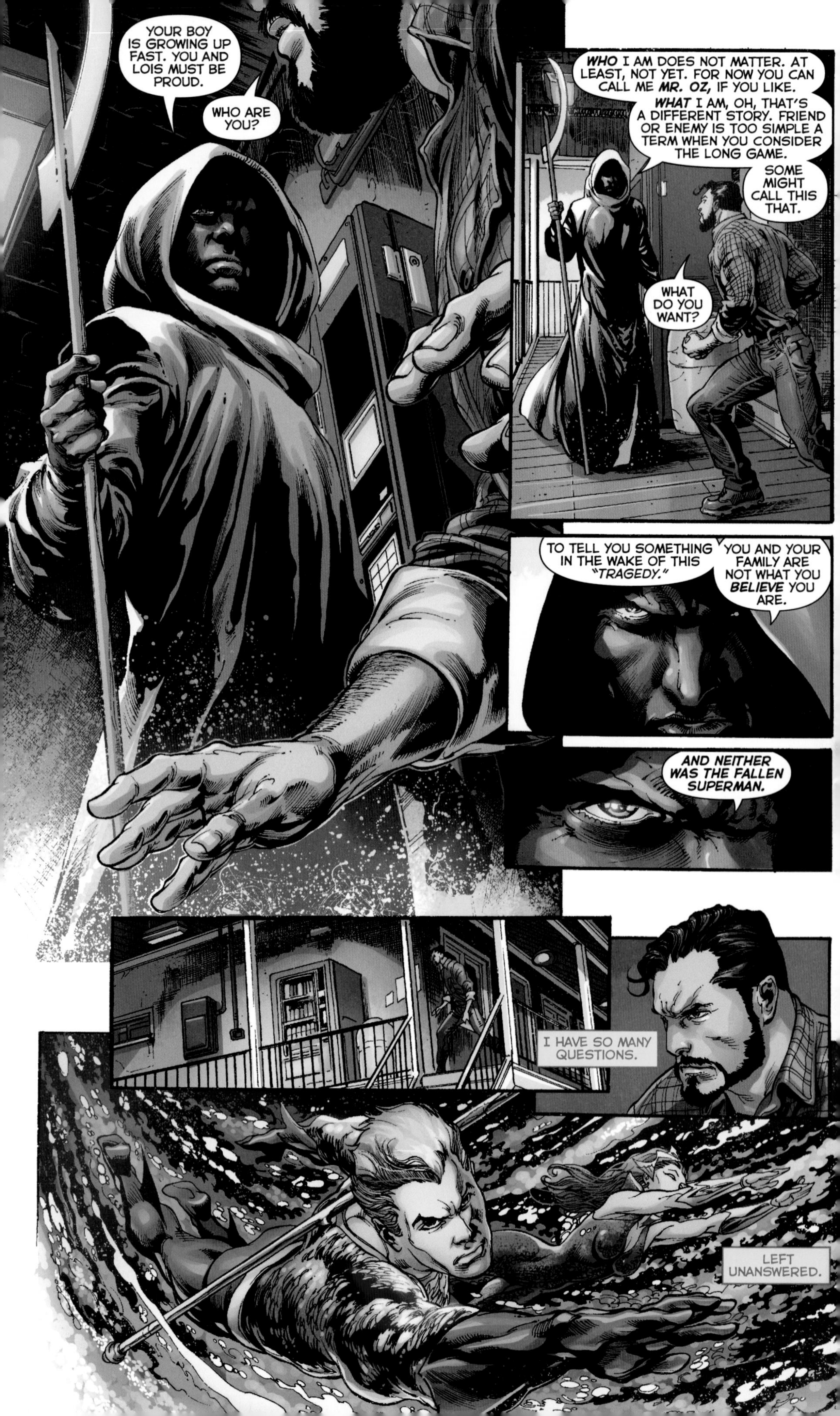
YOUR BOY IS GROWING UP FAST. YOU AND LOIS MUST BE PROUD.
WHO ARE YOU?
WHO I AM DOES NOT MATTER. AT LEAST, NOT YET. FOR NOW YOU CAN CALL ME MR. OZ, IF YOU LIKE.
WHAT I AM, OH, THAT'S A DIFFERENT STORY. FRIEND OR ENEMY IS TOO SIMPLE A TERM WHEN YOU CONSIDER THE LONG GAME.
SOME MIGHT CALL THIS THAT.
WHAT DO YOU WANT?
TO TELL YOU SOMETHING IN THE WAKE OF THIS "TRAGEDY."
YOU AND YOUR FAMILY ARE NOT WHAT YOU BELIEVE YOU ARE.
AND NEITHER WAS THE FALLEN SUPERMAN.
I HAVE SO MANY QUESTIONS.
LEFT UNANSWERED.

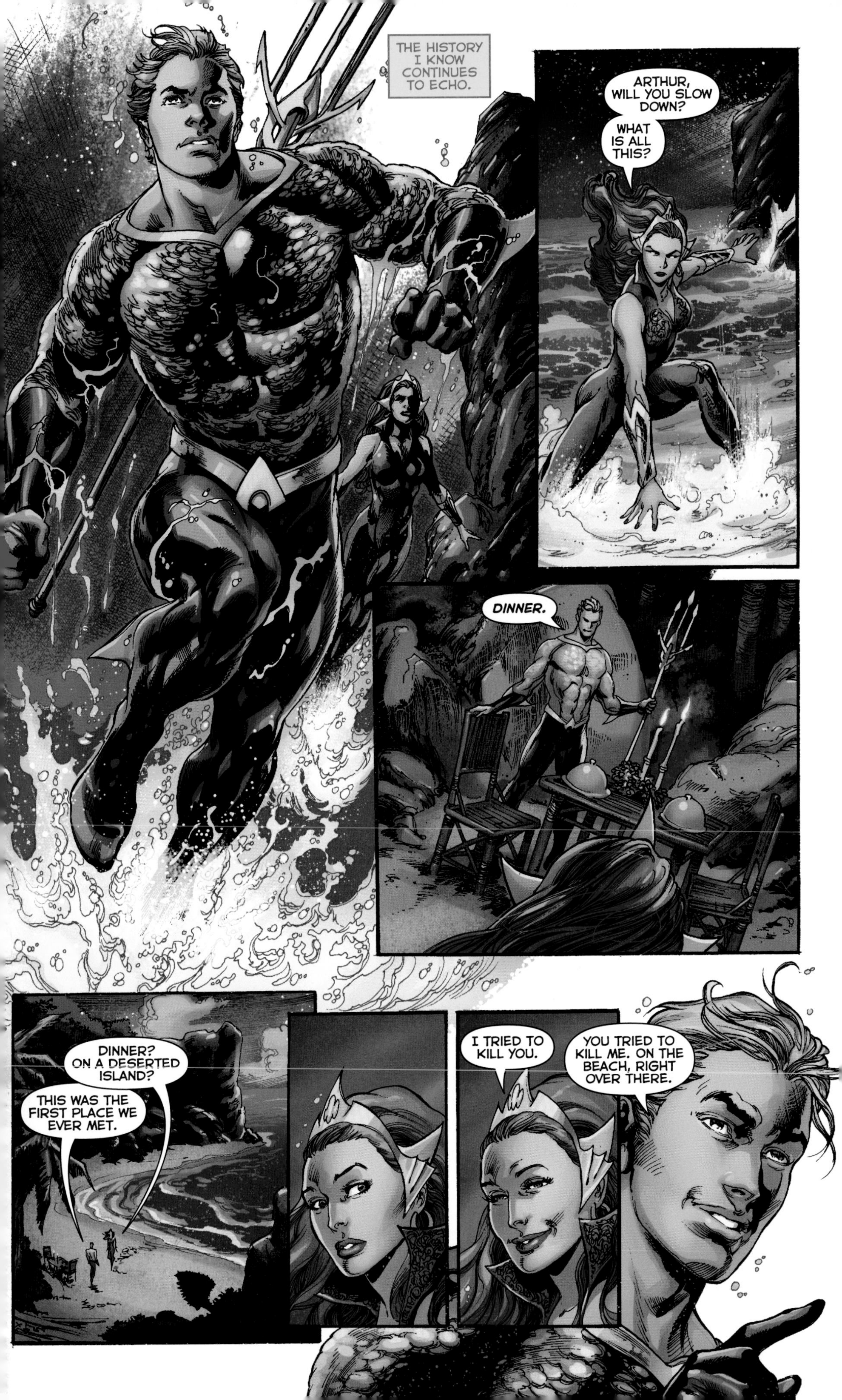
THE HISTORY I KNOW CONTINUES TO ECHO.
ARTHUR, WILL YOU SLOW DOWN?
WHAT IS ALL THIS?
DINNER.
DINNER? ON A DESERTED ISLAND?
THIS WAS THE FIRST PLACE WE EVER MET.
I TRIED TO KILL YOU.
YOU TRIED TO KILL ME. ON THE BEACH, RIGHT OVER THERE.

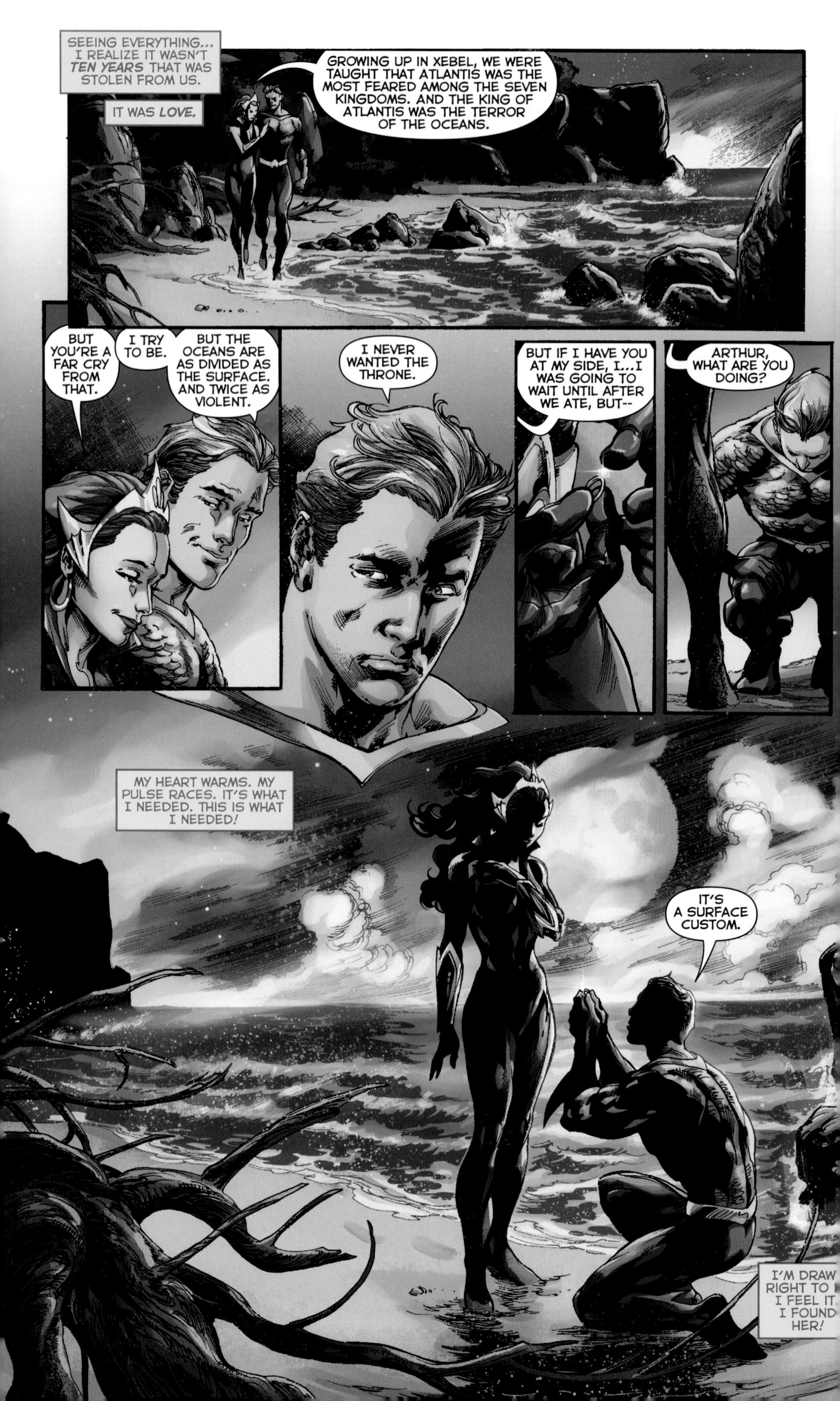

SEEING EVERYTHING... I REALIZE IT WASN'T *TEN YEARS* THAT WAS STOLEN FROM US.
IT WAS *LOVE.*
GROWING UP IN XEBEL, WE WERE TAUGHT THAT ATLANTIS WAS THE MOST FEARED AMONG THE SEVEN KINGDOMS. AND THE KING OF ATLANTIS WAS THE TERROR OF THE OCEANS.
BUT YOU'RE A FAR CRY FROM THAT.
I TRY TO BE.
BUT THE OCEANS ARE AS DIVIDED AS THE SURFACE. AND TWICE AS VIOLENT.
I NEVER WANTED THE THRONE.
BUT IF I HAVE YOU AT MY SIDE, I...I WAS GOING TO WAIT UNTIL AFTER WE ATE, BUT--
ARTHUR, WHAT ARE YOU DOING?
MY HEART WARMS. MY PULSE RACES. IT'S WHAT I NEEDED. THIS IS WHAT I NEEDED!
IT'S A SURFACE CUSTOM.

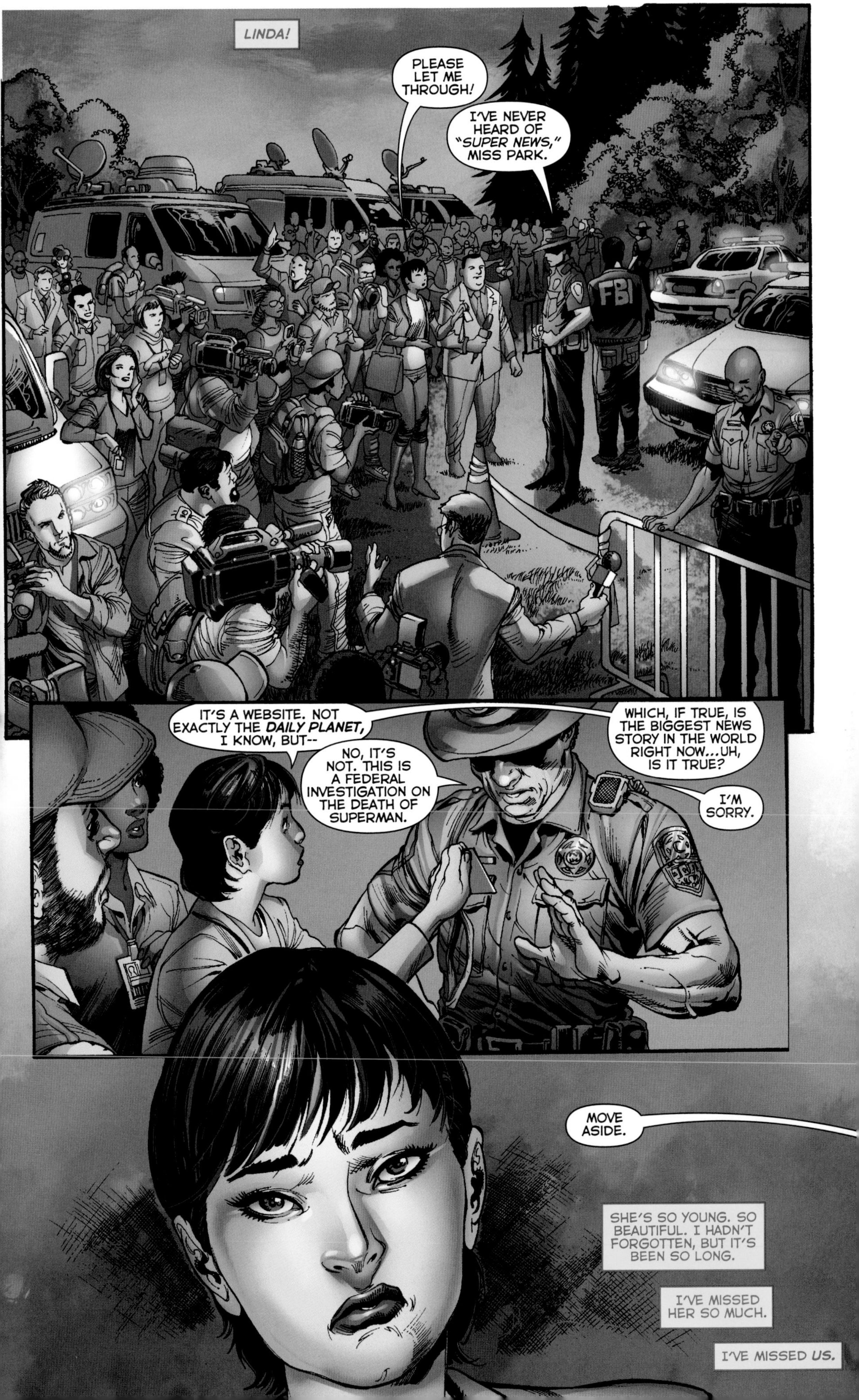
LINDA!
PLEASE LET ME THROUGH!
I'VE NEVER HEARD OF "SUPER NEWS," MISS PARK.
IT'S A WEBSITE. NOT EXACTLY THE DAILY PLANET, I KNOW, BUT--
NO, IT'S NOT. THIS IS A FEDERAL INVESTIGATION ON THE DEATH OF SUPERMAN.
WHICH, IF TRUE, IS THE BIGGEST NEWS STORY IN THE WORLD RIGHT NOW...UH, IS IT TRUE?
I'M SORRY.
FBI
MOVE ASIDE.
SHE'S SO YOUNG. SO BEAUTIFUL. I HADN'T FORGOTTEN, BUT IT'S BEEN SO LONG.
I'VE MISSED HER SO MUCH.
I'VE MISSED US.

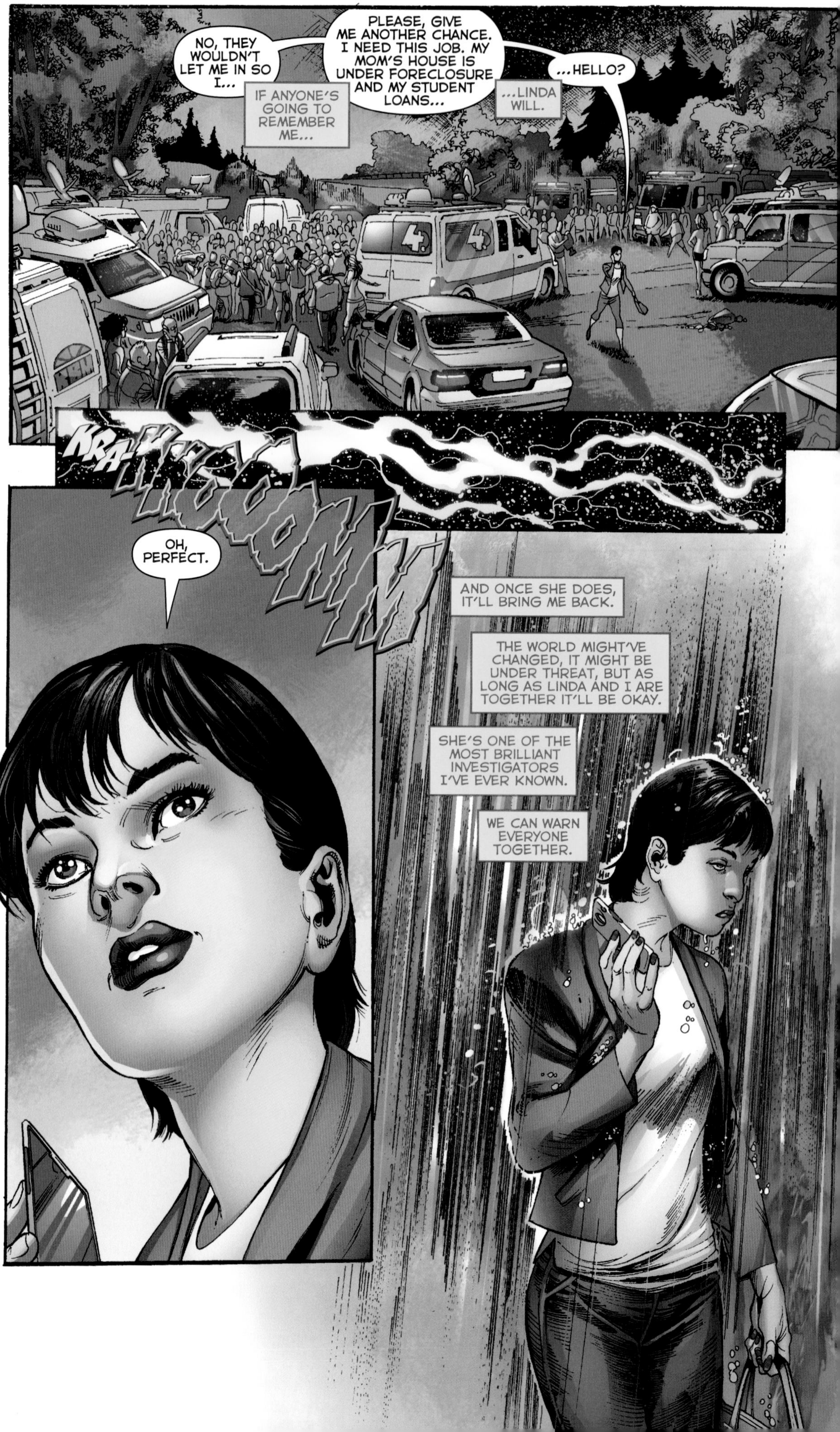
NO, THEY WOULDN'T LET ME IN SO I...
PLEASE, GIVE ME ANOTHER CHANCE. I NEED THIS JOB. MY MOM'S HOUSE IS UNDER FORECLOSURE AND MY STUDENT LOANS...
IF ANYONE'S GOING TO REMEMBER ME...
...LINDA WILL.
...HELLO?
KRA-KOOOMM
OH, PERFECT.
AND ONCE SHE DOES, IT'LL BRING ME BACK.
THE WORLD MIGHT'VE CHANGED, IT MIGHT BE UNDER THREAT, BUT AS LONG AS LINDA AND I ARE TOGETHER IT'LL BE OKAY.
SHE'S ONE OF THE MOST BRILLIANT INVESTIGATORS I'VE EVER KNOWN.
WE CAN WARN EVERYONE TOGETHER.

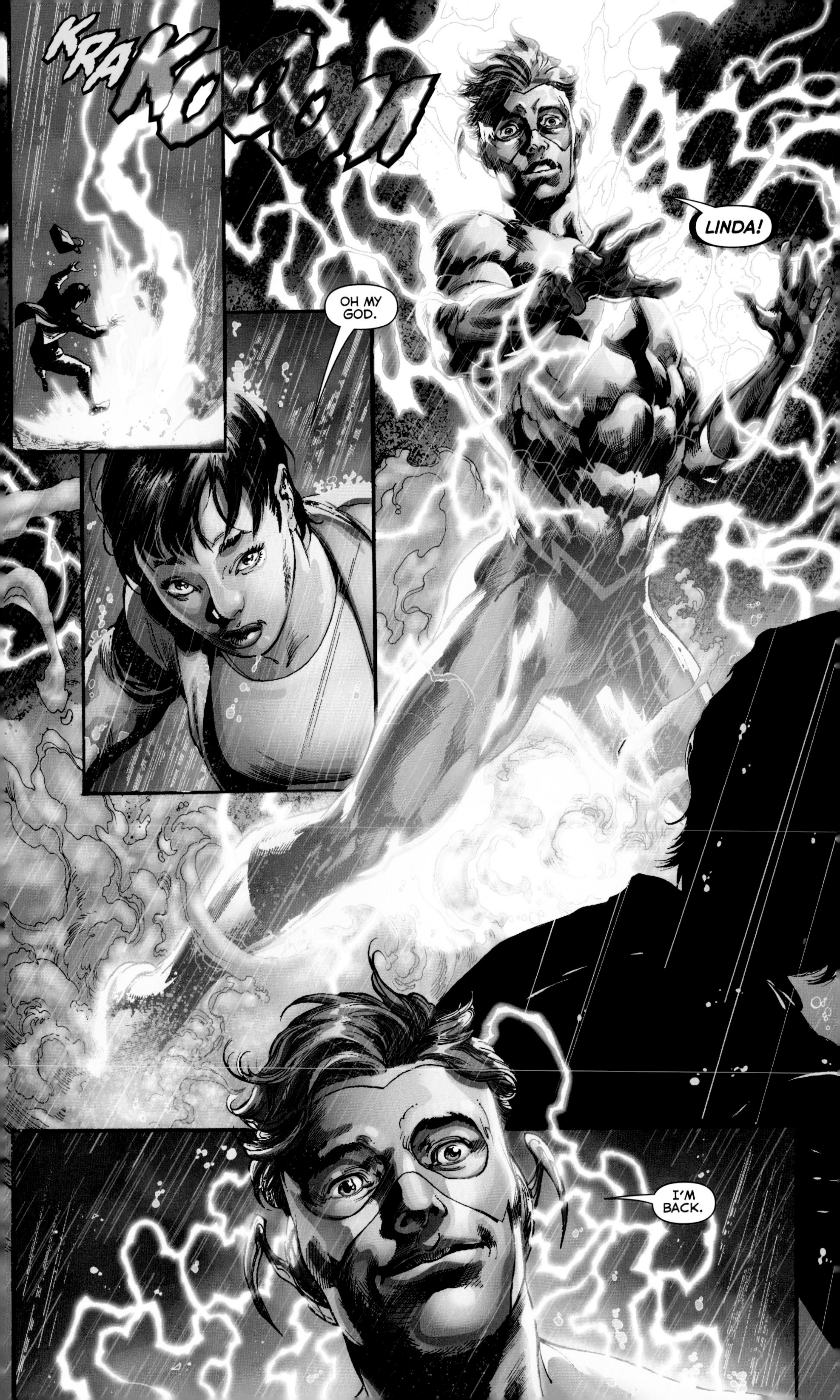
KRAKOOOOM
LINDA!
OH MY GOD.
I'M BACK.

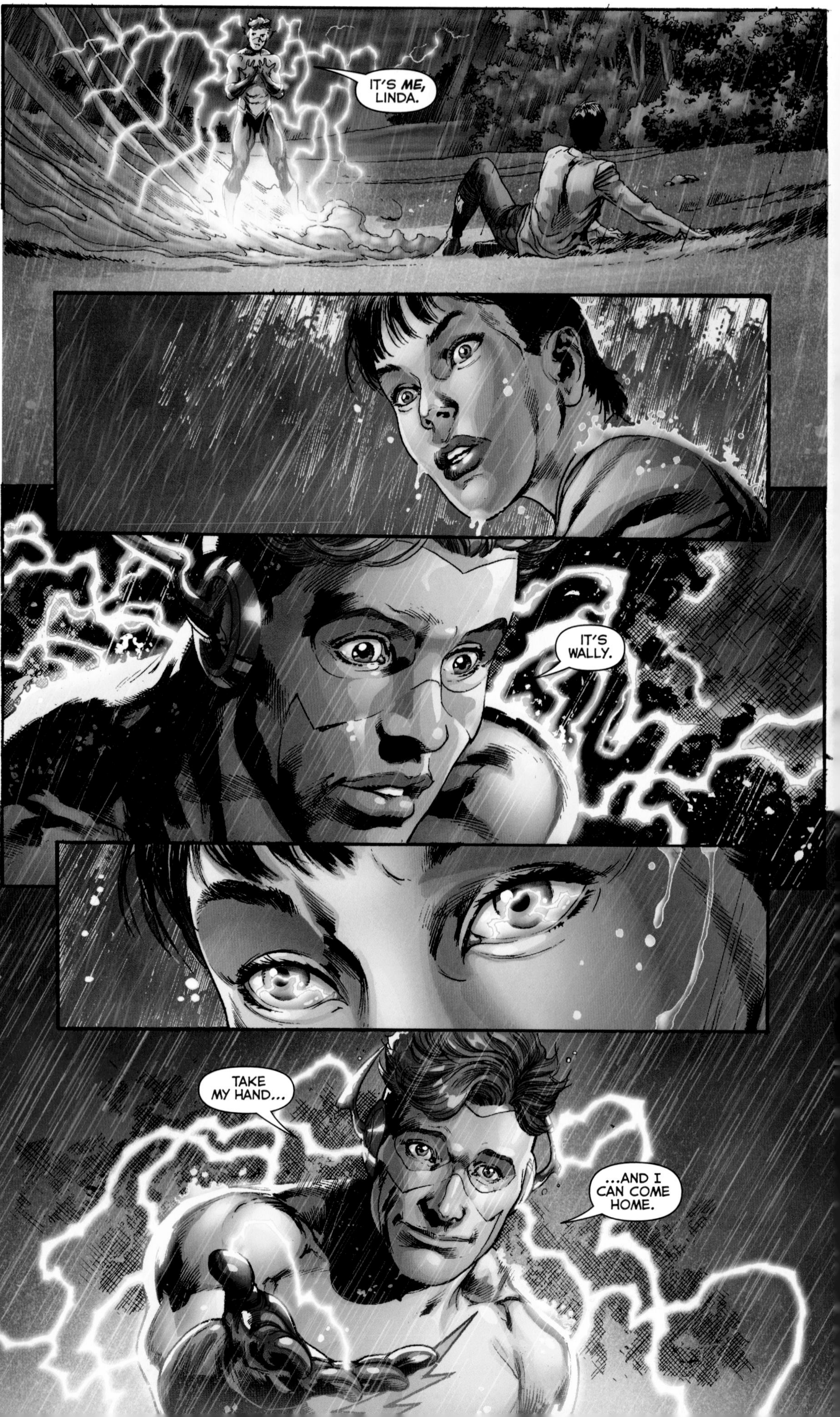
IT'S ME, LINDA.
IT'S WALLY.
TAKE MY HAND...
...AND I CAN COME HOME.

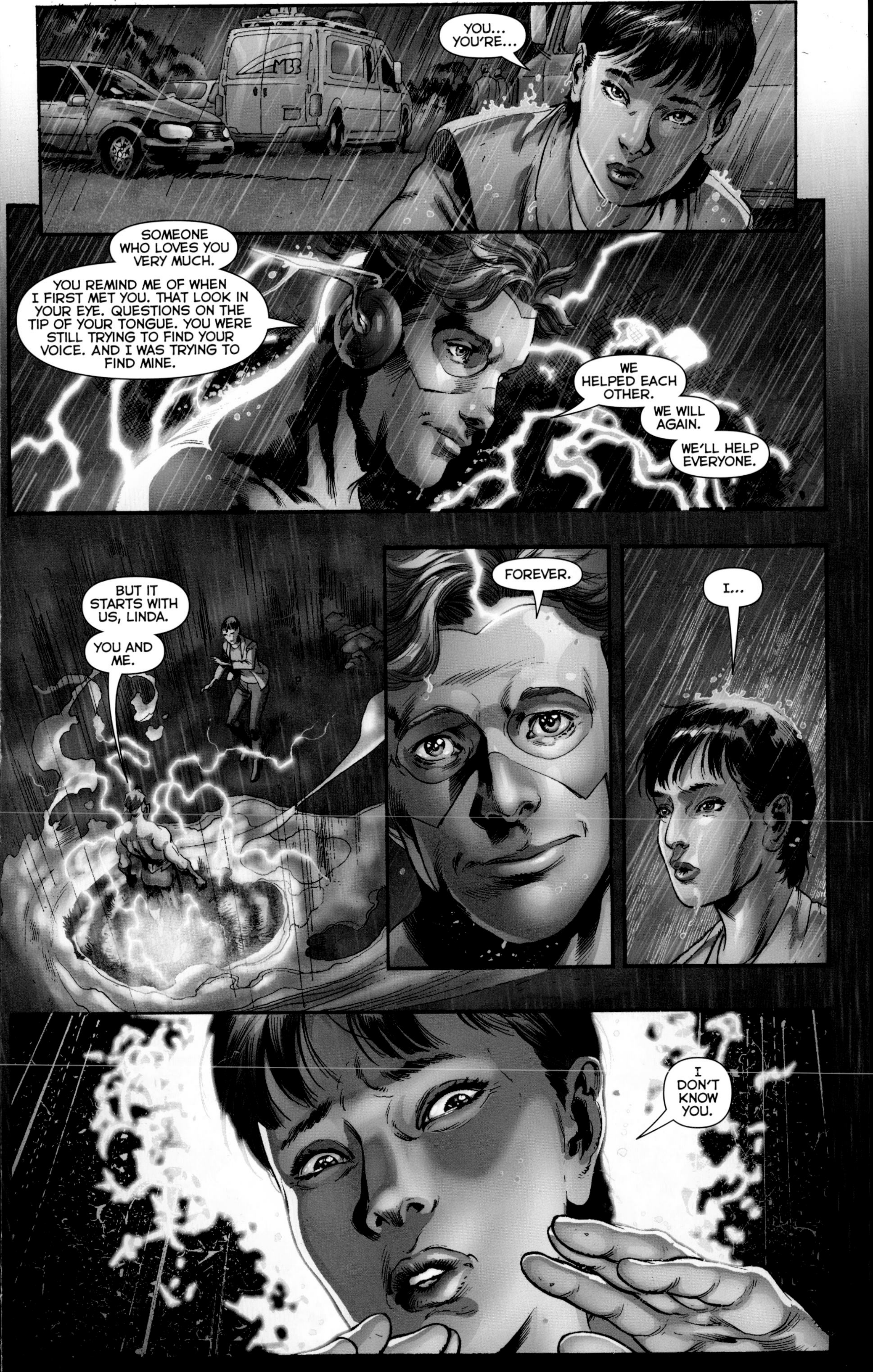
YOU... YOU'RE...
SOMEONE WHO LOVES YOU VERY MUCH.
YOU REMIND ME OF WHEN I FIRST MET YOU. THAT LOOK IN YOUR EYE. QUESTIONS ON THE TIP OF YOUR TONGUE. YOU WERE STILL TRYING TO FIND YOUR VOICE. AND I WAS TRYING TO FIND MINE.
WE HELPED EACH OTHER.
WE WILL AGAIN.
WE'LL HELP EVERYONE.
BUT IT STARTS WITH US, LINDA.
YOU AND ME.
FOREVER.
I...
I DON'T KNOW YOU.

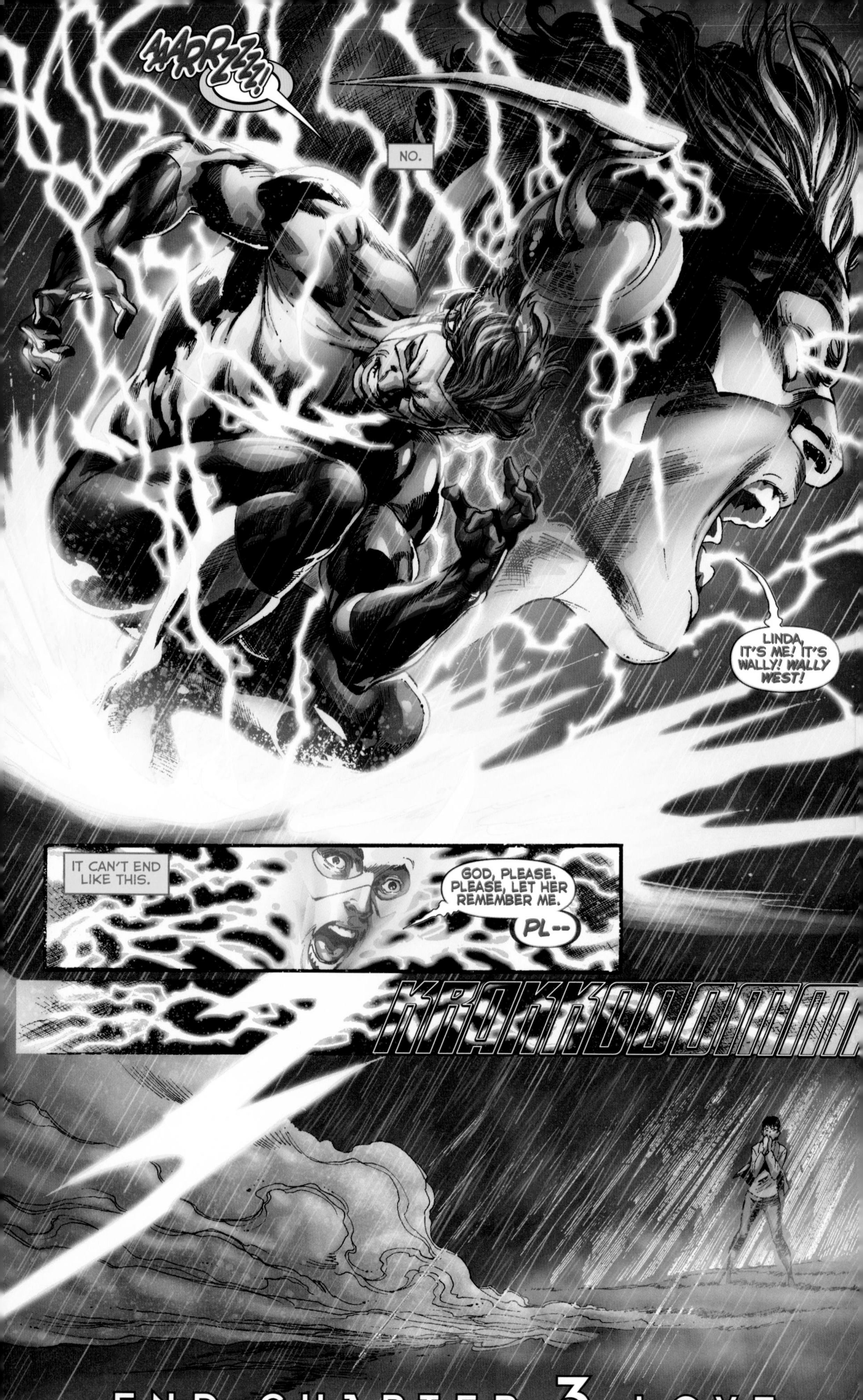

WARRZZZ!
NO.
LINDA, IT'S ME! IT'S WALLY! WALLY WEST!
IT CAN'T END LIKE THIS.
GOD, PLEASE. PLEASE, LET HER REMEMBER ME.
PL--
KRAKKOOOMM

END CHAPTER 3: LOVE

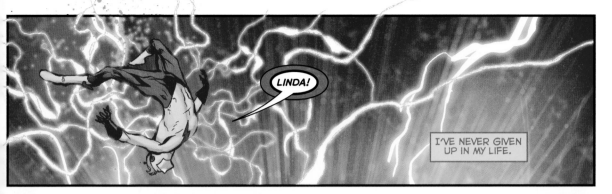

LINDA!

I'VE NEVER GIVEN UP IN MY LIFE.

THE SIGNAL, GOTHAM--

IT'S NOT FOR US. NOT YET.

THERE HAS TO BE SOMETHING ELSE I CAN DO.

YOUR MISSUS IS LONG GONE, CHIEF. ABBY ARCANE IS LOST TO THE DARK SIDE AND WHATNOT.

YOU ASKED FOR MY HELP AGAINST THE CAPES, CONSTANTINE... THAT IS MY PRICE.

YOU'VE ALWAYS BEEN A PAIN IN THE ARSE, YOU BLOODY TURNIP.

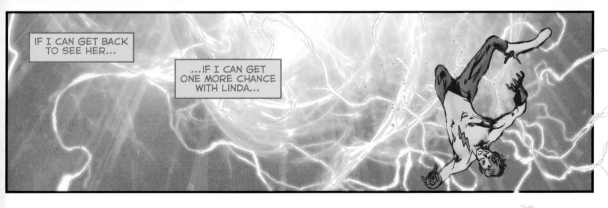

IF I CAN GET BACK TO SEE HER...

...IF I CAN GET ONE MORE CHANCE WITH LINDA...

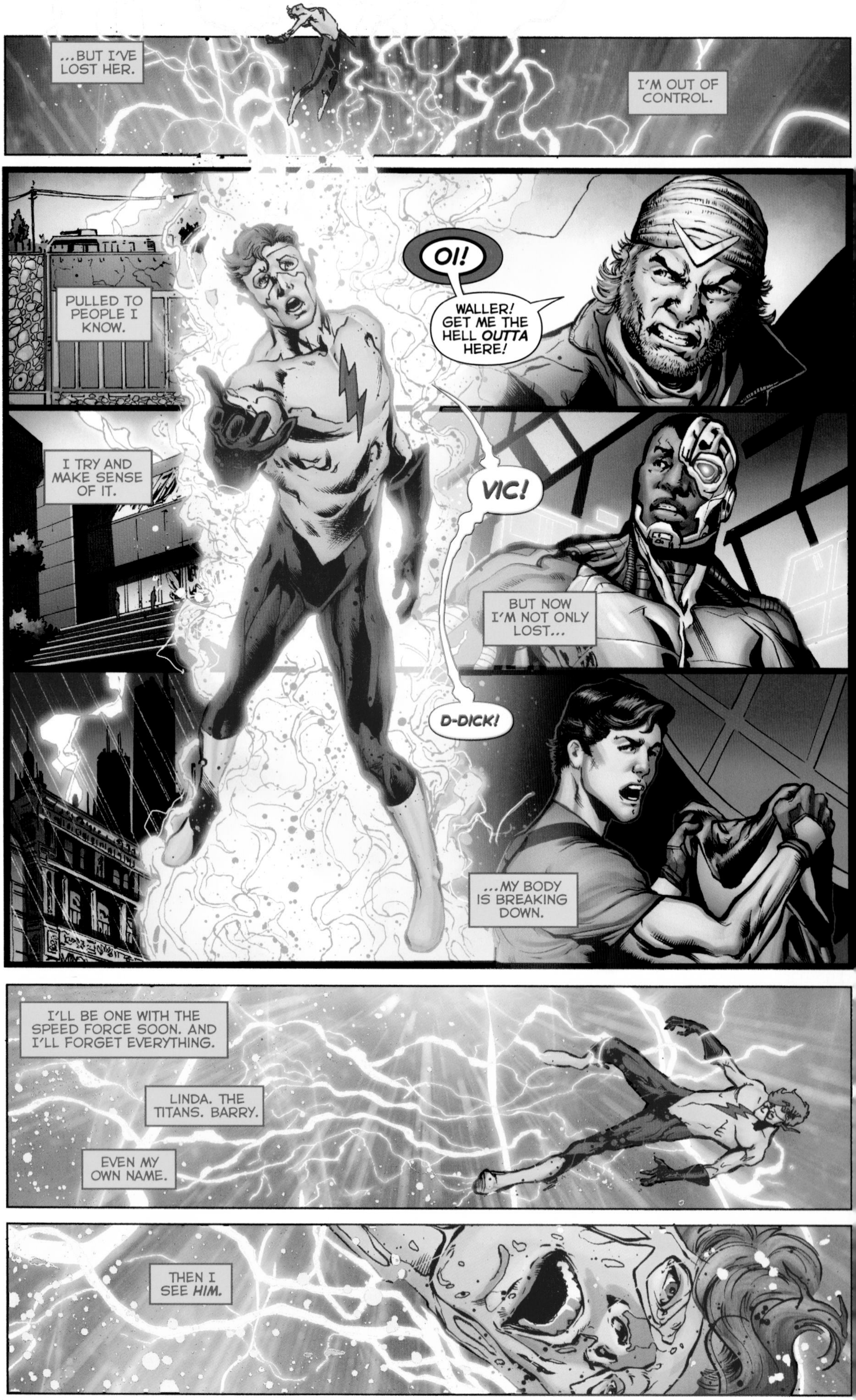
...BUT I'VE LOST HER.
I'M OUT OF CONTROL.
PULLED TO PEOPLE I KNOW.
OI!
WALLER! GET ME THE HELL OUTTA HERE!
I TRY AND MAKE SENSE OF IT.
VIC!
BUT NOW I'M NOT ONLY LOST...
D-DICK!
...MY BODY IS BREAKING DOWN.
I'LL BE ONE WITH THE SPEED FORCE SOON. AND I'LL FORGET EVERYTHING.
LINDA. THE TITANS. BARRY.
EVEN MY OWN NAME.
THEN I SEE HIM.

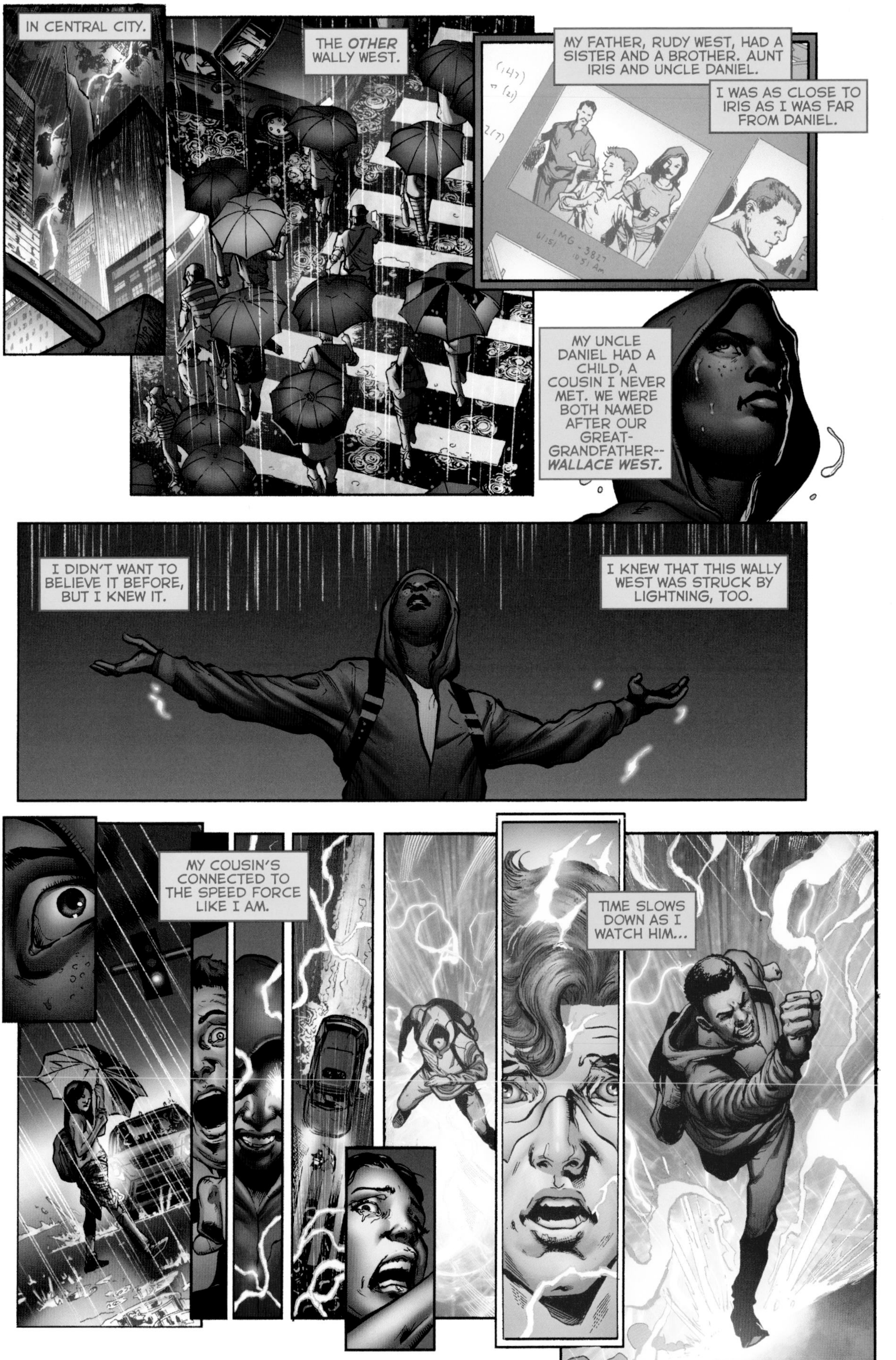
IN CENTRAL CITY.
THE *OTHER* WALLY WEST.
MY FATHER, RUDY WEST, HAD A SISTER AND A BROTHER. AUNT IRIS AND UNCLE DANIEL.
I WAS AS CLOSE TO IRIS AS I WAS FAR FROM DANIEL.
MY UNCLE DANIEL HAD A CHILD, A COUSIN I NEVER MET. WE WERE BOTH NAMED AFTER OUR GREAT-GRANDFATHER-- *WALLACE WEST.*
I DIDN'T WANT TO BELIEVE IT BEFORE, BUT I KNEW IT.
I KNEW THAT THIS WALLY WEST WAS STRUCK BY LIGHTNING, TOO.
MY COUSIN'S CONNECTED TO THE SPEED FORCE LIKE I AM.
TIME SLOWS DOWN AS I WATCH HIM...

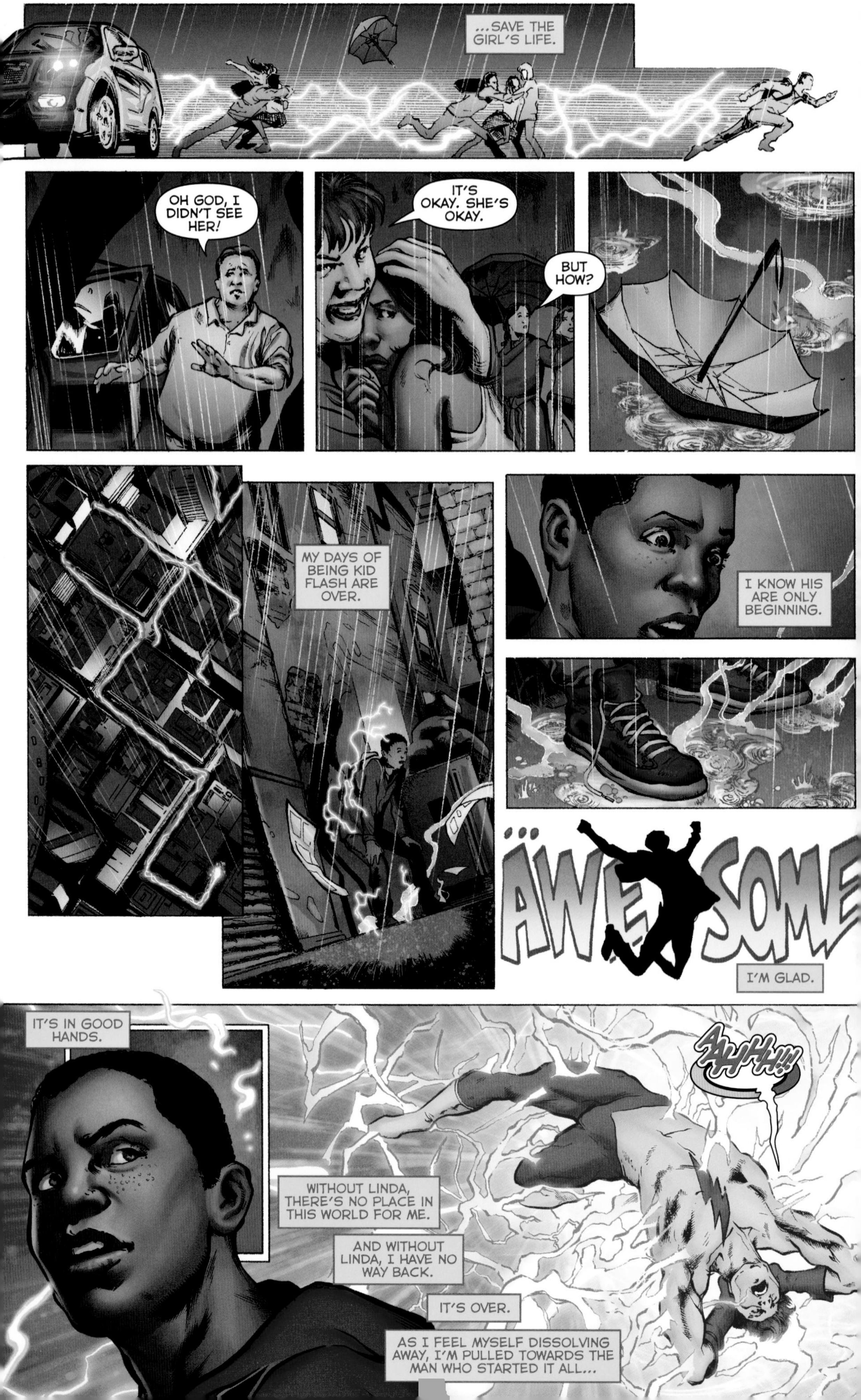

...SAVE THE GIRL'S LIFE.
OH GOD, I DIDN'T SEE HER!
IT'S OKAY. SHE'S OKAY.
BUT HOW?
MY DAYS OF BEING KID FLASH ARE OVER.
I KNOW HIS ARE ONLY BEGINNING.
...AWESOME
I'M GLAD.
IT'S IN GOOD HANDS.
AAHHH!!!
WITHOUT LINDA, THERE'S NO PLACE IN THIS WORLD FOR ME.
AND WITHOUT LINDA, I HAVE NO WAY BACK.
IT'S OVER.
AS I FEEL MYSELF DISSOLVING AWAY, I'M PULLED TOWARDS THE MAN WHO STARTED IT ALL...

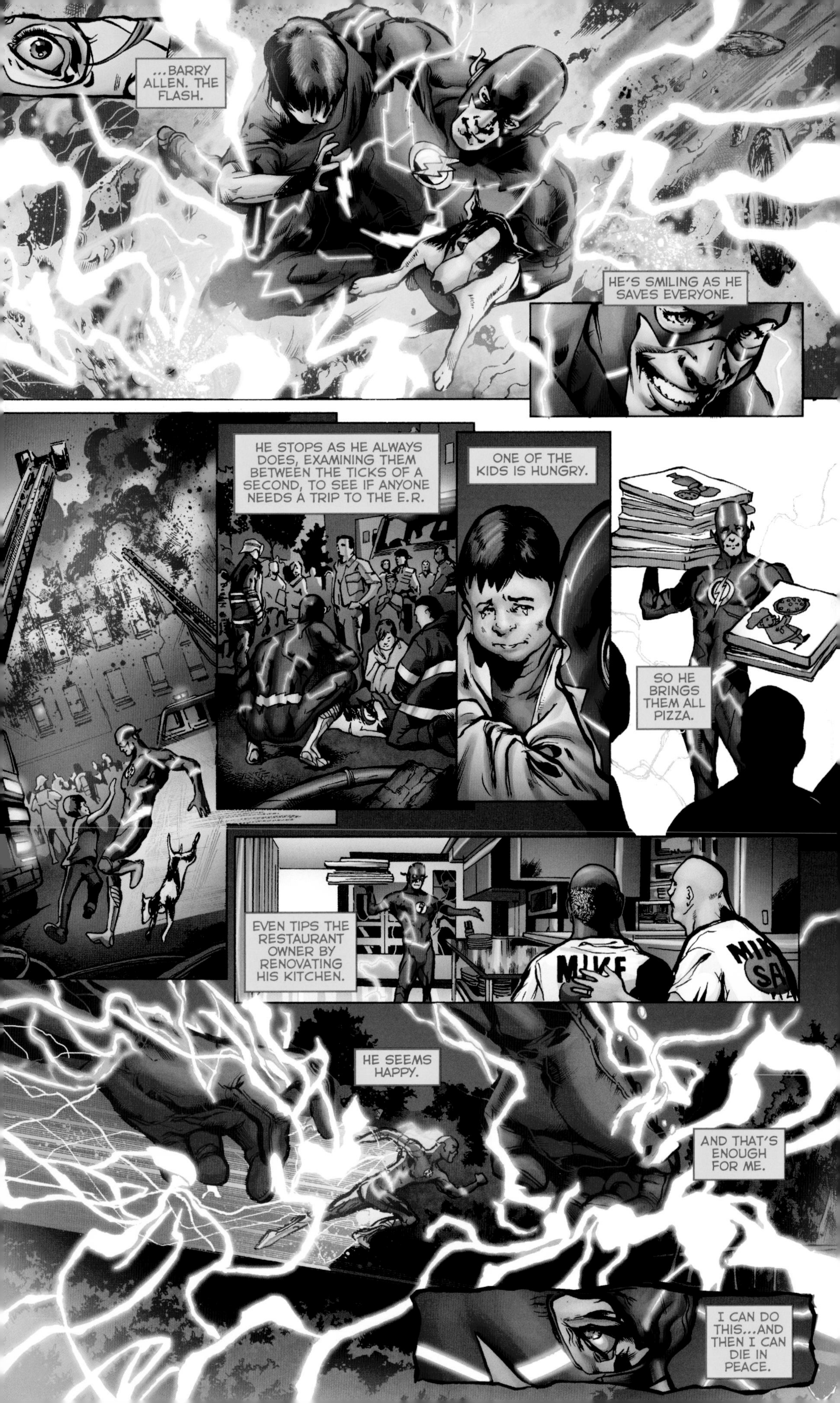
...BARRY ALLEN. THE FLASH.
HE'S SMILING AS HE SAVES EVERYONE.
HE STOPS AS HE ALWAYS DOES, EXAMINING THEM BETWEEN THE TICKS OF A SECOND, TO SEE IF ANYONE NEEDS A TRIP TO THE E.R.
ONE OF THE KIDS IS HUNGRY.
SO HE BRINGS THEM ALL PIZZA.
EVEN TIPS THE RESTAURANT OWNER BY RENOVATING HIS KITCHEN.
MIKE
HE SEEMS HAPPY.
AND THAT'S ENOUGH FOR ME.
I CAN DO THIS...AND THEN I CAN DIE IN PEACE.

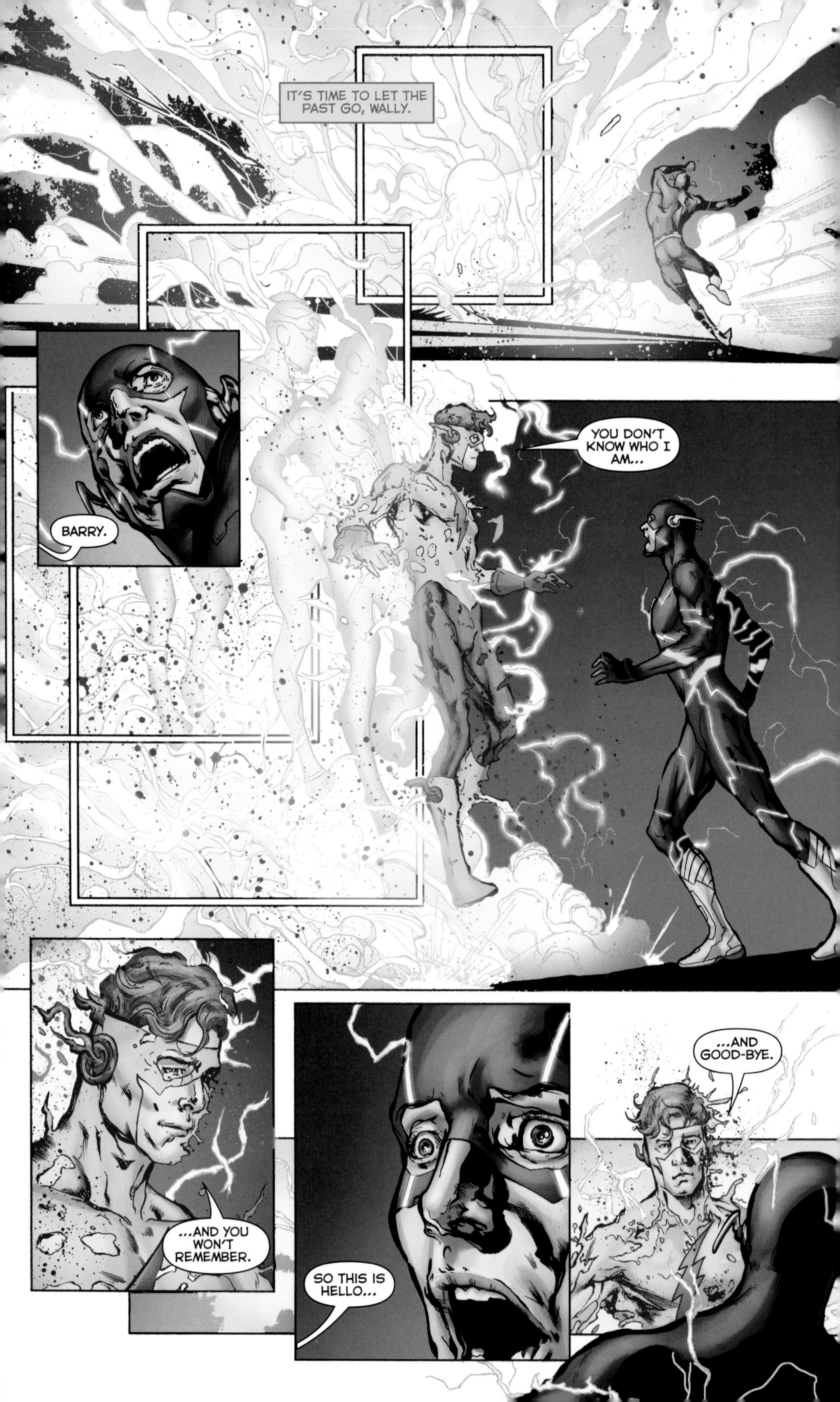
IT'S TIME TO LET THE PAST GO, WALLY.
BARRY.
YOU DON'T KNOW WHO I AM...
...AND YOU WON'T REMEMBER.
SO THIS IS HELLO...
...AND GOOD-BYE.

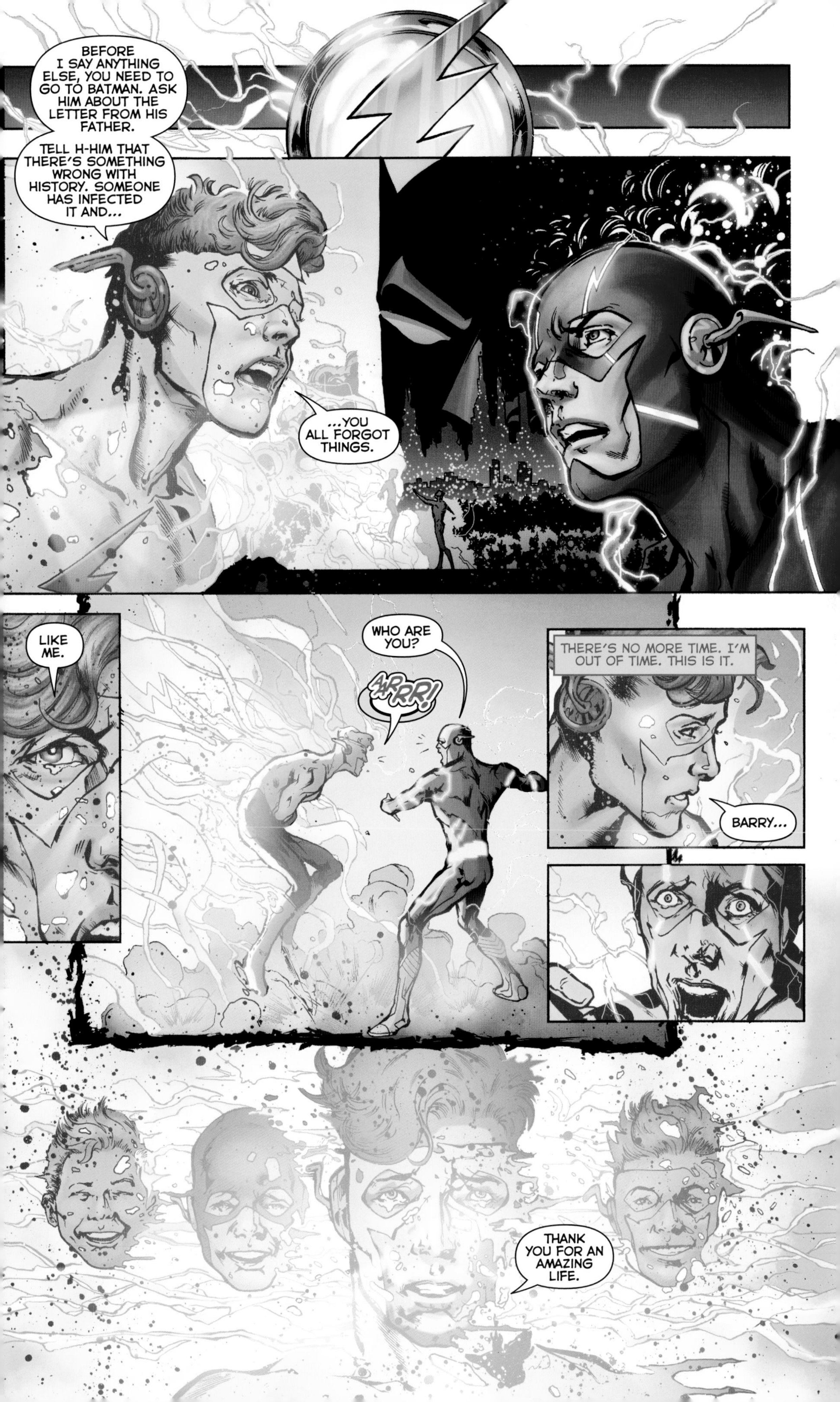

BEFORE I SAY ANYTHING ELSE, YOU NEED TO GO TO BATMAN. ASK HIM ABOUT THE LETTER FROM HIS FATHER.
TELL H-HIM THAT THERE'S SOMETHING WRONG WITH HISTORY. SOMEONE HAS INFECTED IT AND...
...YOU ALL FORGOT THINGS.
LIKE ME.
WHO ARE YOU?
SKRRR!
THERE'S NO MORE TIME. I'M OUT OF TIME. THIS IS IT.
BARRY...
THANK YOU FOR AN AMAZING LIFE.

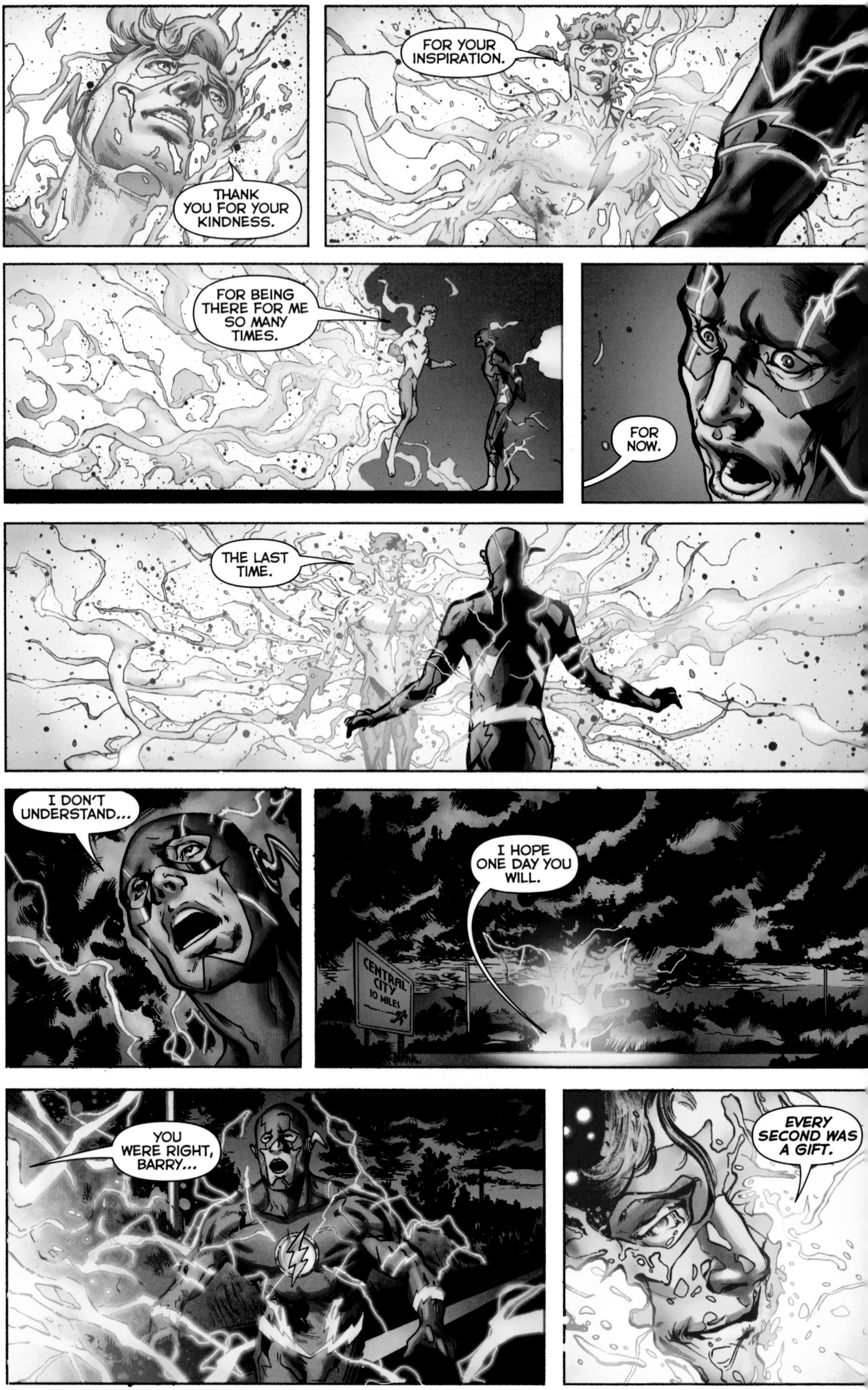
THANK YOU FOR YOUR KINDNESS.
FOR YOUR INSPIRATION.
FOR BEING THERE FOR ME SO MANY TIMES.
FOR NOW.
THE LAST TIME.
I DON'T UNDERSTAND...
I HOPE ONE DAY YOU WILL.
CENTRAL CITY 10 MILES
YOU WERE RIGHT, BARRY...
EVERY SECOND WAS A GIFT.

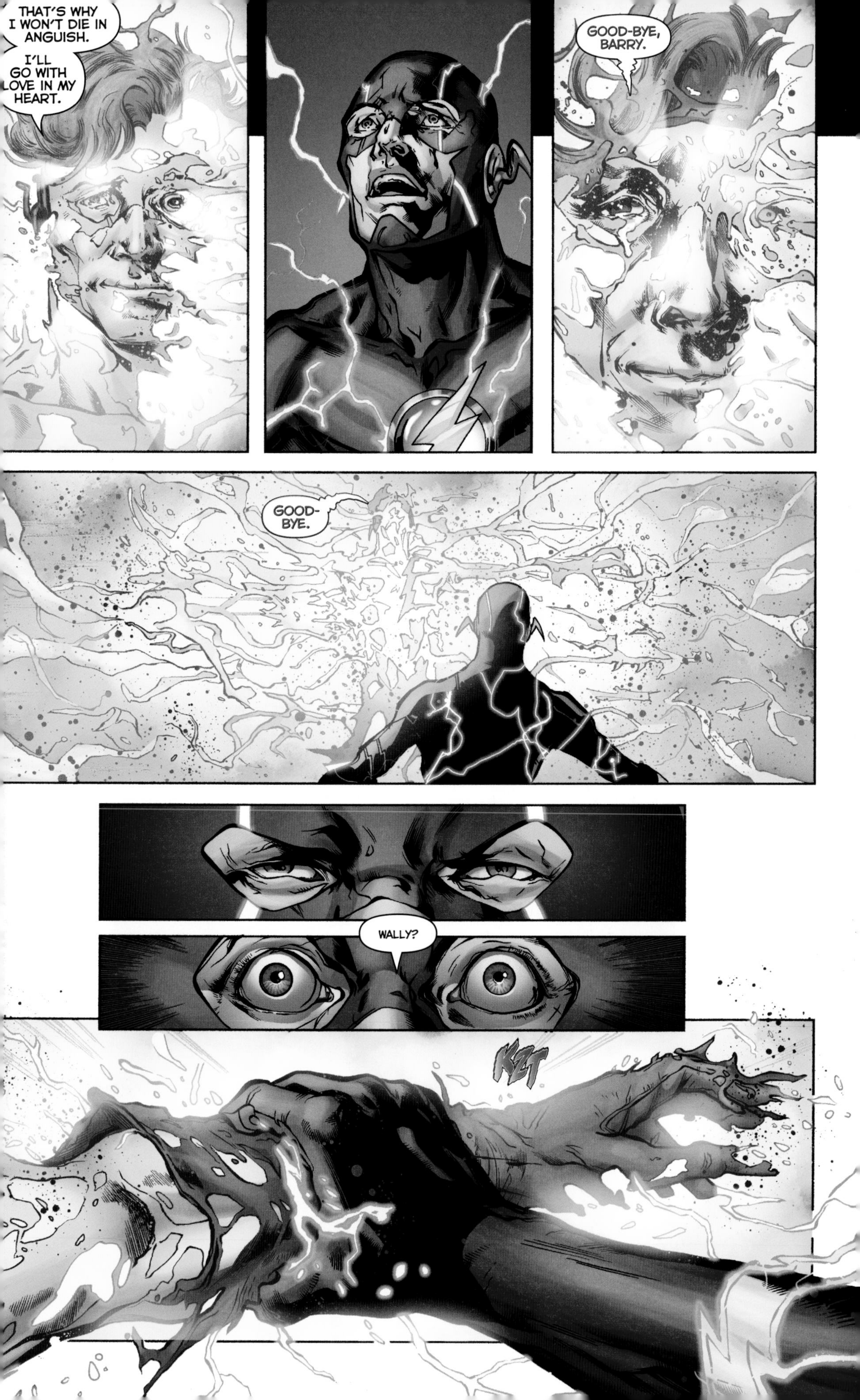
THAT'S WHY I WON'T DIE IN ANGUISH.
I'LL GO WITH LOVE IN MY HEART.
GOOD-BYE, BARRY.
GOOD-BYE.
WALLY?
KZT

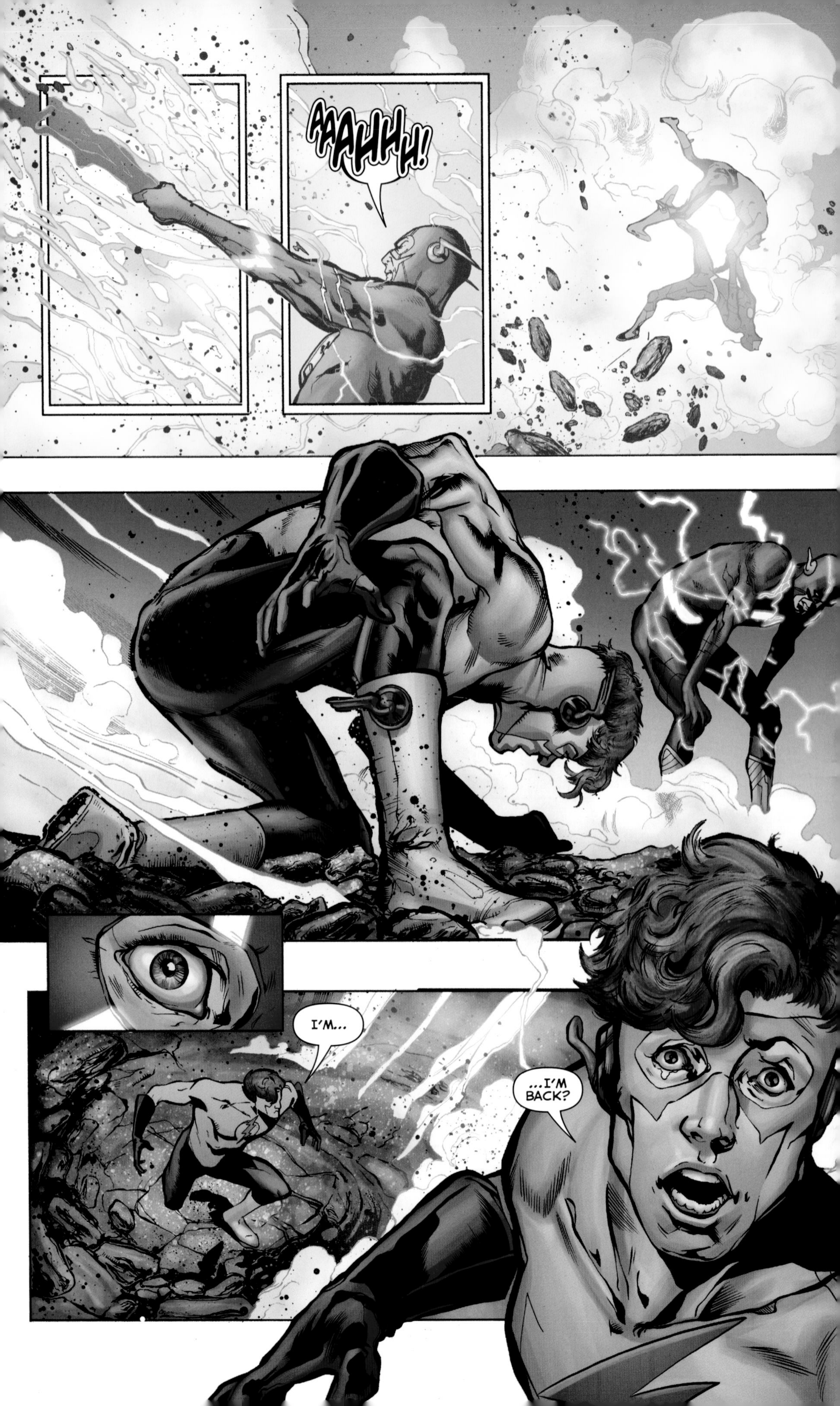
AAAHHH!
I'M...
...I'M BACK?

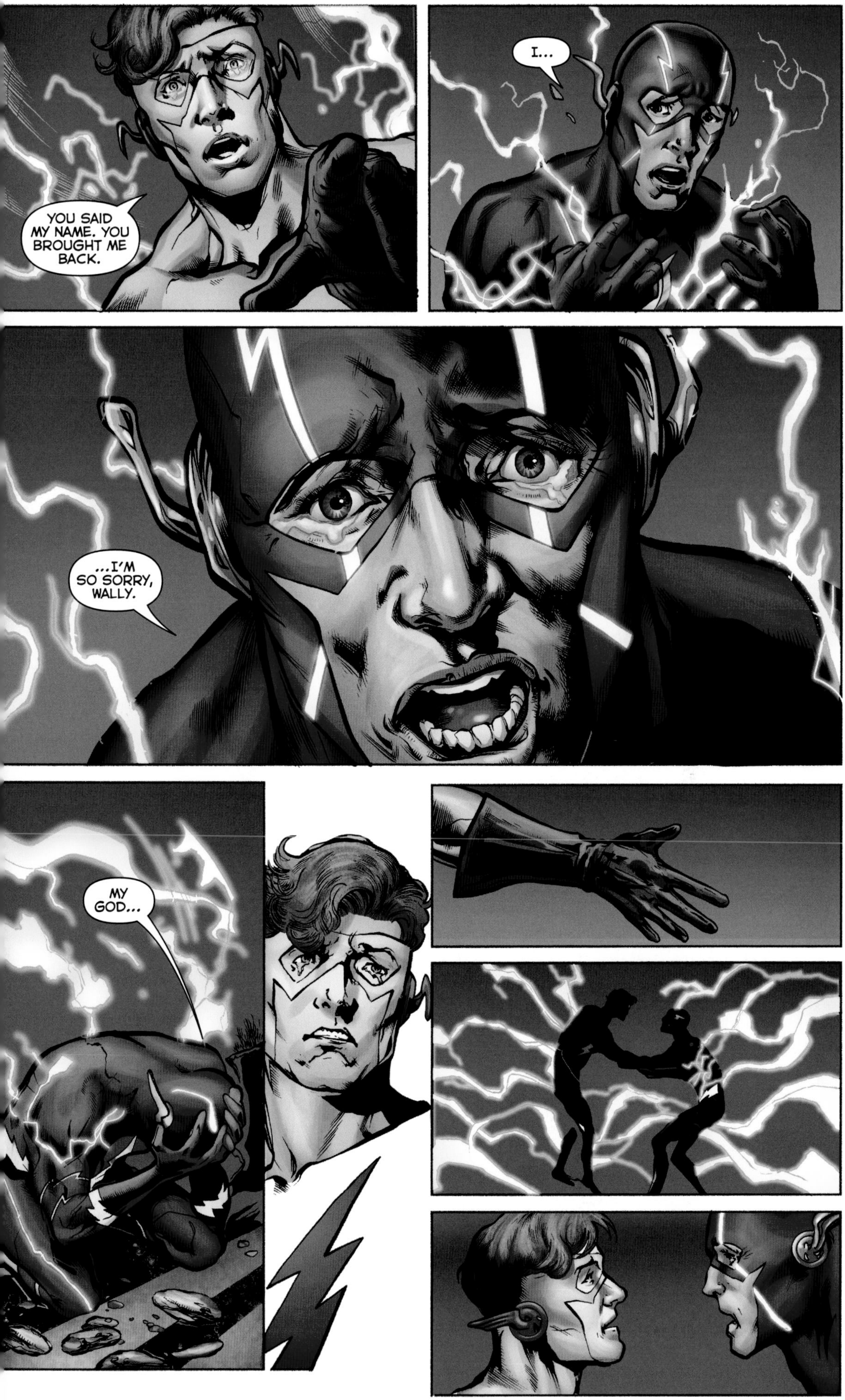
YOU SAID MY NAME. YOU BROUGHT ME BACK.
I...
...I'M SO SORRY, WALLY.
MY GOD...

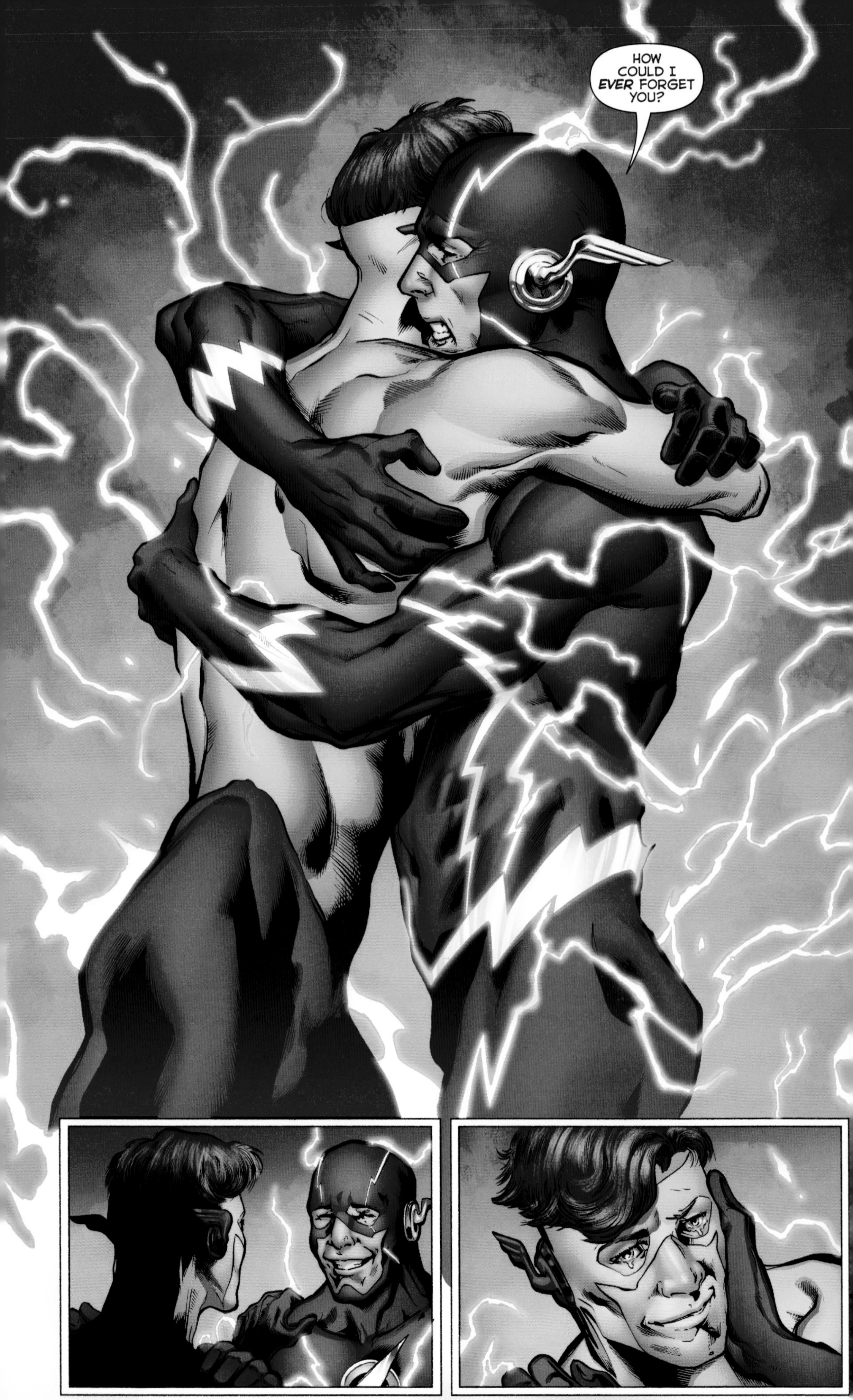
HOW COULD I *EVER* FORGET YOU?

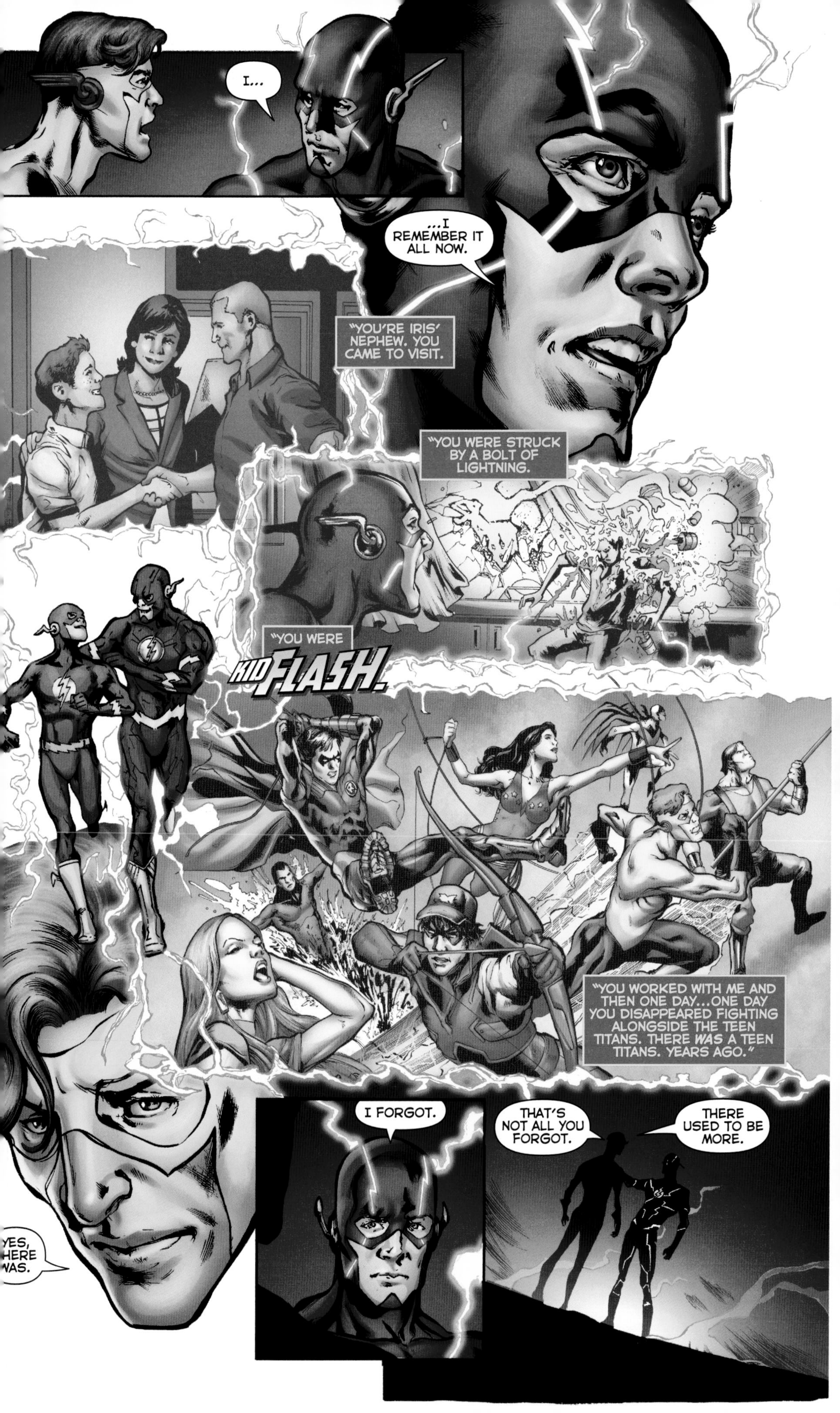

I...
...I REMEMBER IT ALL NOW.
"YOU'RE IRIS' NEPHEW. YOU CAME TO VISIT.
"YOU WERE STRUCK BY A BOLT OF LIGHTNING.
"YOU WERE
KID FLASH.
"YOU WORKED WITH ME AND THEN ONE DAY...ONE DAY YOU DISAPPEARED FIGHTING ALONGSIDE THE TEEN TITANS. THERE WAS A TEEN TITANS. YEARS AGO."
YES, THERE WAS.
I FORGOT.
THAT'S NOT ALL YOU FORGOT.
THERE USED TO BE MORE.

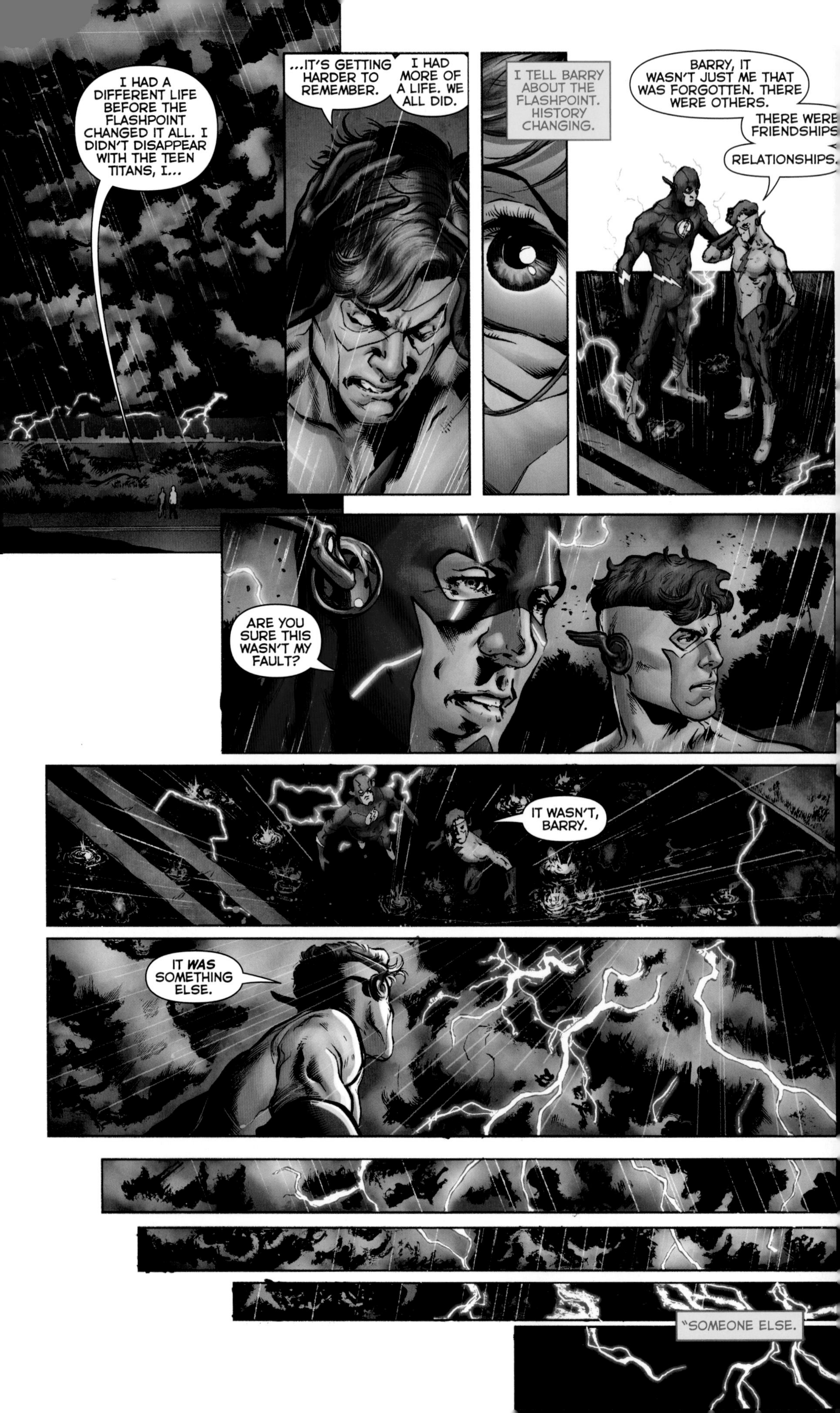
I HAD A DIFFERENT LIFE BEFORE THE FLASHPOINT CHANGED IT ALL. I DIDN'T DISAPPEAR WITH THE TEEN TITANS, I...
...IT'S GETTING HARDER TO REMEMBER.
I HAD MORE OF A LIFE. WE ALL DID.
I TELL BARRY ABOUT THE FLASHPOINT. HISTORY CHANGING.
BARRY, IT WASN'T JUST ME THAT WAS FORGOTTEN. THERE WERE OTHERS.
THERE WERE FRIENDSHIPS
RELATIONSHIPS.
ARE YOU SURE THIS WASN'T MY FAULT?
IT WASN'T, BARRY.
IT *WAS* SOMETHING ELSE.
"SOMEONE ELSE.

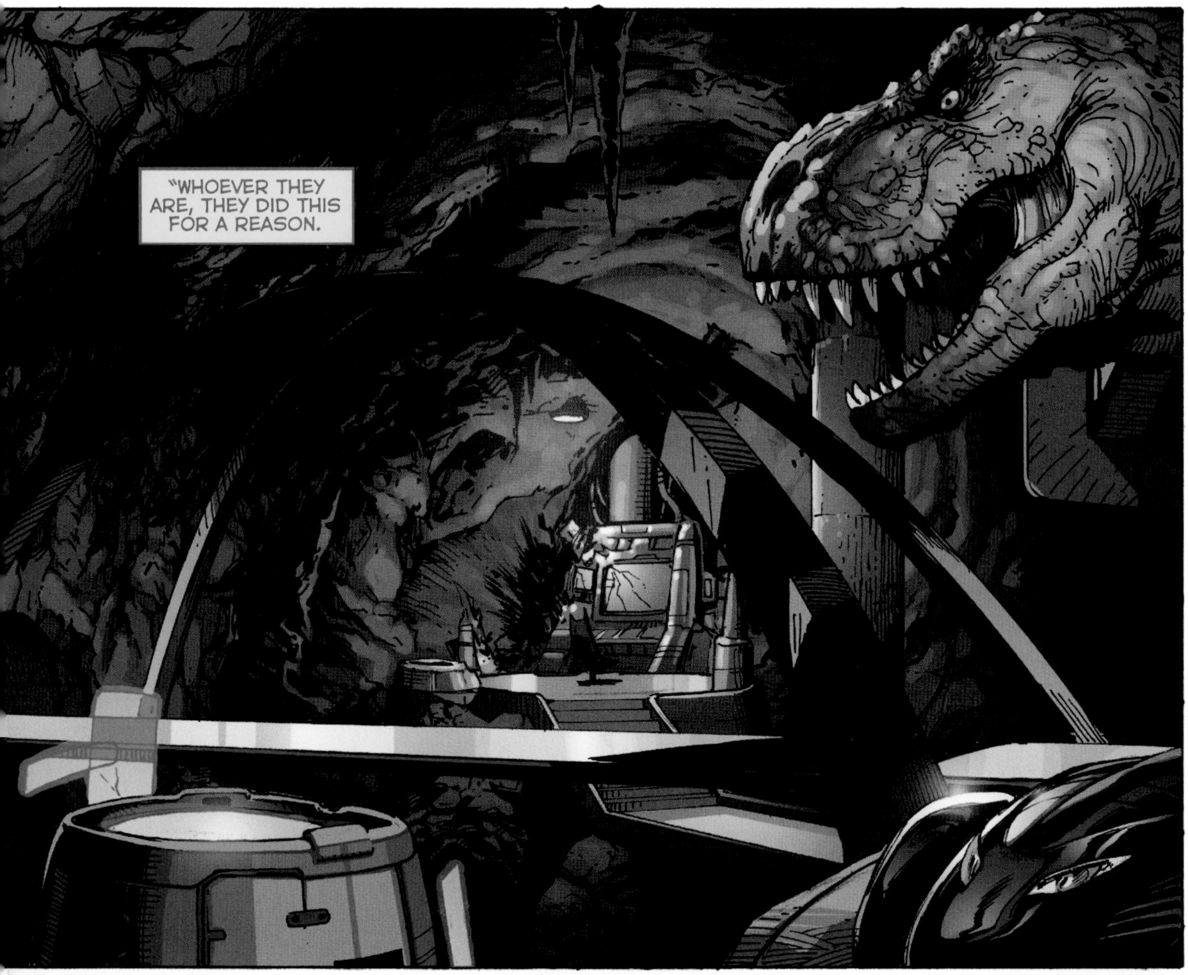
"WHOEVER THEY ARE, THEY DID THIS FOR A REASON.

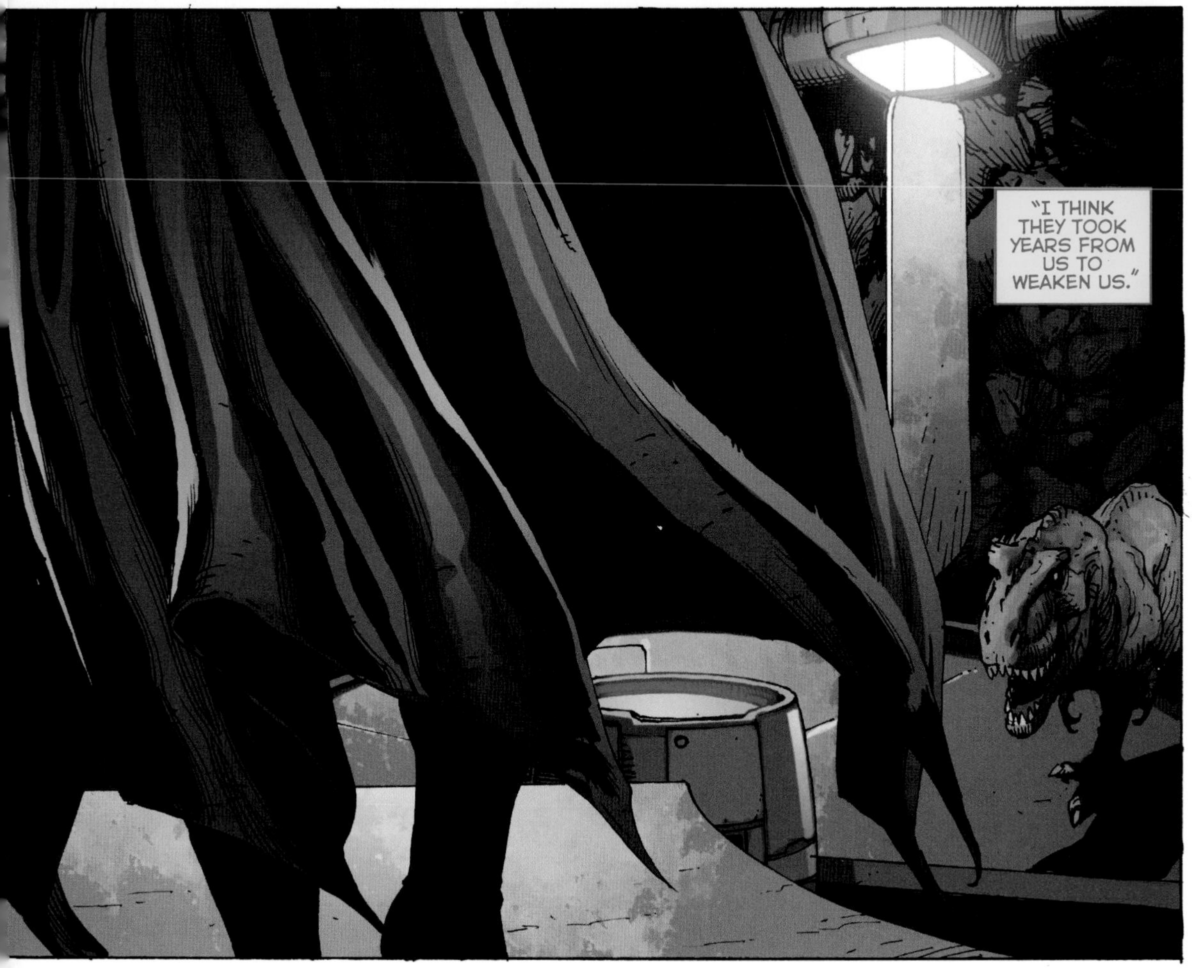
"I THINK THEY TOOK YEARS FROM US TO WEAKEN US."

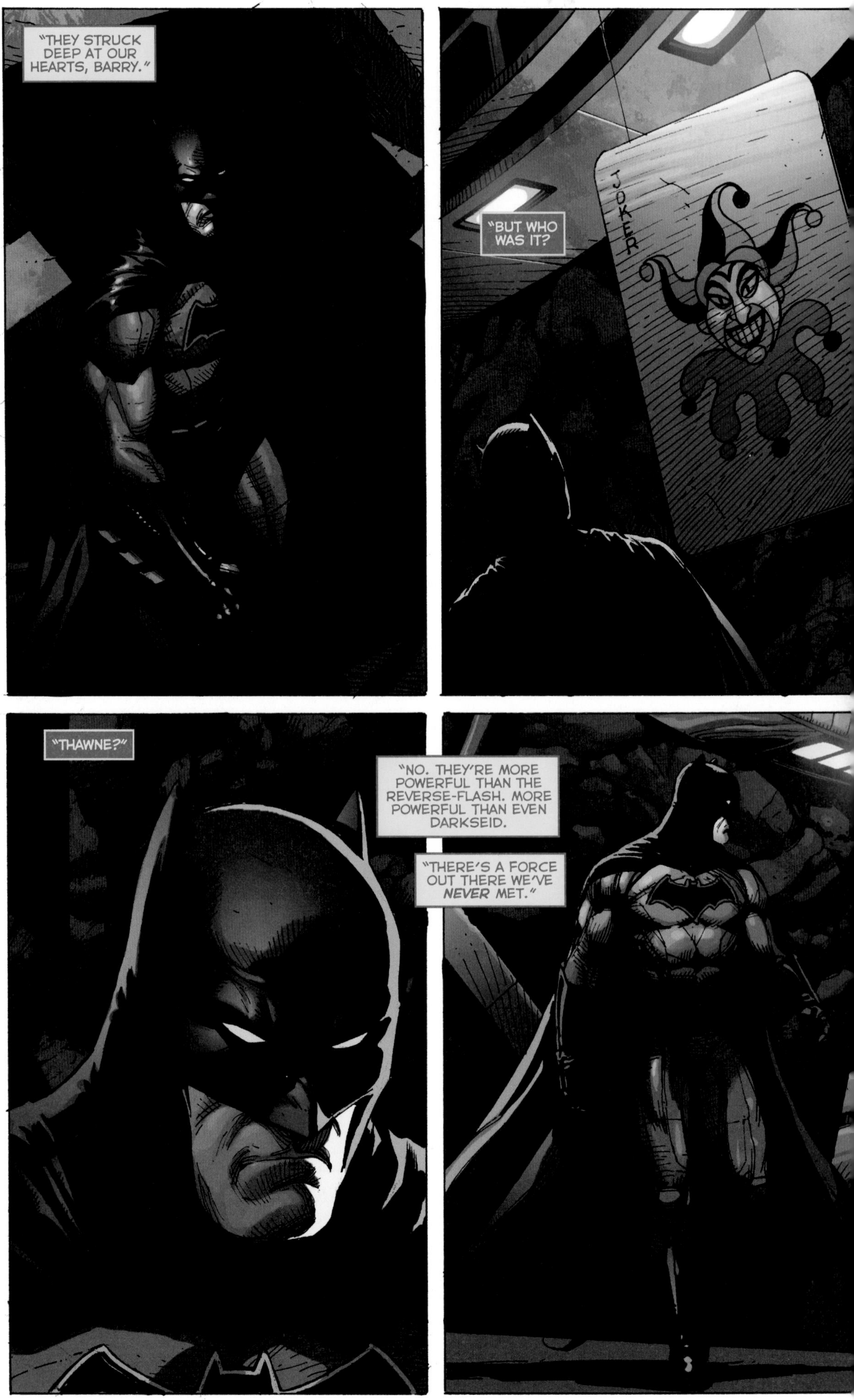

"THEY STRUCK DEEP AT OUR HEARTS, BARRY."
"BUT WHO WAS IT?
JOKER
"THAWNE?"
"NO. THEY'RE MORE POWERFUL THAN THE REVERSE-FLASH. MORE POWERFUL THAN EVEN DARKSEID.
"THERE'S A FORCE OUT THERE WE'VE *NEVER* MET."

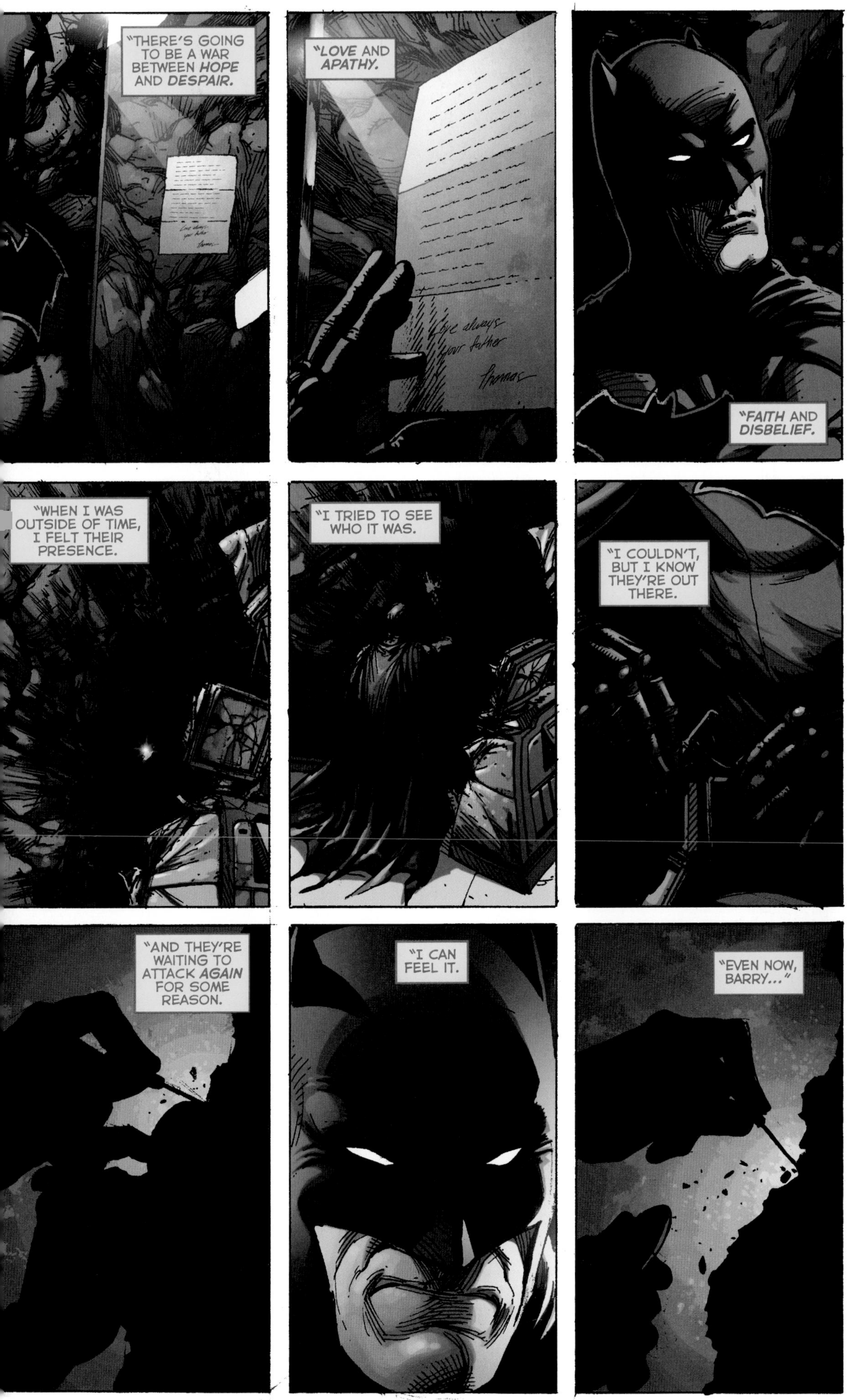
"THERE'S GOING TO BE A WAR BETWEEN *HOPE* AND *DESPAIR.*
"*LOVE* AND *APATHY.*
Love always your father Thomas
"*FAITH* AND *DISBELIEF.*
"WHEN I WAS OUTSIDE OF TIME, I FELT THEIR PRESENCE.
"I TRIED TO SEE WHO IT WAS.
"I COULDN'T, BUT I KNOW THEY'RE OUT THERE.
"AND THEY'RE WAITING TO ATTACK *AGAIN* FOR SOME REASON.
"I CAN FEEL IT.
"EVEN NOW, BARRY..."

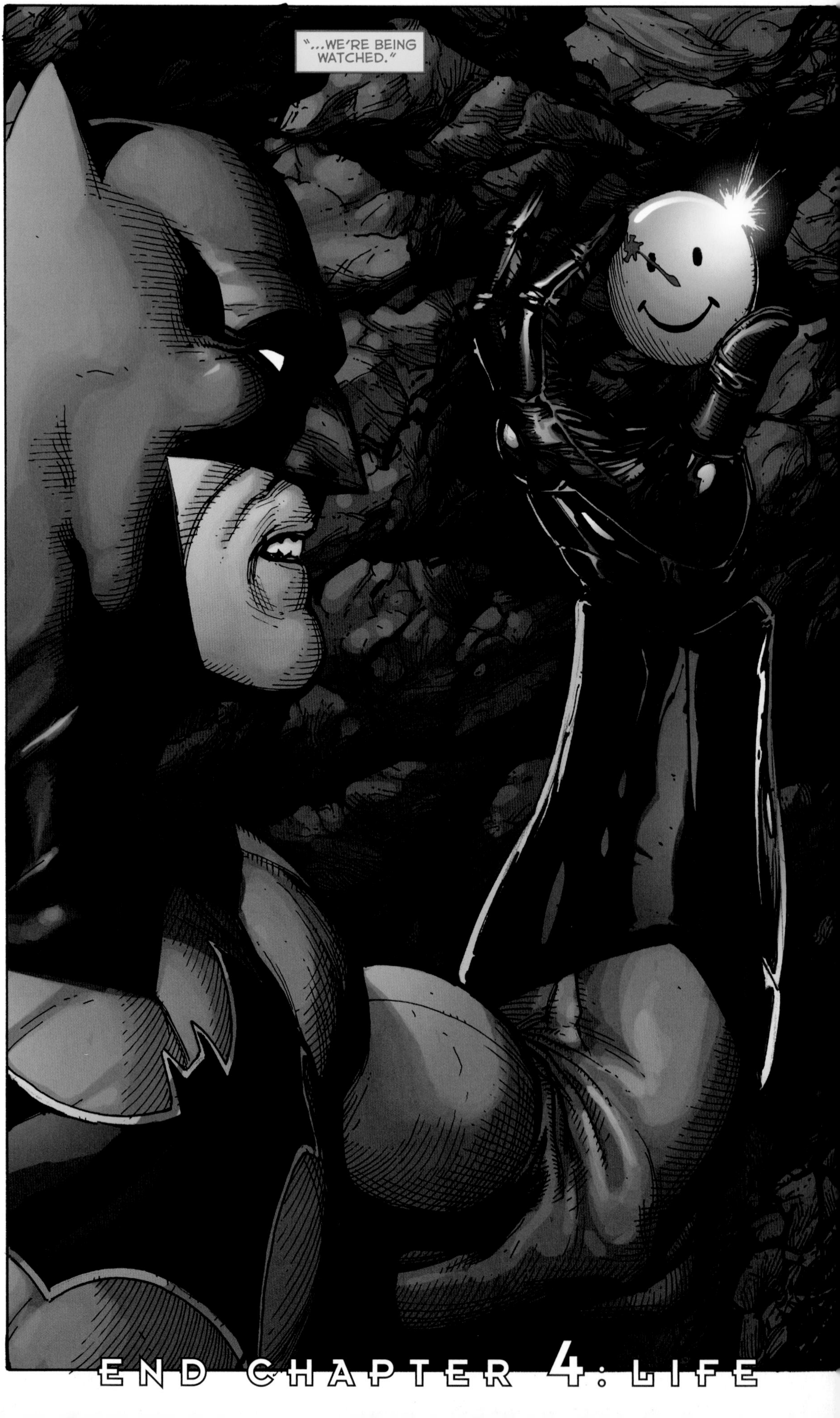
"...WE'RE BEING WATCHED."
END CHAPTER 4: LIFE

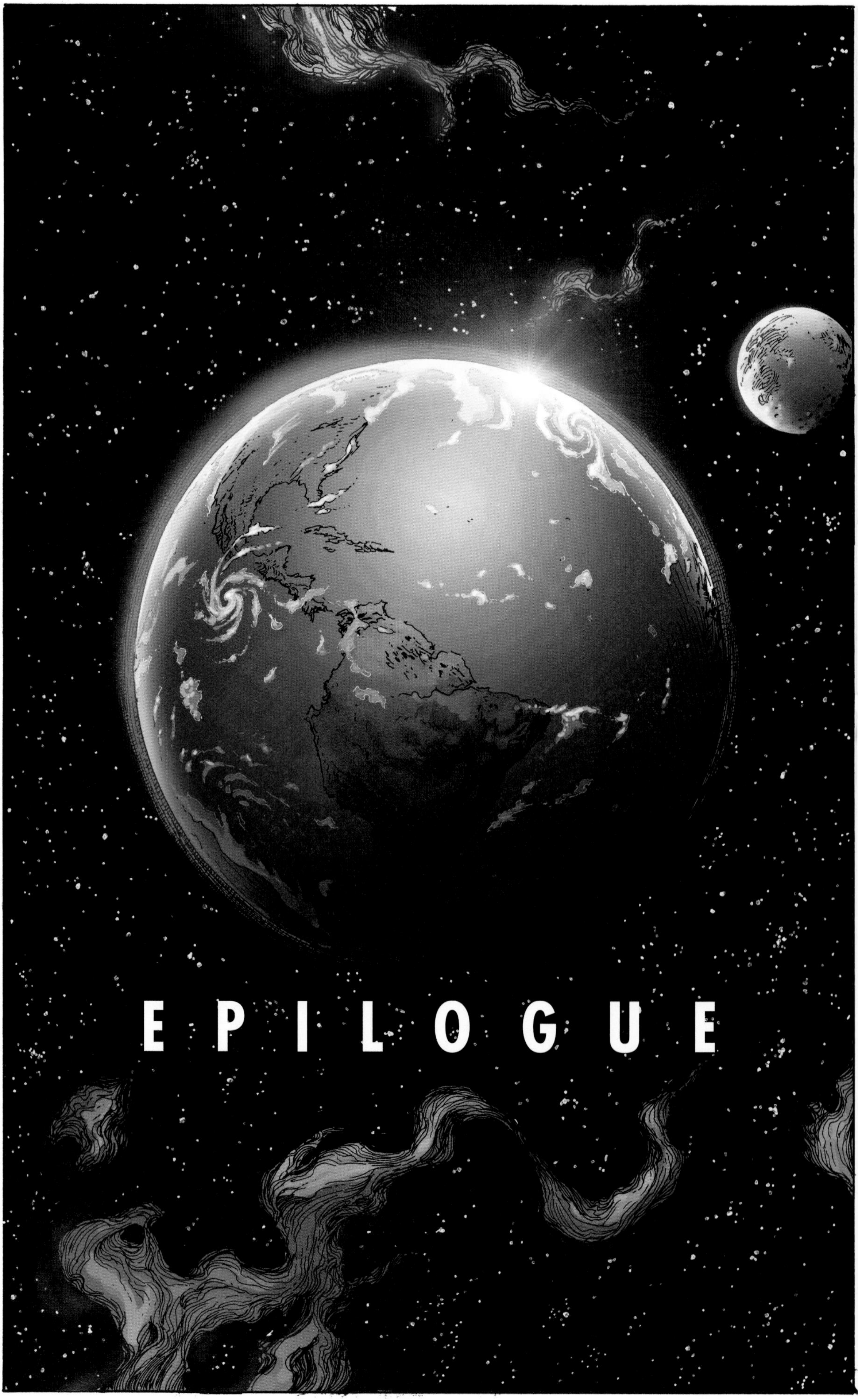
EPILOGUE

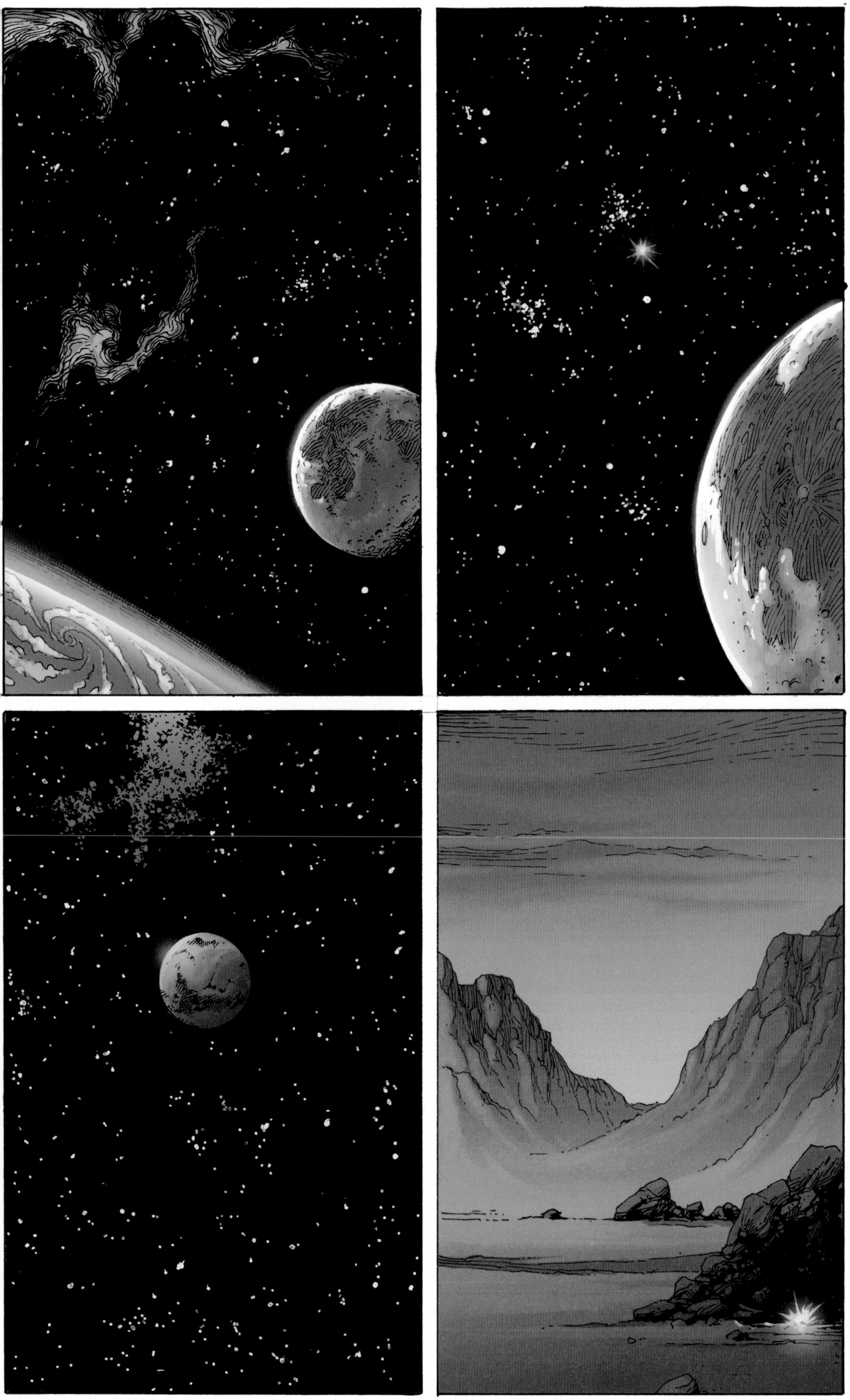

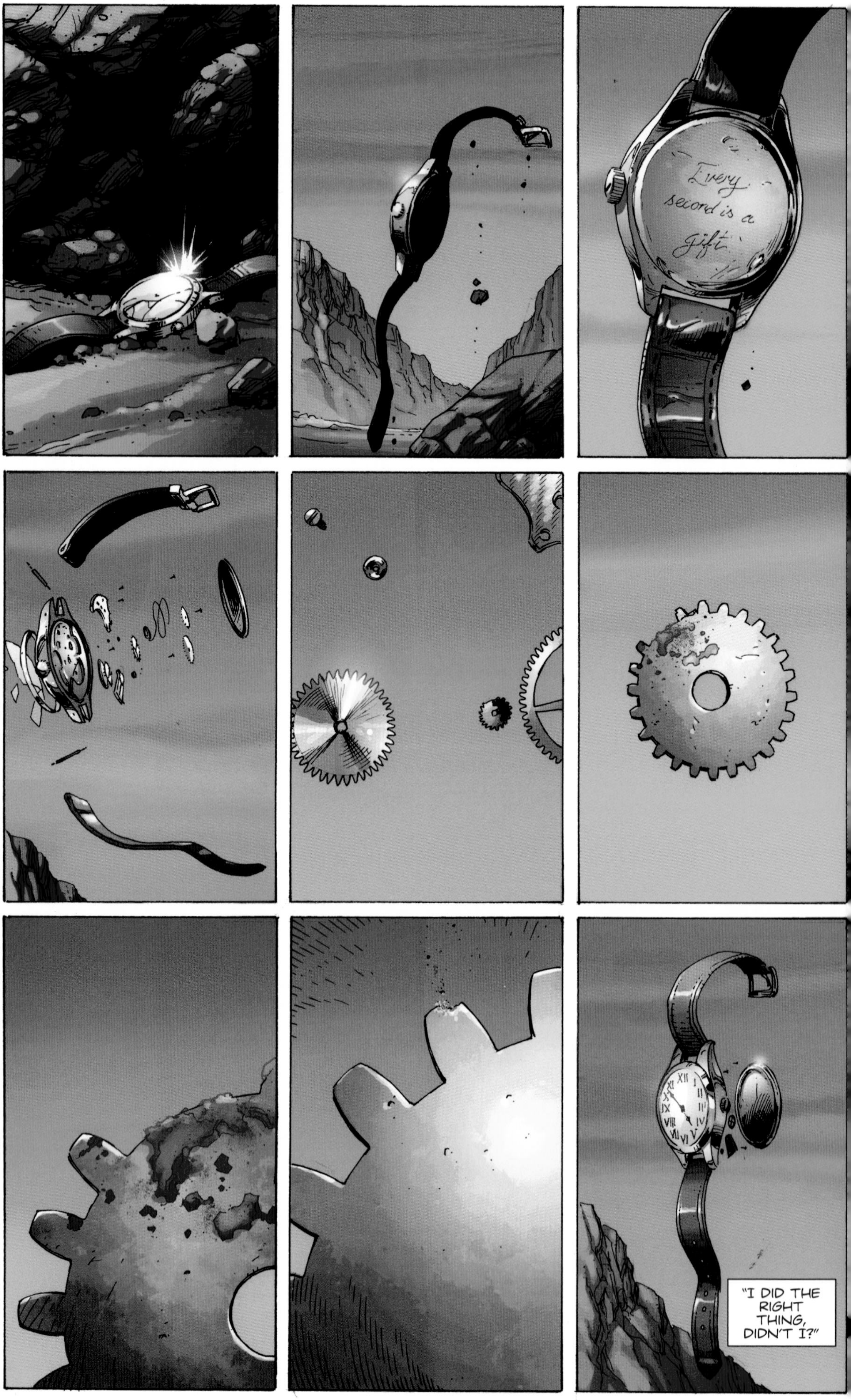
Every second is a gift
"I DID THE RIGHT THING, DIDN'T I?"

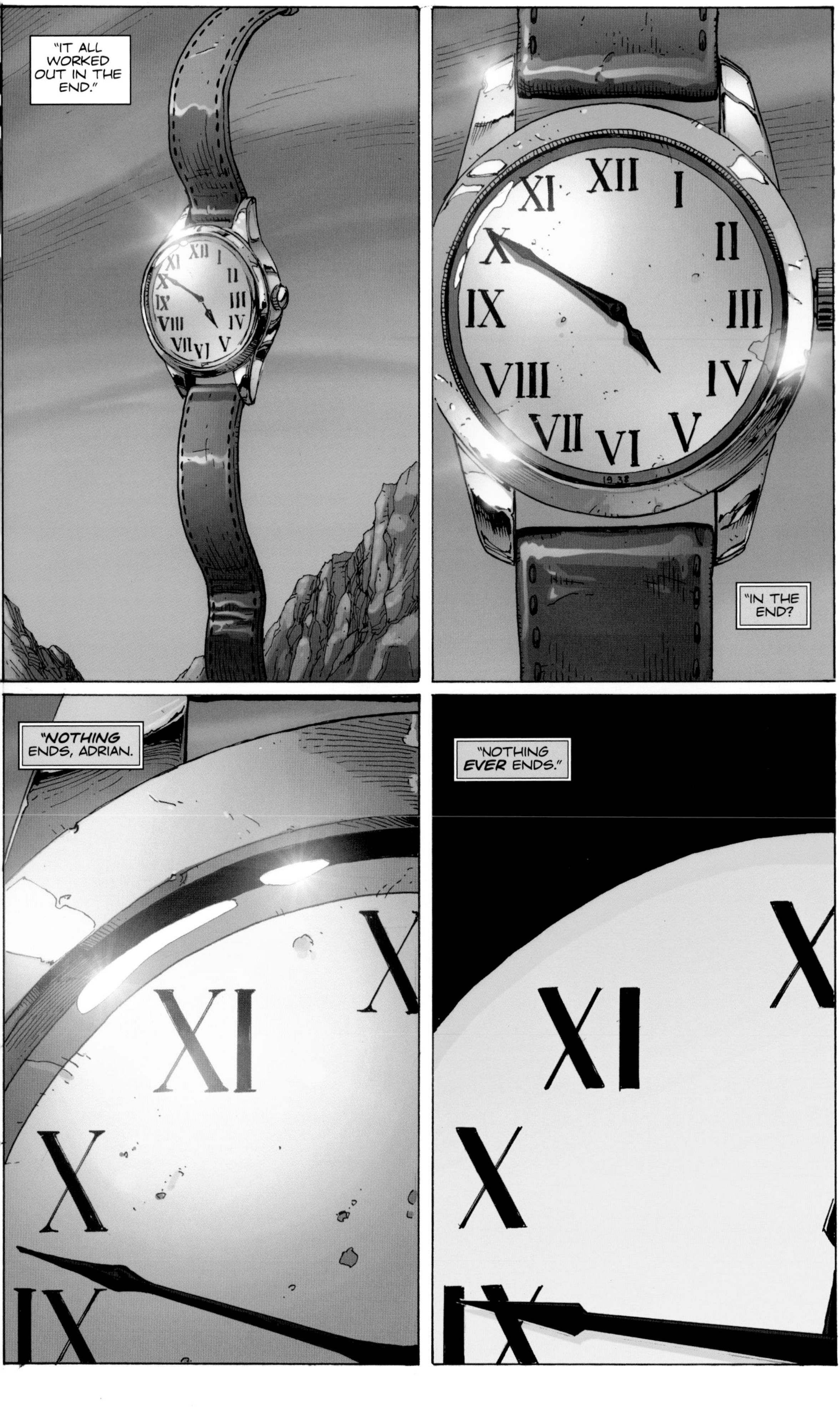
"IT ALL WORKED OUT IN THE END."
"IN THE END?
"NOTHING ENDS, ADRIAN.
"NOTHING EVER ENDS."

THE CLOCK IS TICKING

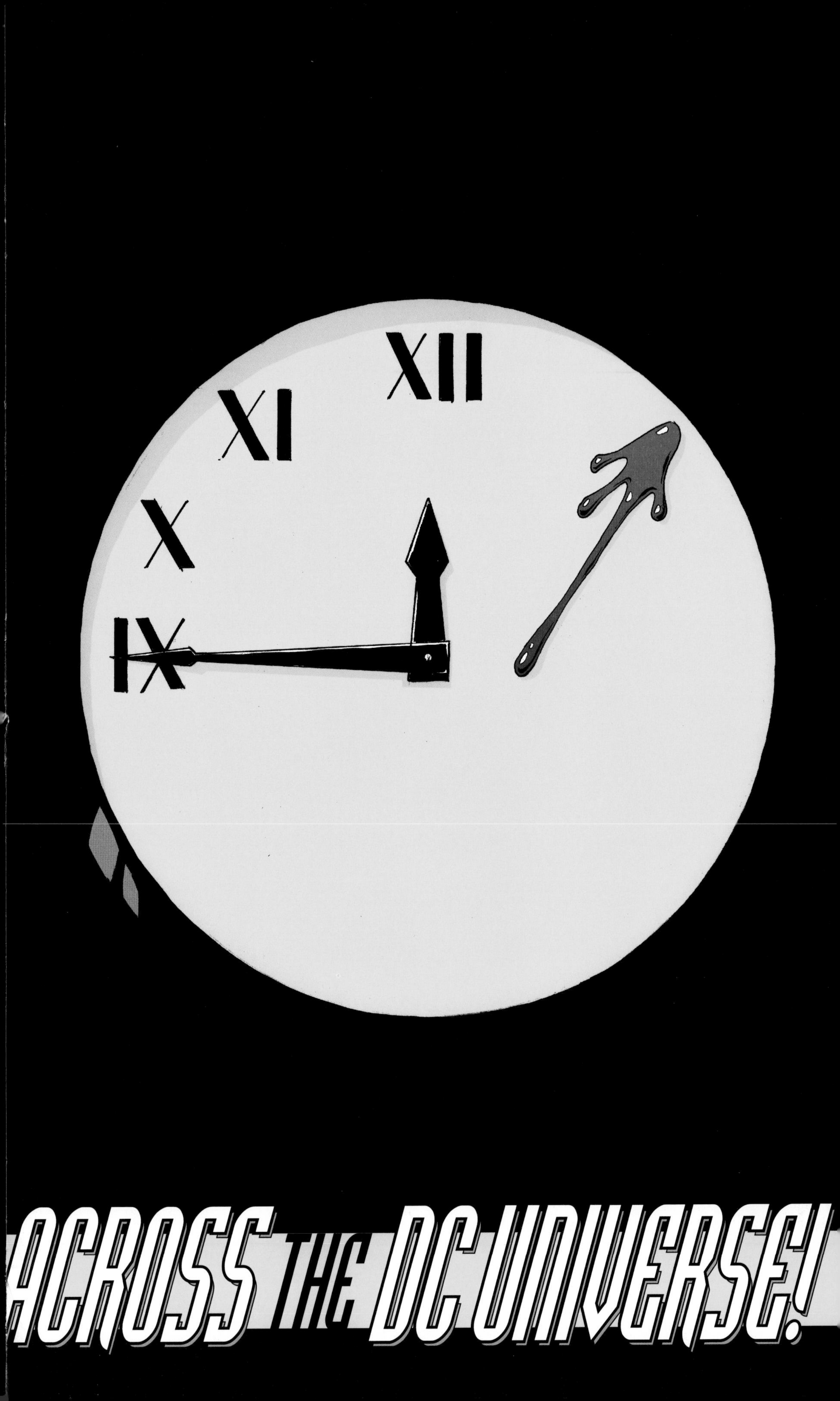
XII
XI
X
IX
ACROSS THE DC UNIVERSE!

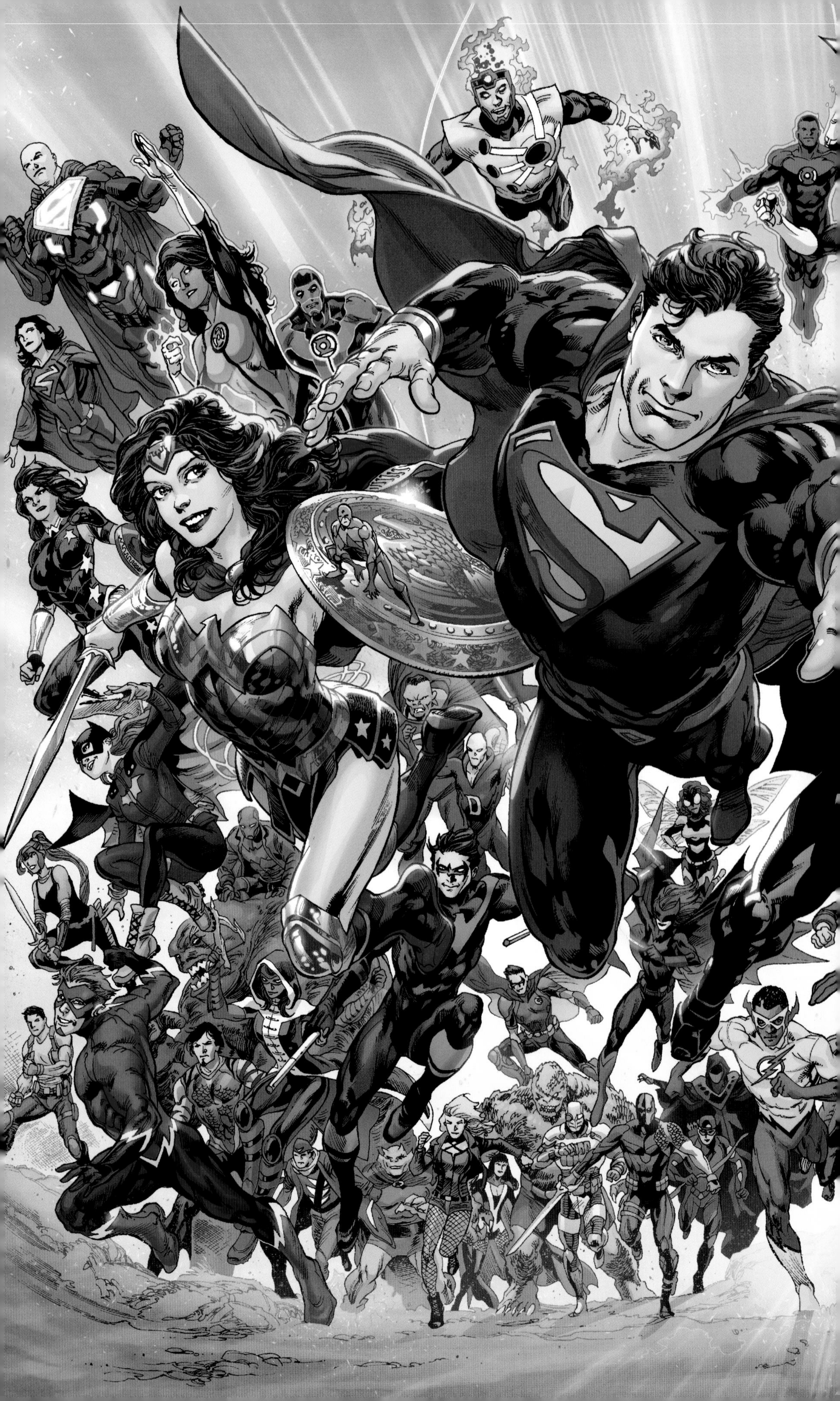

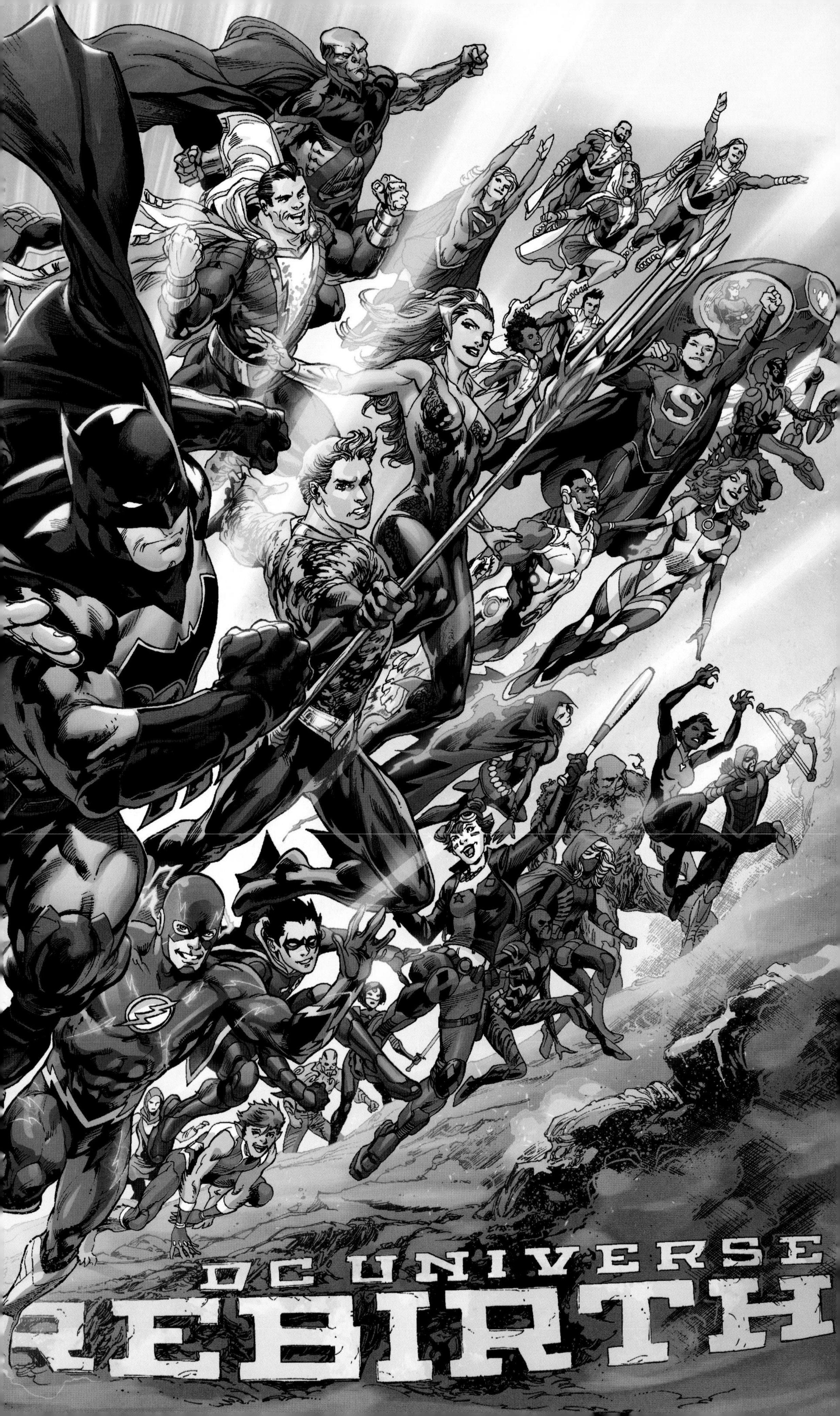
DC UNIVERSE
REBIRTH

DC UNIVERSE: REBIRTH #1 • First Printing Cover
By GARY FRANK and BRAD ANDERSON

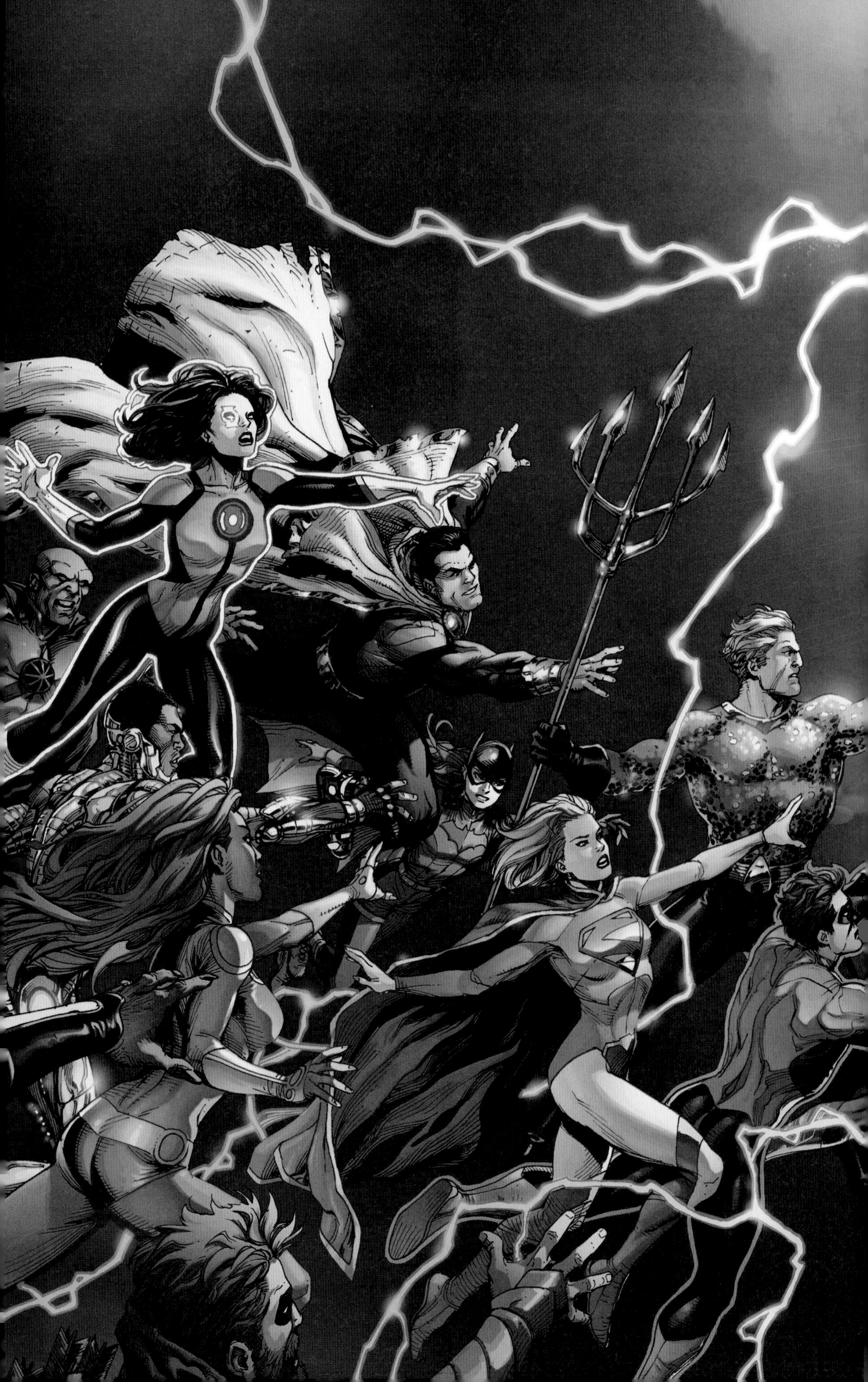

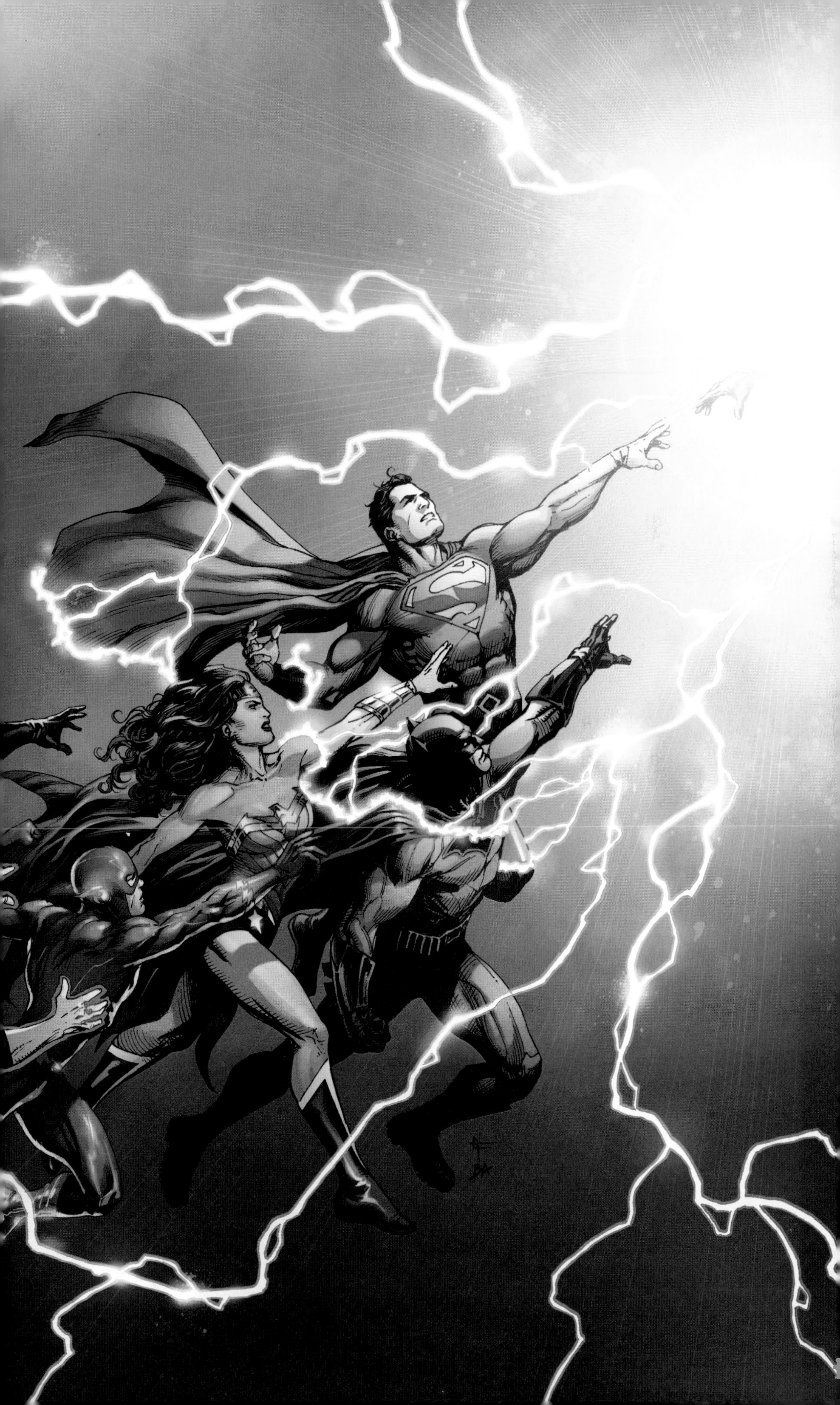

DC UNIVERSE: REBIRTH #1 • Second Printing Cover
By GARY FRANK and BRAD ANDERSON

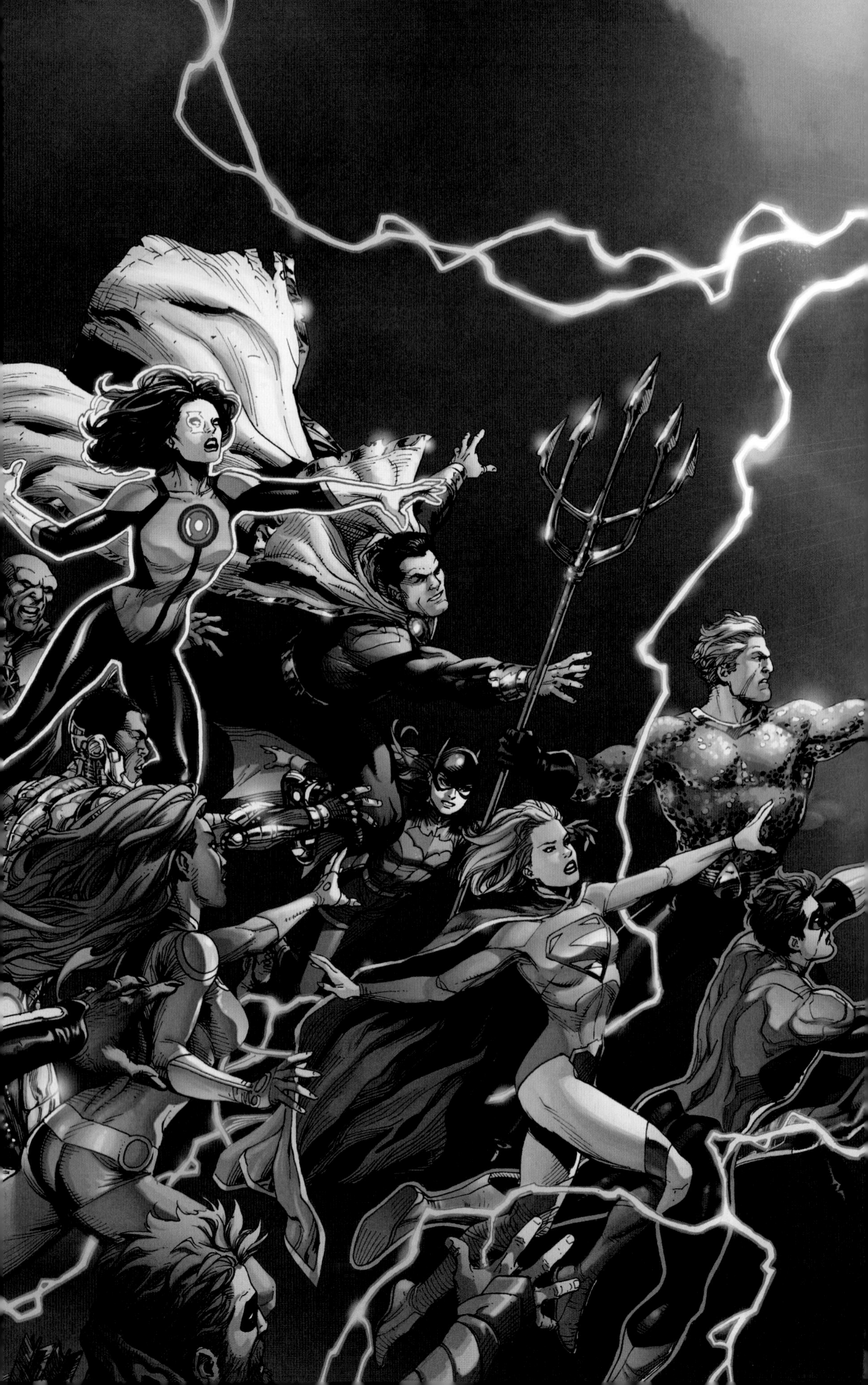

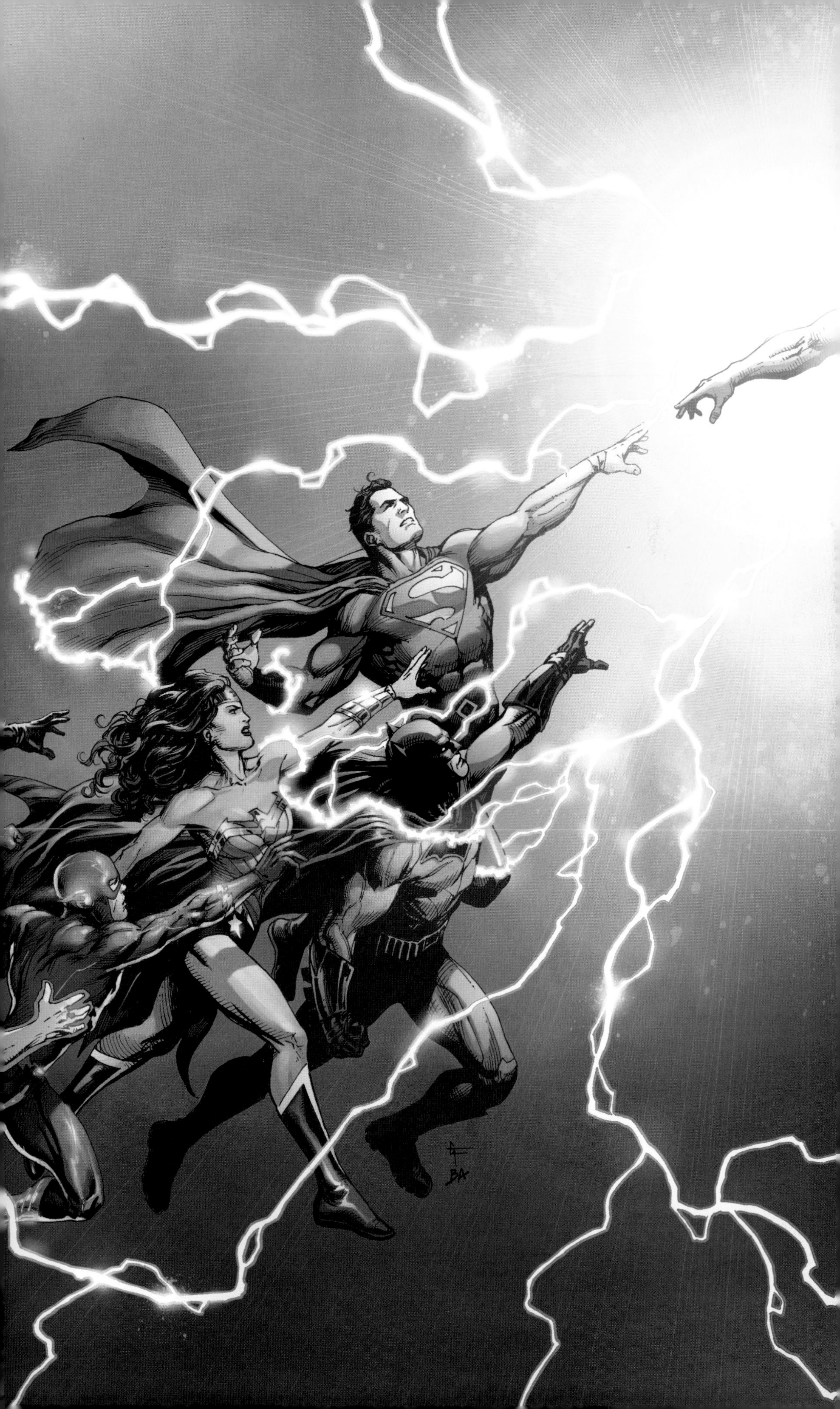

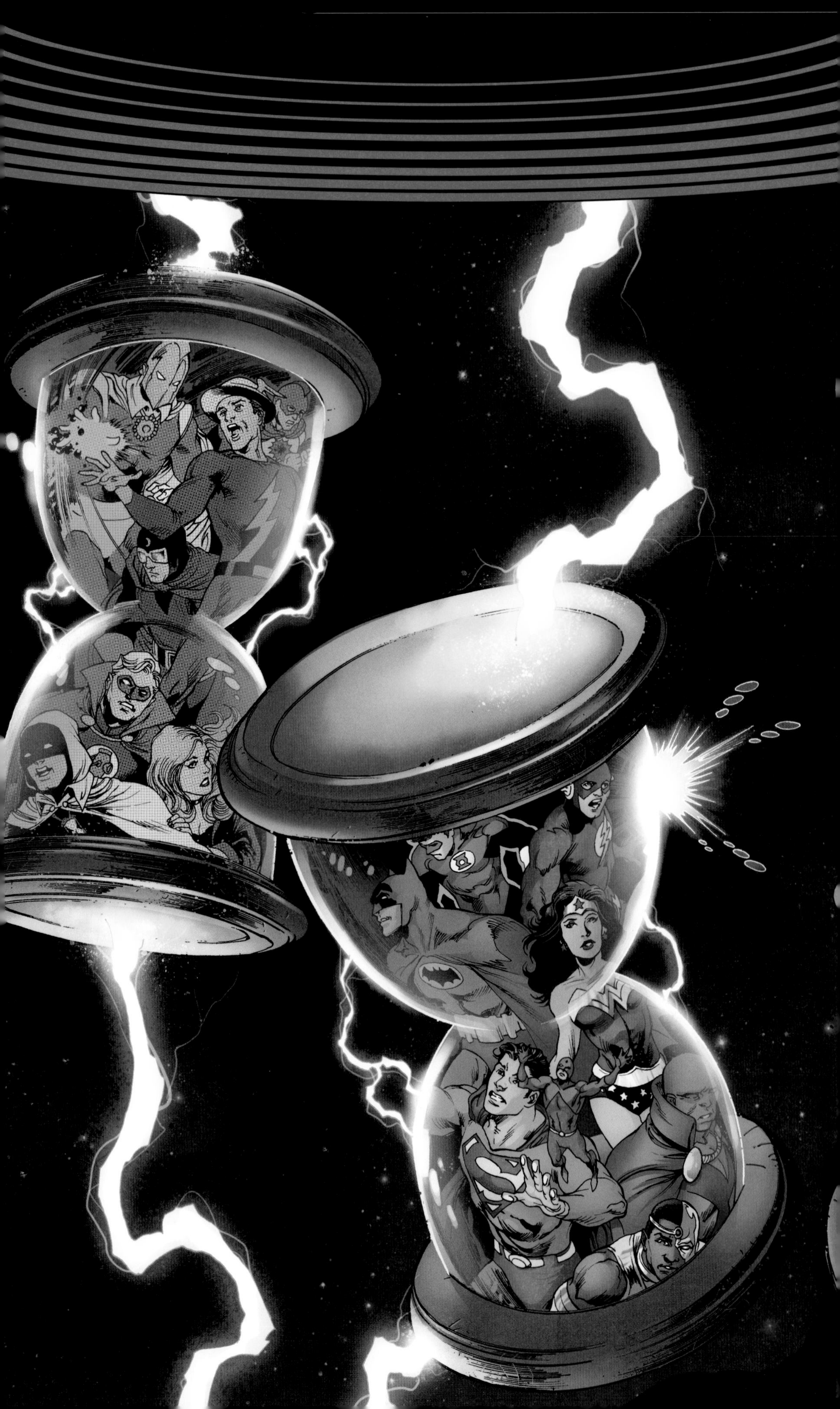

DC UNIVERSE: REBIRTH #1 * Variant Cover
By IVAN REIS, JOE PRADO and ALEX SINCLAIR

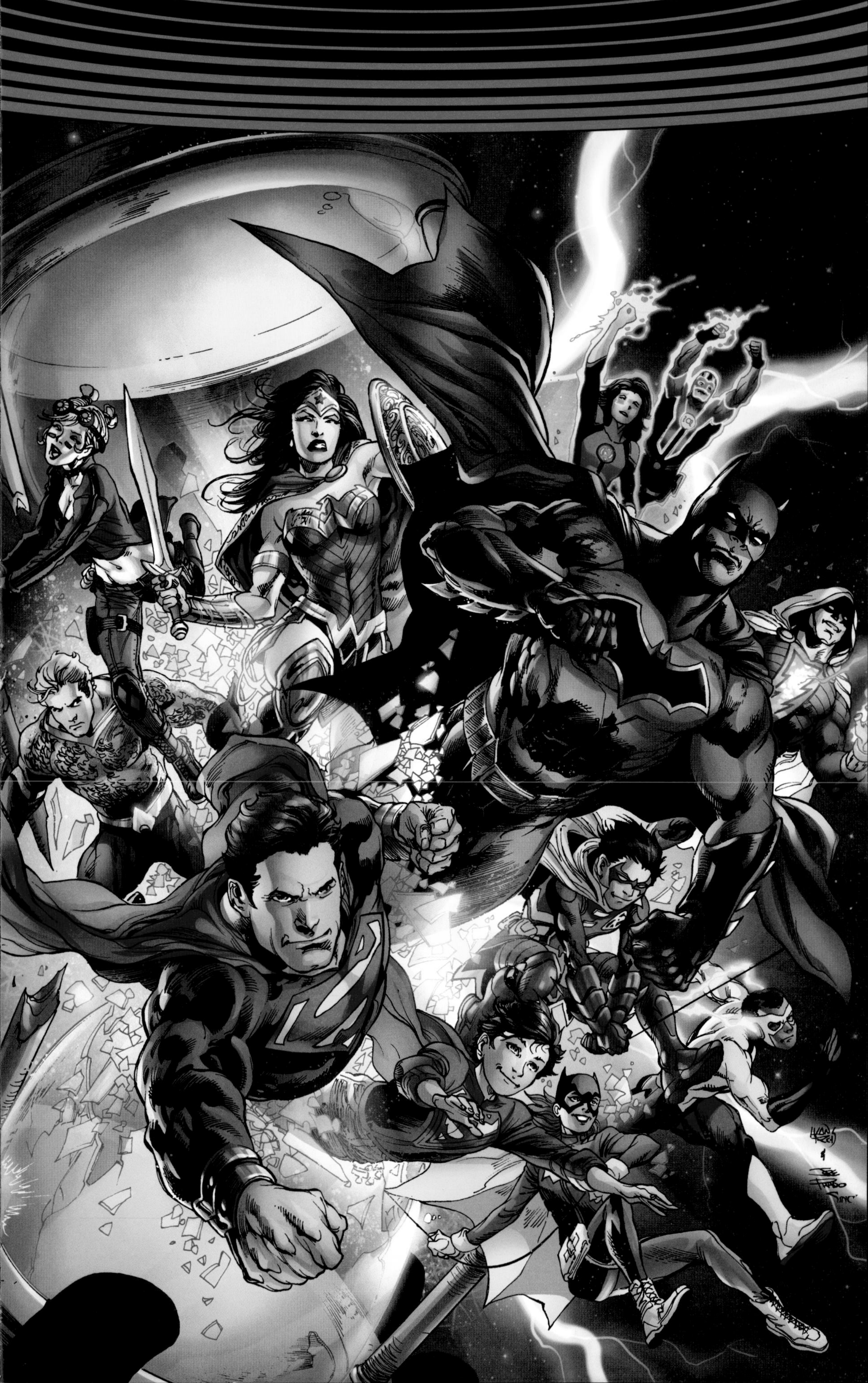

DC UNIVERSE: REBIRTH #1 • Third Printing Cover
By GARY FRANK and ALEX SINCLAIR

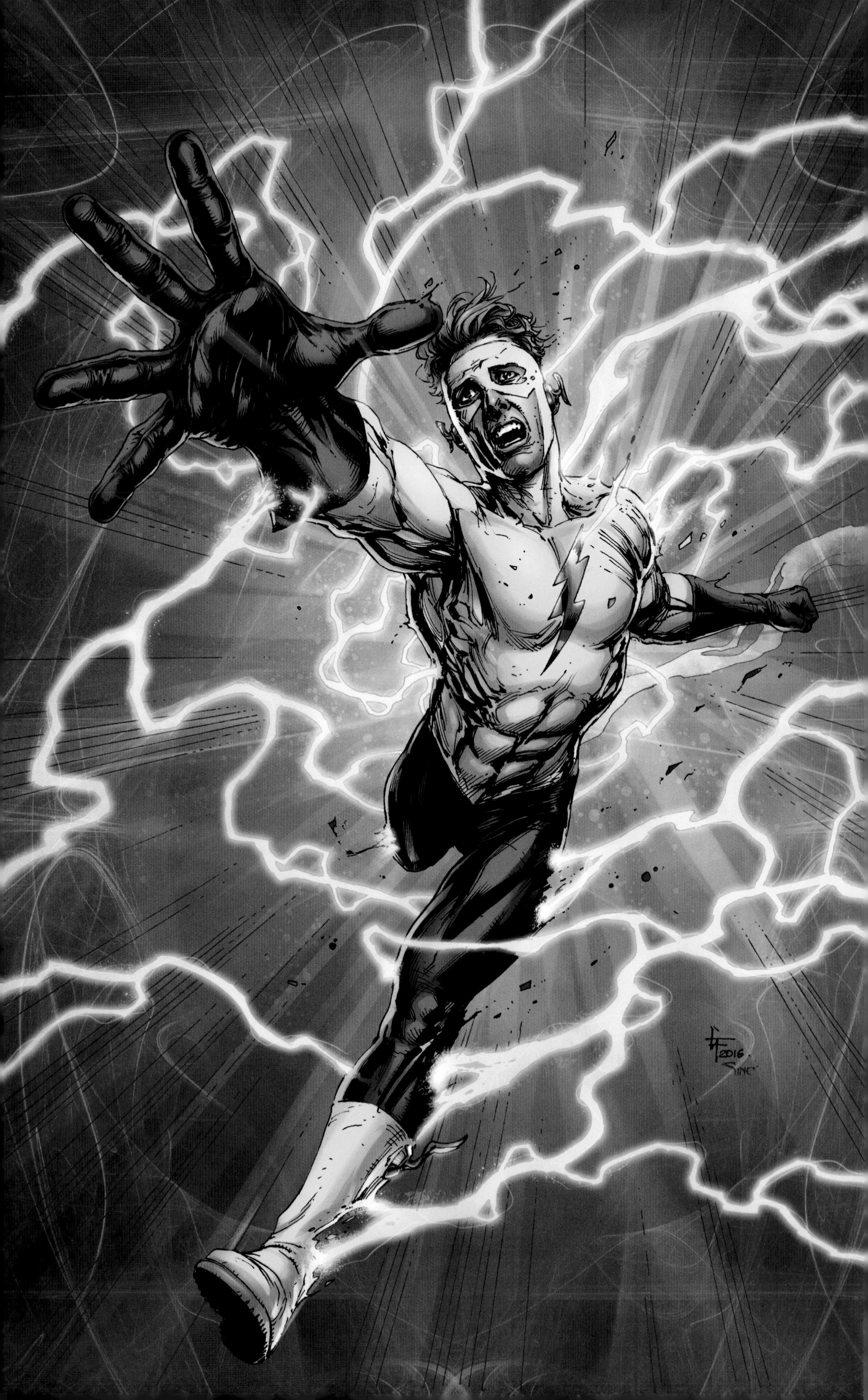

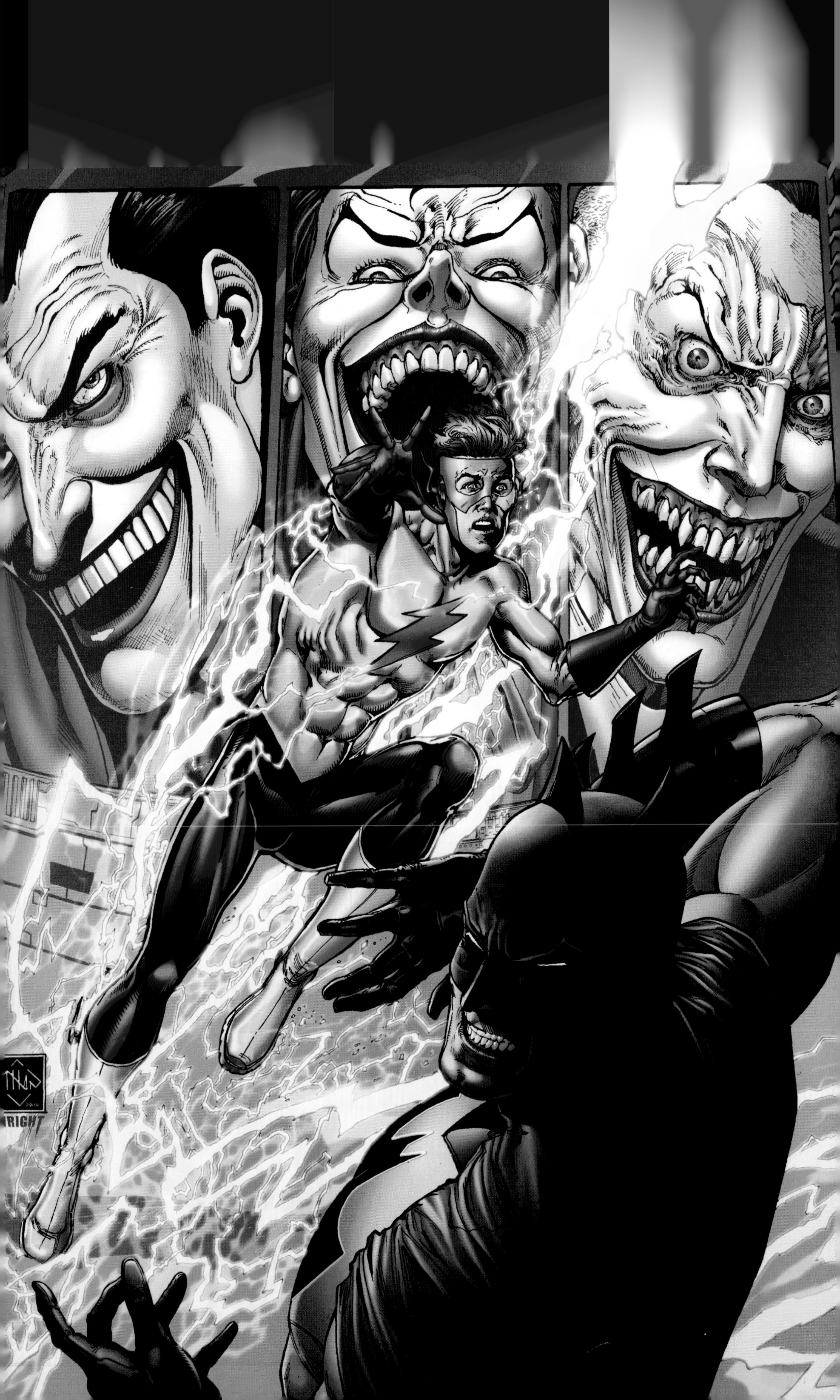

DC UNIVERSE: REBIRTH #1 * Fifth Printing Cover
By PHIL JIMENEZ and ALEX SINCLAIR

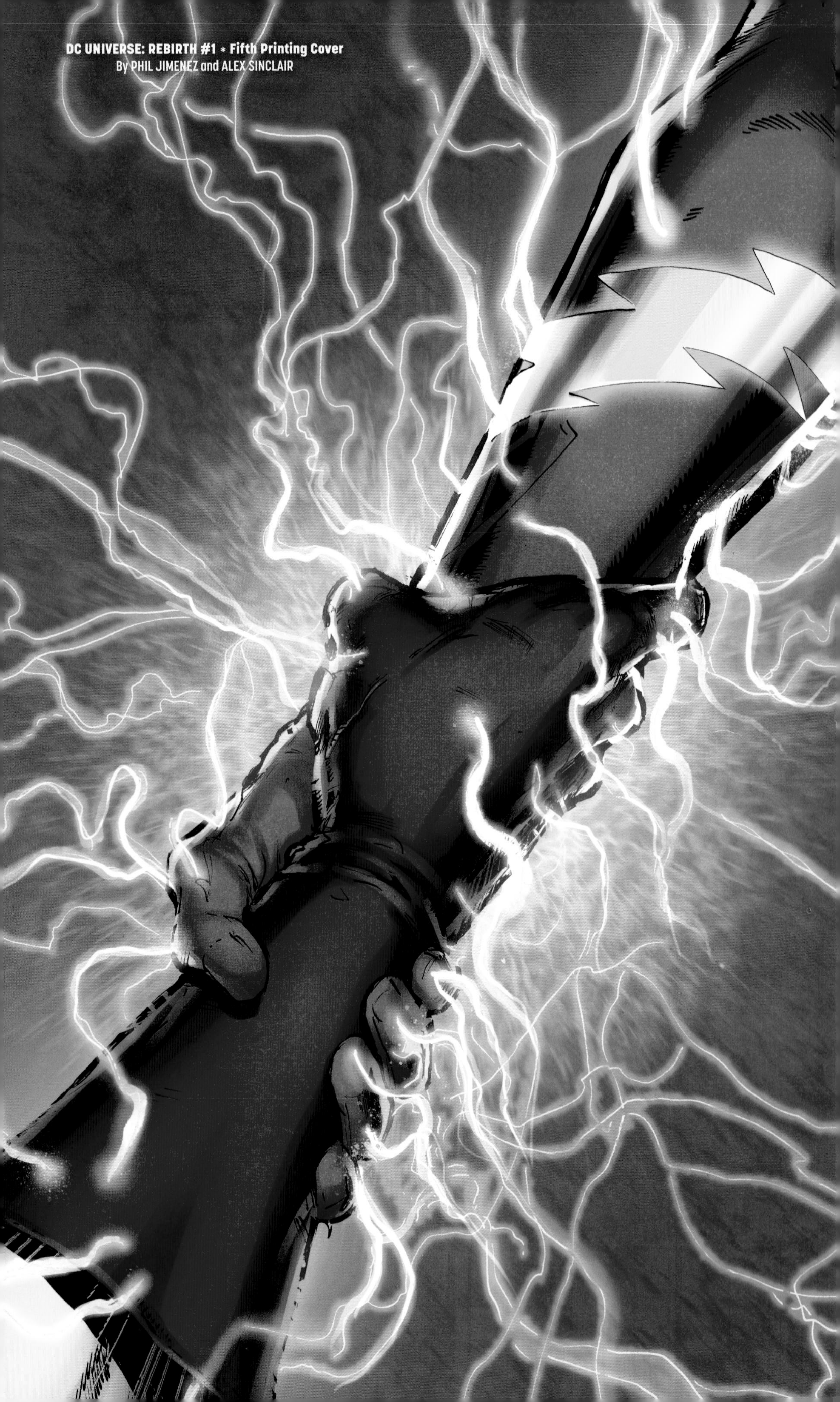

WHO'S WATCHING GEOFF & GARY?

Artist Gary Frank used a nine-panel grid layout on the first page and just before the reveal in the epilogue. This same layout appeared throughout WATCHMEN, specifically when Doctor Manhattan is recounting his past and using a metaphor about the cogs in a watch.

THE DAY I GRADUATED HIGH SCHOOL, MY UNCLE GAVE ME A WATCH.
IT BELONGED TO HIS FATHER.
AND HIS GRANDFATHER BEFORE THAT.
THE WATCH HAD BEEN HANDED DOWN GENERATION AFTER GENERATION WITH AN INSCRIPTION ON THE BACK...
"EVERY SECOND IS A GIFT."
MY UNCLE WAS AN OPTIMIST.
I USED TO BE AN OPTIMIST, TOO.
UNTIL THE DAY THE WATCH BROKE.
AND I LOST IT.
I LOST TIME.
EVERYONE DID.

Every second is a gift
"I DID THE RIGHT THING, DIDN'T I?"

IT IS AUGUST 7TH, 1945. THE BROOKLYN MORNING IS HUMID AND THE FIRE ESCAPE DOOR HAS BEEN LEFT OPEN.
JON? WHERE ARE YOU?
IN HERE. I'M PRACTICING ON YOUR OLD POCKETWATCH, BEFORE IT'S TIME FOR SCHOOL.
FORGET POCKET-WATCHES! HAVE YOU SEEN THE NEWS?
NEWS?
THEY DROPPED THE ATOMIC BOMB ON JAPAN! A WHOLE CITY, GONE!
ACH! THESE ARE NO TIMES FOR A REPAIRER OF WATCHES ...
ATOMIC BOMB DROPPED ON HIROSHIMA
THIS CHANGES EVERYTHING! THERE WILL BE MORE BOMBS. THEY ARE THE FUTURE.
SHALL MY SON FOLLOW ME INTO AN OBSOLETE TRADE?
FATHER? WHAT ARE YOU DOING?
I'M DOING WHAT IS BEST FOR YOU. THIS ATOMIC SCIENCE... THIS IS WHAT THE WORLD WILL NEED! NOT POCKET-WATCHES!
HEY! GIVE ME THAT BACK!
PROFESSOR EINSTEIN SAYS THAT TIME DIFFERS FROM PLACE TO PLACE. CAN YOU IMAGINE?
IF TIME IS NOT TRUE, WHAT PURPOSE HAVE WATCHMAKERS, HEIN?
WAIT! DON'T...
MY PROFESSION IS A THING OF THE PAST. INSTEAD, MY SON MUST HAVE A FUTURE.
FATHER, NO!
FORTY YEARS AGO, COGS RAIN ON BROOKLYN...
ONE HUNDRED AND FIFTEEN MINUTES INTO THE FUTURE, THE METEORITES HAIL DOWN THROUGH THE RAREFIED ATMOSPHERE OF MARS...
IT IS 1948, AND I AM ARRIVING AT PRINCETON UNIVERSITY.
IT IS 1958, AND I AM GRADUATING WITH A PH.D. IN ATOMIC PHYSICS.
THE COGS ARE FALLING...
3

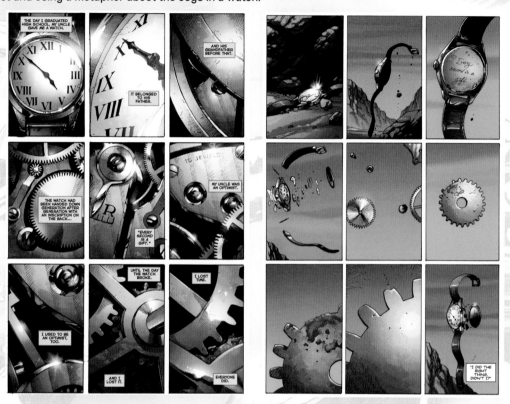

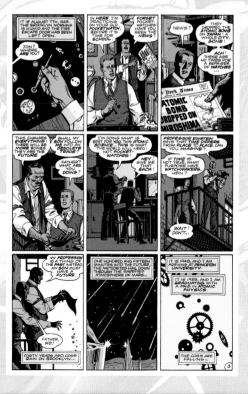

The inclusion of the seminal characters of WATCHMEN in the DC Universe wasn't a task done lightly, but instead a well-thought-out decision. To help ease the readers into this idea, writer Geoff Johns and artist Gary Frank included some subtle (and a few overt) nods to the source material.

THIS WON'T HIDE WHAT YOU'VE DONE.
IT'S BEEN MY BURDEN TO CARRY. MY CURSE TO SUFFER THROUGH.
THE NAIVE LITTLE PANDORA UNLEASHED EVILS UPON THE WORLD.
SKEPTICISM. DOUBT. CORRUPTION. ALL THINGS YOUR COLD HEART BELIEVES IN.
BUT IN THE END, THERE WAS HOPE.
AND THE HEROES OF THIS UNIVERSE EMBODY IT.
THEIR HOPE, THEIR DEVOTION, THEIR LOVE FOR ONE ANOTHER WILL VANQUISH WHAT YOU'VE DONE.
IT MAY BE OVER FOR ME BUT THEY WILL PROVE YOU WRONG.
THEY WILL PROVE YOU ARE NOTHING BUT A LONELY, CRUEL MONST--

HUHHH.
OF COURSE. MUST PROTECT VEIDT'S NEW UTOPIA. ONE MORE BODY AMONGST FOUNDATIONS MAKES LITTLE DIFFERENCE.
WELL? WHAT ARE YOU WAITING FOR?
DO IT.
RORSCHACH...
DO IT!
24

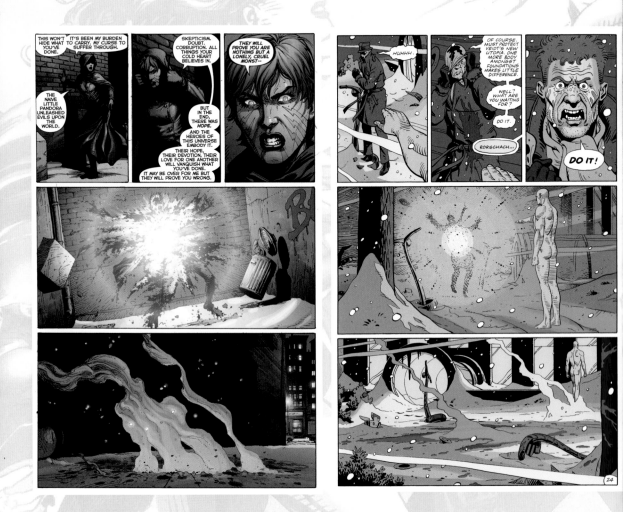

At the end of Chapter 2: "Legacy," Pandora is disintegrated by an unknown assailant. If you compare it to the death of Rorschach from WATCHMEN #12, the page is almost a replica, with the exclusion of Doctor Manhattan himself.

"IT ALL WORKED OUT IN THE END."
"IN THE END?
"NOTHING ENDS, ADRIAN.
"NOTHING EVER ENDS."

The last lines of dialogue from DC UNIVERSE: REBIRTH also came from Doctor Manhattan and Adrian Veidt in WATCHMEN #12.

YES, I HAVE. I THINK PERHAPS I'LL CREATE SOME.
GOODBYE, ADRIAN.
JON, WAIT, BEFORE YOU LEAVE...
I DID THE RIGHT THING, DIDN'T I? IT ALL WORKED OUT IN THE END.
"IN THE END"?
NOTHING ENDS, ADRIAN. NOTHING EVER ENDS.
JON? WAIT! WHAT DO YOU MEAN BY...

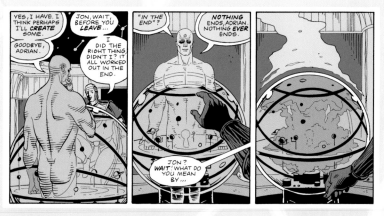

The Rebirth of the DC Universe has brought more than just the WATCHMEN universe to the DCU—it has given new life to the characters, including their costumes. The sketches on the following pages illustrate how certain DC characters changed from their New 52 appearances to their post-Rebirth lives.

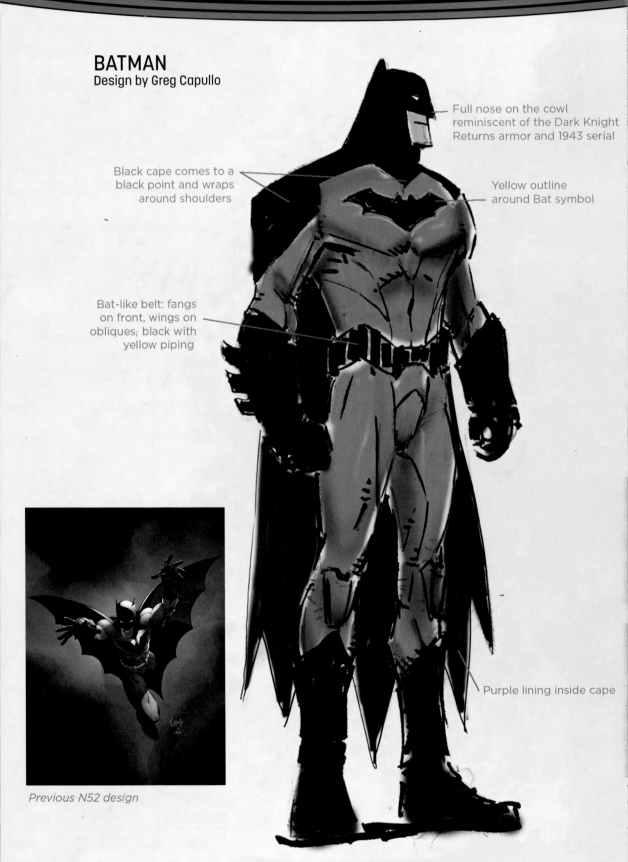

BATMAN
Design by Greg Capullo

Full nose on the cowl reminiscent of the Dark Knight Returns armor and 1943 serial
Black cape comes to a black point and wraps around shoulders
Yellow outline around Bat symbol
Bat-like belt: fangs on front, wings on obliques; black with yellow piping
Purple lining inside cape

Previous N52 design

Illustration by Greg Capullo

SUPERMAN
Design by Patrick Gleason

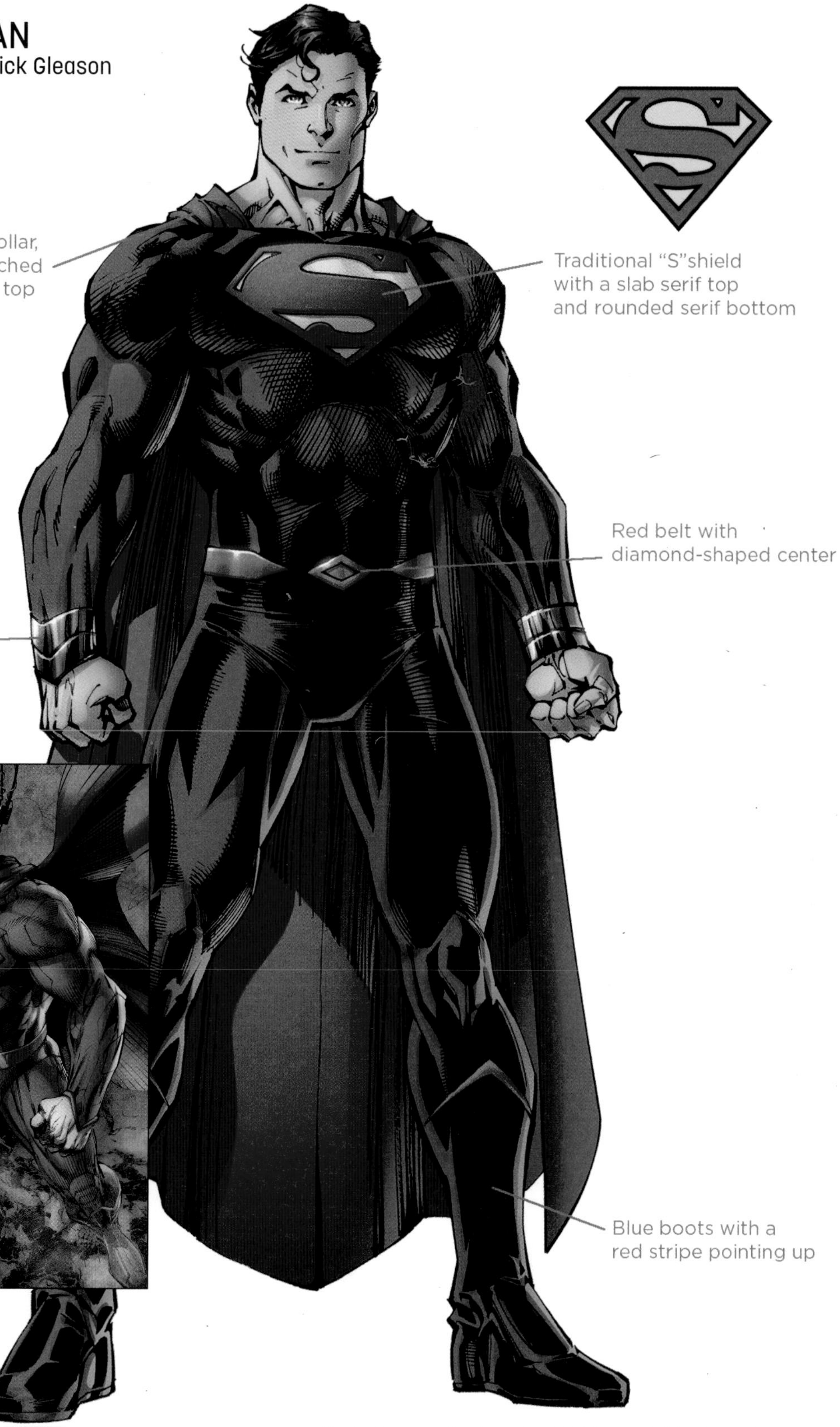

No collar, cape attached to the top
Traditional "S"shield with a slab serif top and rounded serif bottom
Red belt with diamond-shaped center
Blue metallic cuffs
Blue boots with a red stripe pointing up

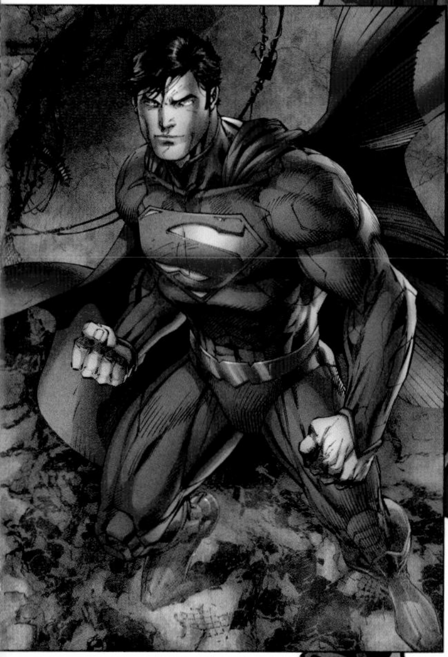

Previous N52 design

Illustration by Jim Lee, Scott Williams & Alex Sinclair

WONDER WOMAN
Design by Tony S. Daniel

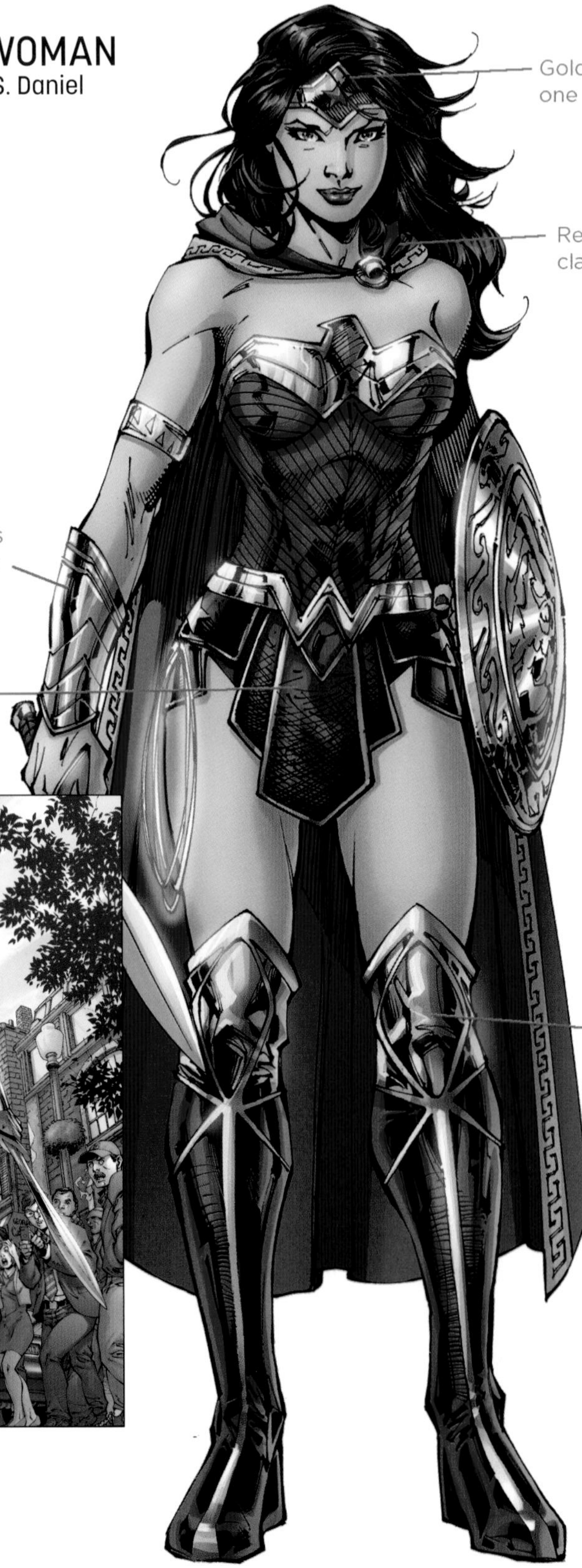

Gold tiara with one red star
Red cape with gold clasp and edge
Silver forearm guards with recessed detailing
Blue leather skirt with gold edges and two stars
Red knee-high boots with gold knee guards and accents

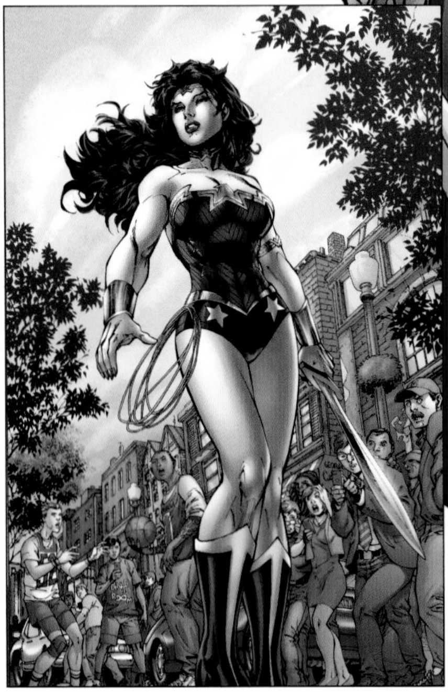

Previous N52 design

Illustration by Jim Lee, Scott Williams & Alex Sinclair

NIGHTWING
Design by Javier Fernandez

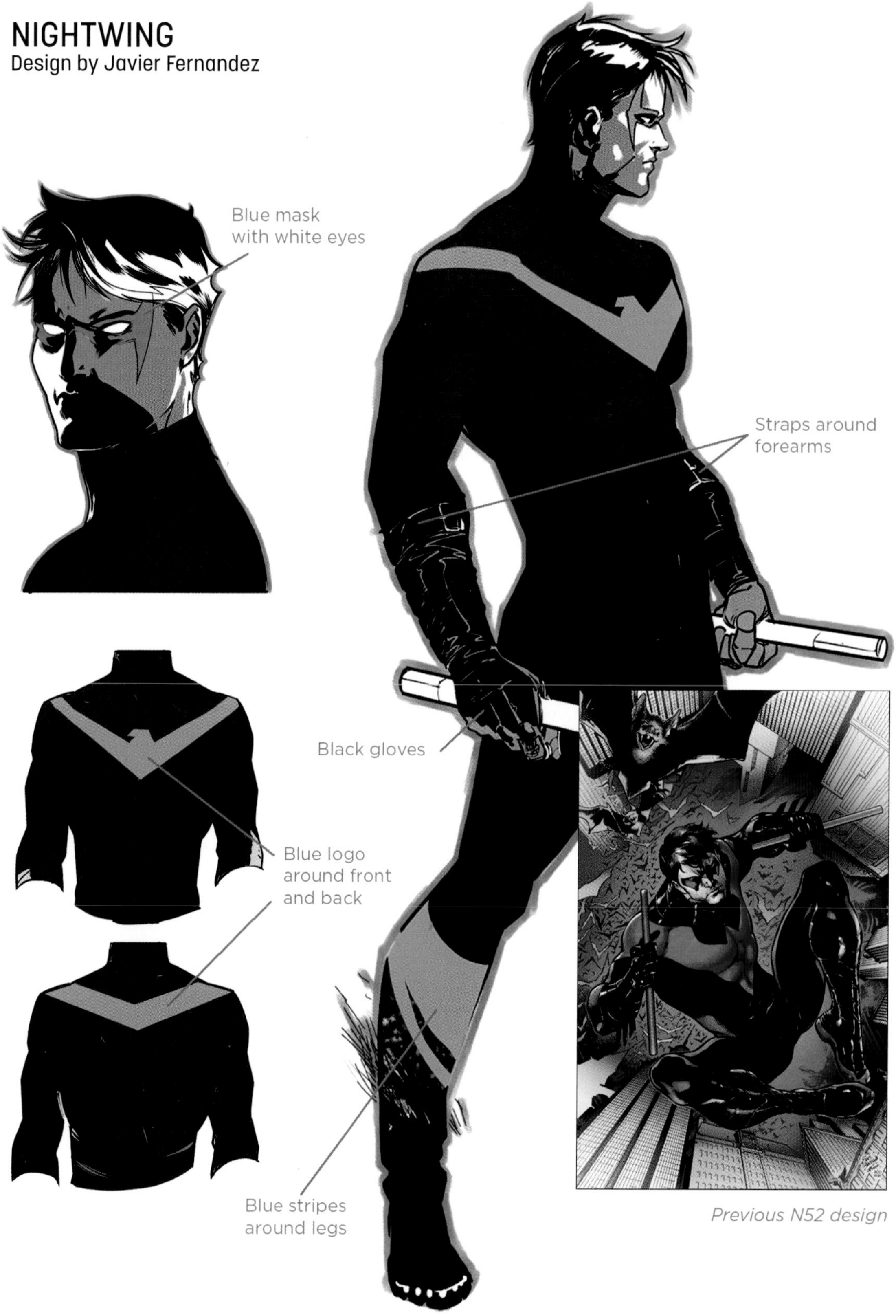
Blue mask
with white eyes
Straps around
forearms
Black gloves
Blue logo
around front
and back
Blue stripes
around legs

Previous N52 design

Illustration by Javier Fernandez

SUPERBOY
Design by Jorge Jimenez

NEW CHARACTER

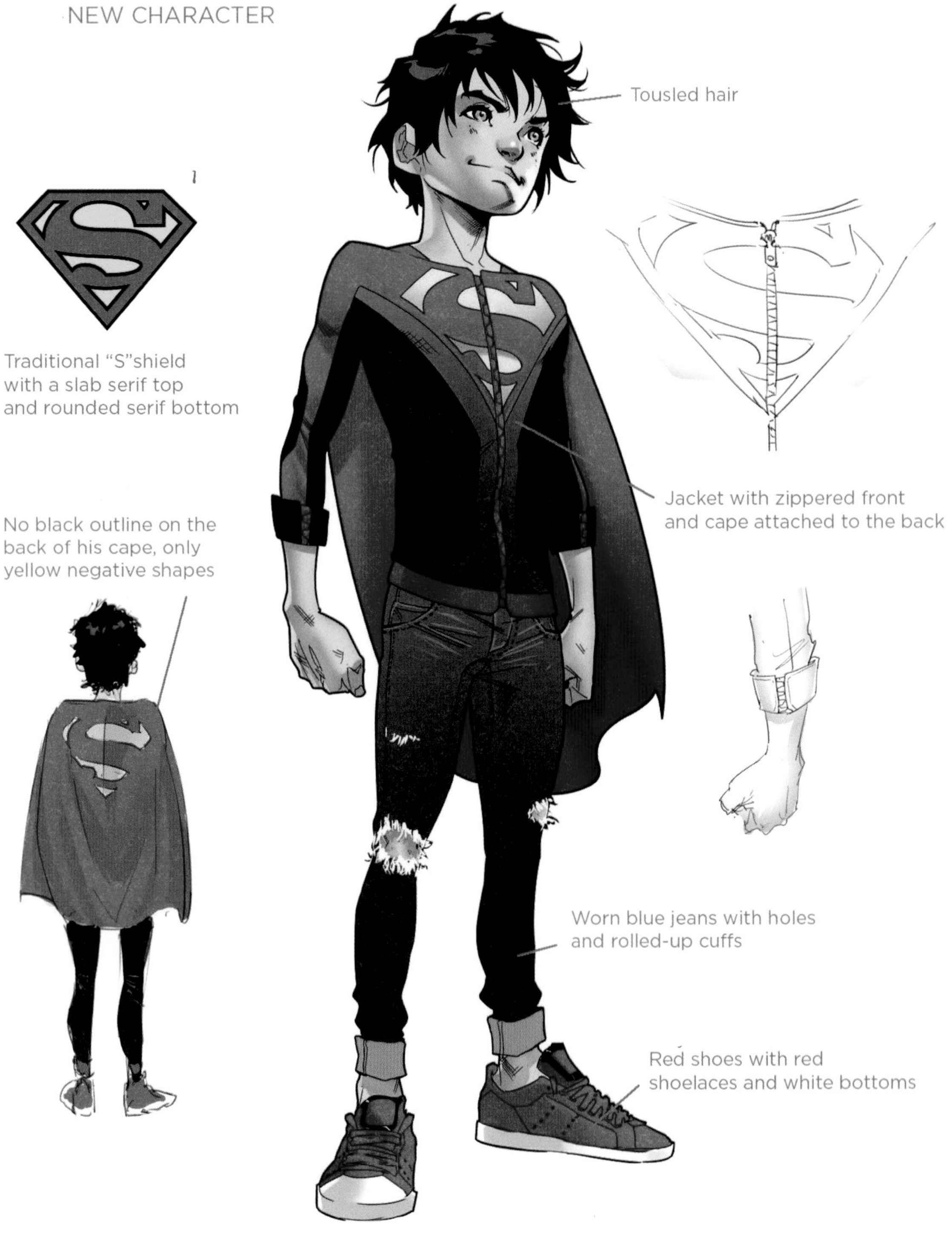
Tousled hair
Traditional "S"shield with a slab serif top and rounded serif bottom
Jacket with zippered front and cape attached to the back
No black outline on the back of his cape, only yellow negative shapes
Worn blue jeans with holes and rolled-up cuffs
Red shoes with red shoelaces and white bottoms

Illustration by Jorge Jimenez

DONNA TROY
Design by Brett Booth

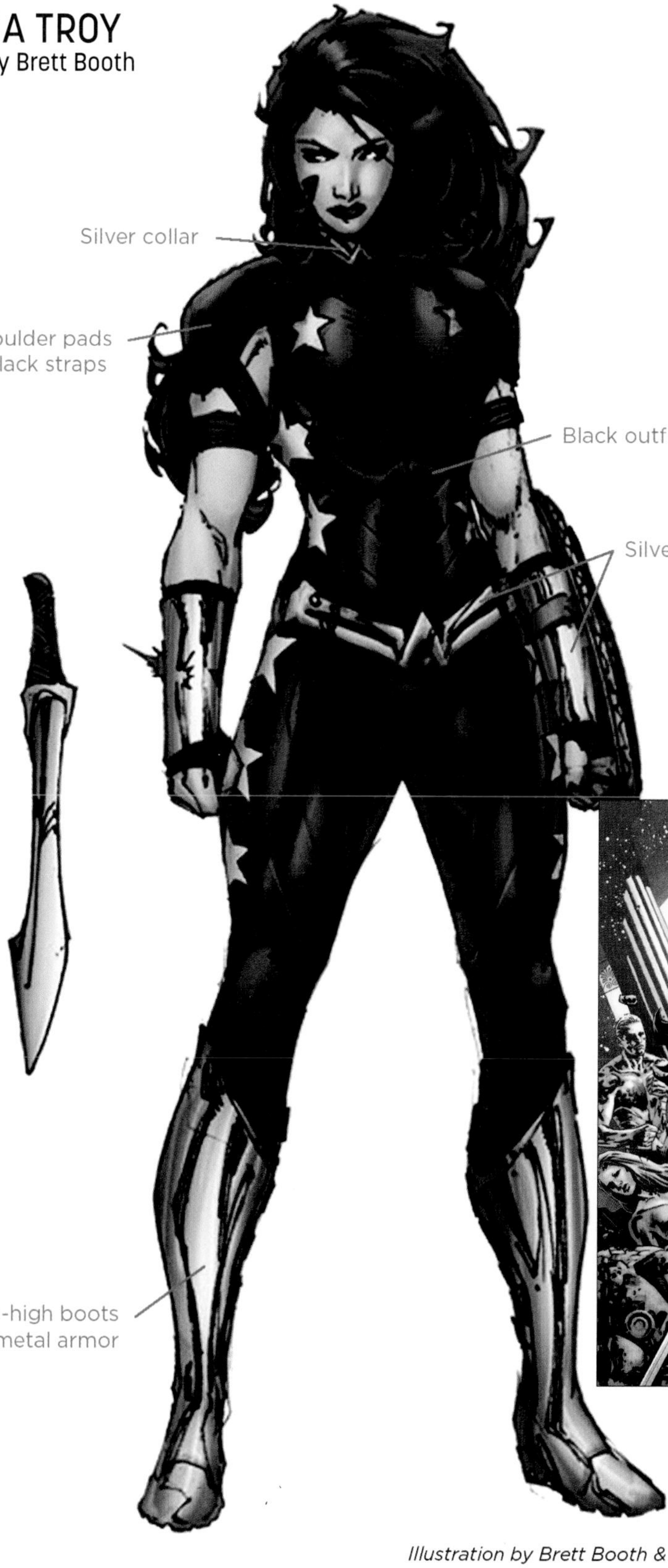
Silver collar
Black shoulder pads with black straps
Black outfit with white stars
Silver gauntlets and belt
Silver thigh-high boots with metal armor

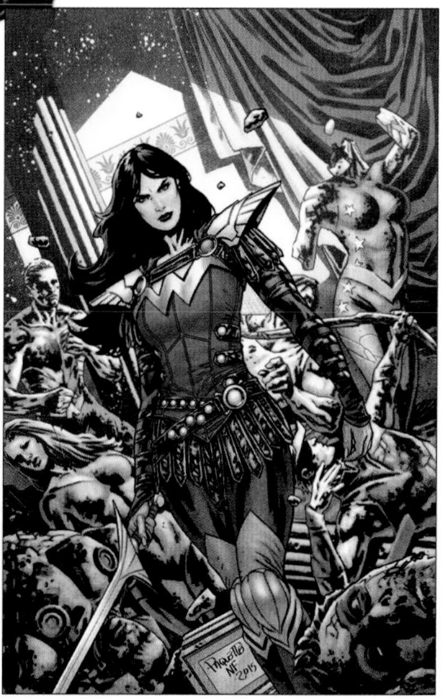

Previous N52 design

Illustration by Brett Booth & Andrew Dalhouse

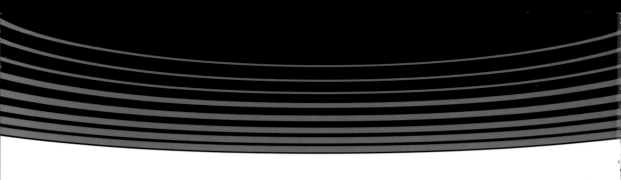

WALLY WEST FLASH
Design by Brett Booth

White lightning when
he's using his powers,
silver when he isn't;
also reflective

Suit should be shiny and
slightly reflective overall

Green eyes

White lightning outlining
his underarms and sides

Burgundy

Additional lightning bolt
lines on the boot exterior

Illustration by Brett Booth & Andrew Dalhouse

AQUAMAN
Design by Brad Walker

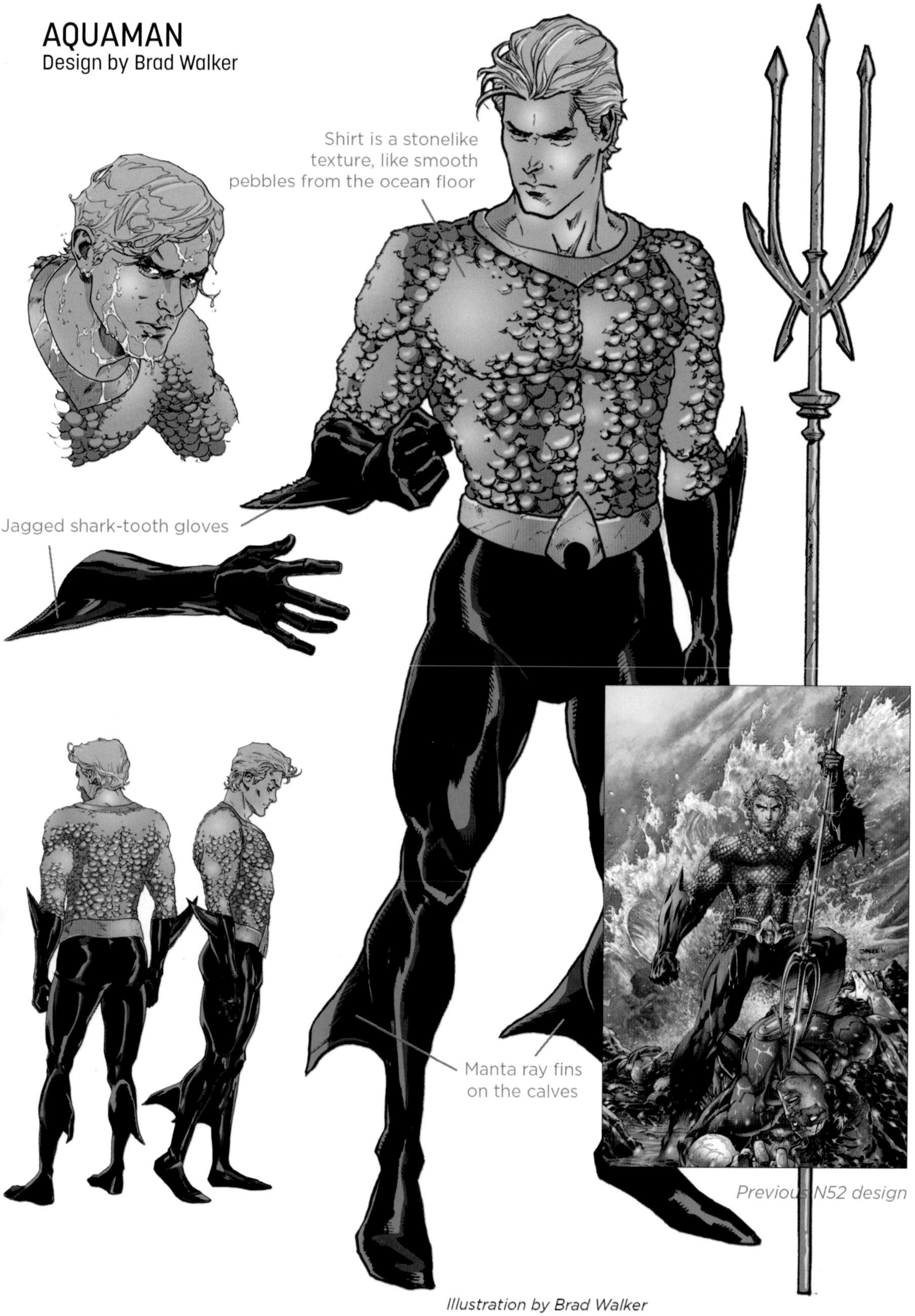

Shirt is a stonelike texture, like smooth pebbles from the ocean floor
Jagged shark-tooth gloves
Manta ray fins on the calves

Previous N52 design

Illustration by Brad Walker

GREEN ARROW
Design by Otto Schmidt

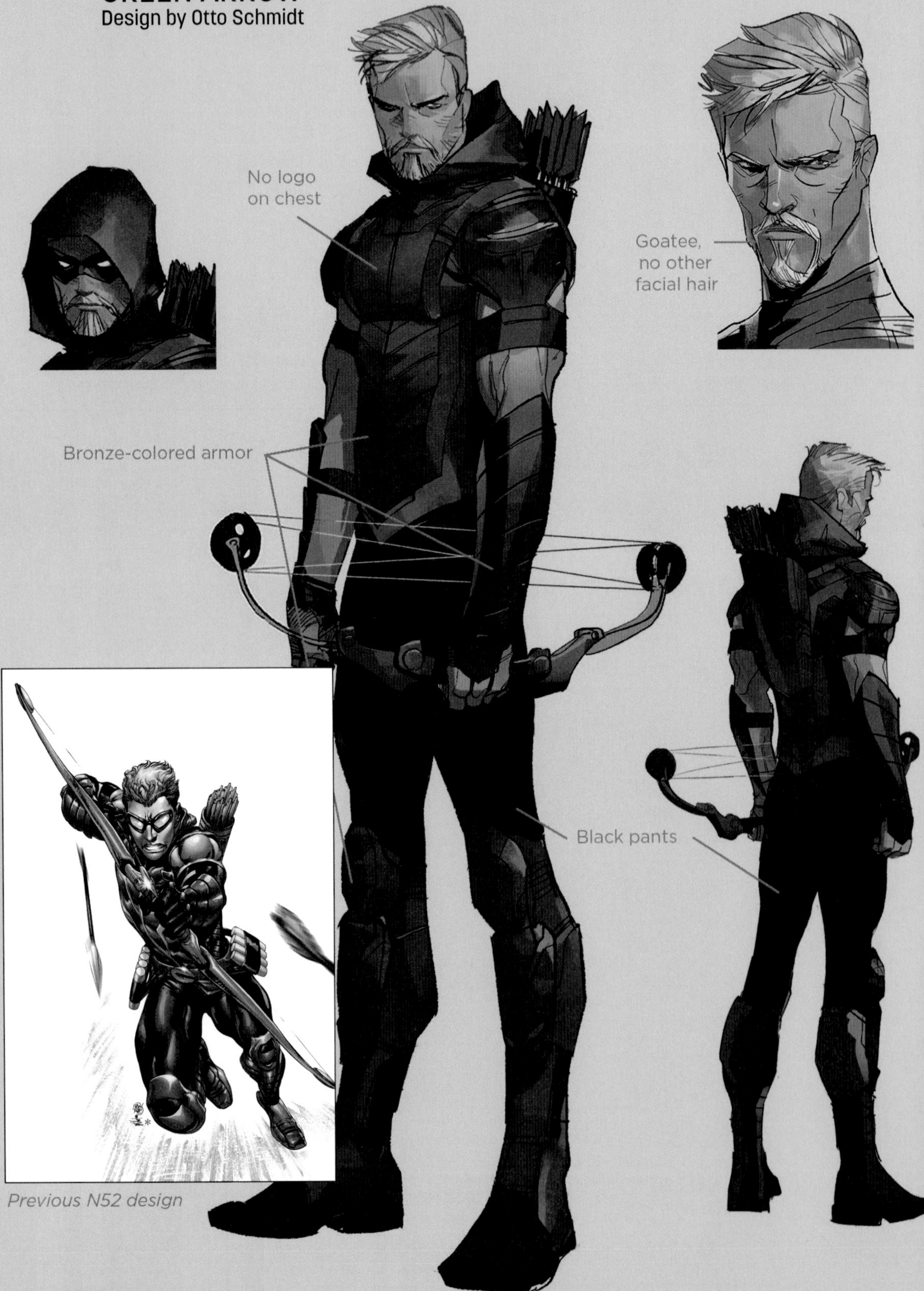
No logo on chest
Goatee, no other facial hair
Bronze-colored armor
Black pants

Previous N52 design

Illustration by Otto Schmidt